THE GODDESS ANAT
IN UGARITIC MYTH

SOCIETY OF BIBLICAL LITERATURE

DISSERTATION SERIES

Number 135

THE GODDESS ANAT
IN UGARITIC MYTH

by
Neal H. Walls

Neal H. Walls

THE GODDESS ANAT IN UGARITIC MYTH

Scholars Press
Atlanta, Georgia

THE GODDESS IN UGARITIC MYTH

Neal H. Walls

Ph.D., 1991
The Johns Hopkins University

Advisor:
P. Kyle McCarter, Jr.

Library of Congress Cataloging in Publication Data
Walls, Neal H., 1962-
The goddess Anat in Ugaritic myth / Neal H. Walls.
p. cm. — (Dissertation series; no. 135)
Originally presented as author's thesis (Ph.D.)—Johns Hopkins University, 1991.
Includes bibliographical references.
ISBN 1-55540-794-3. — ISBN 1-55540-795-1 (pbk.)
1. Anat (Ugaritic deity) 2. Mythology, Ugaritic. I. Title.
II. Series: Dissertation series (Society of Biblical Literature); no. 135.
BL1645.A53W35 1992
299'.26—dc20

92-33416
CIP

Printed in the United States of America
on acid-free paper

Acknowledgements

This study was completed in September, 1990, and formally accepted by the Johns Hopkins University in January, 1991. In accordance with the guidelines of the SBL Dissertation Series, I have revised neither the text nor bibliography beyond the correction of typographical errors. Recent studies of Hindu and Mesopotamian goddess traditions date the bibliography somewhat, but the only recent work on Anat of which I am aware are two forthcoming articles by Peggy Day.

It is a pleasure to express my sincere thanks to Professors P. Kyle McCarter, Jr., Delbert R. Hillers, and Jerrold S. Cooper of The Johns Hopkins University for their tutelage in Semitic languages and ancient Near Eastern studies. Their rigorous attention to scholarly detail provides an unfailing example of academic excellence. I am especially grateful to Professor McCarter, who guided me through both a Masters degree in the History of Religions at the University of Virginia and the doctoral program in Northwest Semitic Philology (Hebrew Bible) at Johns Hopkins. Were it not for his patience, support, and careful mentorship I could not have succeeded in such an unorthodox program of study.

Hans H. Penner and the faculty of the Department of Religion at Dartmouth College provided a most congenial and stimulating atmosphere in which I wrote the bulk of this dissertation. Their warmth and encouragement during my year in their midst is recalled with much fondness.

Lastly, I wish to express my appreciation for my wife, Patricia, for her long-suffering support and endurance. Although working on her own dissertation, she always had time to proofread my chapters and offer constructive criticism. Most importantly, she provided a much needed link with reality during an otherwise maniacal period. This book is dedicated to her as a small token of my love.

NHW
Colby College
Waterville, Maine

Table of Contents

Abbreviations

AB	Anchor Bible
AcOr	*Acta orientalia*
AHw	W. von Soden, *Akkadisches Handwörterbuch*, 3 vols. (Weisbaden: Otto Harrassowitz, 1965-81)
AJSL	*American Journal of Semitic Languages and Literature*
ANET	J. Pritchard (ed.), *Ancient Near Eastern Texts Relating to the Old Testament*, 3rd ed. (Princeton: Princeton University, 1969)
AnOr	Analecta orientalia
AOAT	Alter Orient und Altes Testament
AOS	American Oriental Series
BA	*Biblical Archaeologist*
BASOR	*Bulletin of the American Schools of Oriental Research*
BH	Biblical Hebrew
BM	Cuneiform Tablets in the British Museum
BZAW	Beihefte zur *Zeitschrift für die altestamentliche Wissenschaft*
CAD	*The Assyrian Dictionary of the Oriental Institute of the University of Chicago*
CBQMS	Catholic Biblical Quarterly Monograph Series
CRAIBL	*Comptes rendus de l'Académie des inscriptions et belles-lettres*
CTA	A. Herdner, *Corpus des tablettes en cunéiformes alphabétiques* (Paris: Imprimerie Nationale, 1963)
EncRel	M. Eliade (ed.), *Encyclopedia of Religion*, 16 vols. (New York: Macmillan, 1987)
GKC	E. Kautzsch (ed.), *Gesenius' Hebrew Grammar*, trans. A. E. Cowley, 2nd English ed. (Oxford: Clarendon, 1985)
HR	*History of Religions*
HSM	Harvard Semitic Monographs
HTR	*Harvard Theological Review*
JANES	*Journal of the Ancient Near Eastern Society of Columbia University*
JAOS	*Journal of the American Oriental Society*
JCS	*Journal of Cuneiform Studies*

JEA	*Journal of Egyptian Archaeology*
JHS	*Journal of Hellenic Studies*
JNES	*Journal of Near Eastern Studies*
JNSL	*Journal of Northwest Semitic Languages*
JSS	*Journal of Semitic Studies*
KTU	M. Dietrich, O. Loretz, and J. Sanmartín (eds.), *Die Keilalphabetischen Texte aus Ugarit* (Neukirchen-Vluyn: Neukirchener, 1976)
LÄ	W. Helck and W. Westendorf (eds.), *Lexikon der Ägyptologie* (Wiesbaden: Otto Harrassowitz, 1972—)
LXX	Septuagint
MARI	*Mari: annales de Recherches interdisciplinaires*
MT	Masoretic Text
MUSJ	*Mélanges de l'université Saint-Joseph*
MVAG	Mitteilungen der vorderasiatisch-ägyptischen Gesellschaft
Ni	Cuneiform Tablets from Nippur in the Istanbul Museum of the Ancient Orient
OBO	Orbis biblicus et orientalis
OLP	Orientalia lovaniensia periodica
Or	*Orientalia*
OTS	*Oudtestamentische Studiën*
PE	Eusebius, *Praeparatio Evangelica*
PRU	*Le palais royale d'Ugarit*
RHR	*Revue de l'histoire des religions*
RlA	E. Ebeling et al. (eds.), *Reallexikon der Assyriologie* (Berlin: Walter de Gruyter, 1928—)
RS	Ras Shamra excavation/tablet number
SBLDS	Society of Biblical Literature Dissertation Series
SBLMS	Society of Biblical Literature Monograph Series
SJLA	Studies in Judaism in Late Antiquity
SEL	*Studi Epigrafici e Linguistici*
TDOT	G. J. Botterweck and H. Ringgren (eds.), *Theological Dictionary of theOld Testament*, trans. J. T. Willis (Grand Rapids: Eerdmans, 1974—)
TO	A. Caquot, M. Sznycer, and A. Herdner (eds.), *Textes Ougaritiques*. Tome 1: *Mythes et Légendes* (Paris: Les Éditions du Cerf, 1974)

TWAT	G. J. Botterweck and H. Ringgren (eds.), *Theologisches Wörterbuch zum Alten Testament* (Stuttgart: W. Kohlhammer, 1973)
UF	*Ugarit-Forschungen*
Ug. V	J. Nougayrol et al. (eds.), *Ugaritica V* (Paris: Geuthner, 1968)
UT	C. Gordon, *Ugaritic Textbook* (Rome: Pontifical Biblical Institute, 1965)
VT	*Vetus Testamentum*
VTSup	Vetus Testamentum, Supplements
WMyth	H. W. Haussig (ed.), *Wörterbuch der Mythologie* (Stuttgart: Ernst Klett Verlag, 1961—)
WO	*Die Welt des Orients*
ZA	*Zeitschrift für Assyriologie*
ZAW	*Zeitschrift für die altestamentliche Wissenschaft*

CHAPTER 1
Introduction

Largely unknown prior to the discovery of the alphabetic cuneiform texts from the ruins of Late Bronze Age Ugarit, the goddess Anat is a striking figure from ancient Syrian mythology. An independent and unrestrained female in the divine realm, the Maiden Anat plays an active role in the Ugaritic myths. Although she is described as a nubile female, Anat aggressively engages in the masculine pursuits of hunting and warfare. Undoubtedly, Anat's most infamous characteristic is her fierce and violent temperament. She is portrayed as a ruthless warrior who glories in bloodshed and exults in slaughter. Anat boasts of her conquests of Baal's monstrous enemies and threatens the grey-haired father of the gods with physical violence if he does not grant her requests. She causes the death of the hunter and crown prince Aqhat when he denies her desire for his divine bow. Ugaritic myth provides the grisly image of Anat adorning herself with the decapitated heads and severed limbs of her defeated enemies. Delighting in the carnage of battle, Anat wades in blood up to her thighs. She is indeed a most fearsome and aggressive character in Ugaritic myth. Yet, Anat's violence also serves a positive function in the Baal Cycle. Anat's hostile actions contribute to the balance of cosmic power and the establishment of Baal as the king of the gods. Indeed, her vigorous extirpation of Death allows fertility to return to the earth. Thus, Anat is an ambivalent force in Ugaritic myth.

Yet, Anat is more than a simple warrior deity. Ugaritic myth also portrays her as a compassionate goddess who pathetically grieves over the death of her brother, Baal. Anat is a pubescent female who serves as a wet nurse to humans of royal descent. While her primary epithet is "Maiden," *btlt*, modern scholars frequently identify her as an erotic goddess of love and fertility. The enigmatic quality of her symbolic identity well typifies the complexities of ancient myths and mythic characters. In particular, the combination of feminine and masculine attributes in Anat's mythic character demonstrates her ambiguous identity. Anat's apparent disdain for domestic responsibility and rejection of an exclusively feminine social identity demonstrates the importance of gender to her symbolic identity. Indeed, as this study argues, Anat holds a liminal position with respect to the gender system and social ideology of the ancient patriarchal culture.

The present study examines the mythological character of the goddess Anat as a means better to appreciate the mythic symbolism of the Ugaritic texts. While defending readings of disputed passages concerning Anat, the study will concentrate more on the symbolic role of Anat in Ugaritic myth than on the presentation of yet another philological commentary. Attention is given to both the narrative acts and poetic descriptions of the goddess Anat, with particular emphasis on her epithets as evidence of her mythic persona. Given the paucity of information concerning Anat's mythic character apart from the Ugaritic texts, the primary focus of this study remains on the Ugaritic myths.[1] The Mesopotamian evidence for the goddess Anat is limited to onomastics and cultic pantheon lists that provide no information relevant to her mythic character. Perhaps the most important information from cuneiform sources is the appearance of Anat (written Anat or Ḫanat) as a distinct goddess rather than a western manifestation of Ishtar (Huffmon 1965:200-1). Similarly, Anat's appearance in Egyptian texts, discussed briefly below, offers little evidence for Anat's mythic identity in the Ugaritic tradition. Hence, focusing upon Anat's symbolic character within the Ugaritic texts provides a more vivid and accurate portrait of the goddess Anat within one mythological system.

The analysis of Anat's mythic identity necessitates a fresh translation of the relevant Ugaritic texts with particular attention devoted to Anat's sexual and gender identity. The voluminous philological commentary is not usually noted since the interested reader may refer to the standard references for bibliography and other scholars' opinions.[2] However, the

---

1 See Eaton (1964:9-52) and Bowman (1978:202-59) for the history of Anat's cult and its dispersion in the ancient Near East.

2 See, among others, Gordon (1965; 1977), del Olmo Lete (1981a; 1984), *TO* (1974), de Moor (1971; 1987), Margalit 1980; 1989b), Gibson (1978), Aistleitner

controversial passages concerning Anat's alleged sexual activity require special philological attention in Chapter 3. Unless otherwise specified, this study follows *KTU* for numbering Ugaritic tablets, columns, and lines. The transcription of the Ugaritic texts generally follows *KTU*. Finally, tablets 1.1 through 1.6 are conveniently labelled the Baal Cycle.

The Study of Ugaritic Myth

Since their unexpected discovery in 1929, the alphabetic cuneiform tablets from the ancient Syrian city of Ugarit, modern Ras Shamra, have undergone intense linguistic scrutiny by Semitic philologists. While this analysis resulted in a reliable foundation for the translation of the Ugaritic texts, similar attention has not been given to the problems of mythological interpretation. The necessity of philological training in Northwest Semitic languages has precluded substantative study of the Ugaritic myths by non-specialists while scholars trained in Semitic philology are often unfamiliar with contemporary theories of myth interpretation. Thus, recent methodological advances in mythic analysis within other traditions have had little impact upon Ugaritic studies. Furthermore, many scholars who have approached the Ugaritic literary texts have done so only to note their relation to the poetry of the Hebrew Bible. Primarily interested in the light which Ugaritic texts could shed upon the biblical tradition, scholars have often neglected the religious value of these Late Bronze Age mythological speculations. These difficulties and scholarly biases have hindered the mythological analysis of the Ugaritic literature. Scholars commonly reduce gods and goddesses to Frazerian types without reference to the varying roles they play in the actual texts. Anat is often classified as a "virgin-warrior type" and Baal is defined simply as a "storm god" or "dying-rising god," as though these were well-established categories capable of explaining the mythic identity of these deities. While these typologies are easily systematized for comparative use, they misrepresent the complexity of the divine symbols and structural relations within the mythic pantheon.

Oden (1979) and M. Smith (1986b) have presented excellent articles on methodological flaws common to the interpretation of Ugaritic

---

(1969), Gray (1965), and Ginsberg (1959).

mythology in the last fifty years. The thorough study of Rogerson (1974), *Myth in Old Testament Research*, also surveys the major schools of thought in interpreting biblical and Ugaritic myth. Each discussion concludes that scholars continue to assume that Ugaritic myth and religion are obsessed with fertility. Such an interpretive approach dates back to the texts' discovery in the early twentieth century when fertility concerns dominated the discussions of the early anthropologists. This assumption is often justified by a myth-ritual interpretation, reducing Ugaritic myth to the level of primitive science and nature symbolism. This interpretative bias represents the heavy influence of W. Robertson-Smith, the Cambridge circle, and Sir James G. Frazer, whose presence is still felt in many academic fields (see Vickery 1973). The central importance of Frazer to the study of Ugaritic myth, however, rests in the continuing influence of his thought to the present day. In particular, his views on the fertility function of primitive religion, his implicit theories of myth and ritual, and his concept of the dying-rising vegetation god haunt Ugaritic interpretation long after these ideas have been abandoned by historians of religion as essentially groundless.[3] This fact contributes greatly to the outdated quality of much contemporary Ugaritic myth interpretation.

The myth-ritual school of myth interpretation continues to have a profound impact on Ugaritic mythography.[4] Misrepresenting the Ugaritic myths as purely ritual texts, the myth-ritual approach attempts to reconstruct the Ugaritic cult based upon the actions of the gods in the mythic narratives. The hypothetical rituals are then used as the basis for interpreting the myths. Fontenrose (1971) treats these fundamental methodological flaws in a scathing critique of the myth-ritual position, so it is unnecessary to repeat the many arguments here (see also Kirk 1970:12-31). Closely associated with the myth-ritual position is the seasonal interpretation of Ugaritic myth (see M. Smith 1986b:314-6). The most comprehensive defense of this view is that of de Moor (1971),

3 For example, J. Z. Smith (1969; 1973) and Fontenrose (1971:36-49).

4 Following the lead of S. Hooke (1933, 1935, 1958) in biblical studies, Hvidberg (1962), Engnell (1945), James (1958), and especially Gaster (1966) have been strong proponents of the liturgical function of Ugaritic myth. On the myth-ritual school see especially Kirk (1970:8-31) and Rogerson (1974:66-84). Oden (1979:46-9) discusses the extent to which the myth-ritual interpretation permeates Ugaritic mythography, and M. Smith (1986b:316-8) summarizes the bibliography important to this position.

who provides a detailed correlation between the Baal Cycle and the Canaanite seasonal and agricultural calendar. The seasonal interpretation rests firmly upon a cultic basis (e.g. de Moor 1971:16, 30), often associated with the New Year celebration as reconstructed by the Scandinavian tradition of Mowinckel (see de Moor 1972; Gray 1965:33-4). While there is certainly seasonal imagery in the Baal Cycle, Grabbe (1976) demonstrates the methodological weaknesses of this universal approach and, hence, there is no need to recount its faults.

An important component of both the seasonal and ritual interpretations is the description of Baal as a dying and rising god. Based upon the brilliant synthetic work of Frazer and aided by Hooke and the myth-ritualists, the concept of "dying and rising gods" has found its way into modern scholarly discussions concerning the mythic representation of annual agricultural cycles. These youthful gods from the Mediterranean region, commonly identified as Tammuz, Adonis, Attis, and Osiris, are described as fertility or vegetation gods who annually descend to the Netherworld and rise with the vegetation in the Spring (see Baudissin 1911). The introduction of Ugaritic Baal into this category facilitates his identification with the Canaanite fertility cycle, as well as provides him a convenient place within the ancient Near Eastern pattern of myth and ritual. Under the influence of Hooke, Engnell, and other proponents of ancient Near Eastern patternism, the description of Baal as one of many dying and rising gods has become an unquestioned assumption for many writers.

In fact, there are no clear and reliable data for an indigenous belief in a male god who dies and rises on an annual basis in any myth or ritual from the ancient Near East. Returning to the sources used by Frazer in his presentation of cultic and mythic evidence, modern reappraisals of this theory have reached negative conclusions concerning the tradition of a risen god.[5] Indeed, J. Z. Smith (1987:521) states that the category of dying and rising gods "must now be understood to have been largely a misnomer based on imaginative reconstructions and exceedingly late or

---

5 Reappraisals of this theory can be conveniently found in J. Z. Smith (1987), Burkert (1979:99-102), de Vaux (1972:210-37), and Wagner (1967:89-267). Discussions on the Mesopotamian deities Tammuz (Gurney 1962; Alster 1972) and Marduk (von Soden 1955; Frymer-Kensky 1984) arrive at either negative or uncertain conclusions. For a more recent attempt at reconstructing rituals from myths, see Robertson (1982).

highly ambiguous texts." Similarly, Burkert (1979:100) states, "Frazer's 'god of vegetation' is post-classic allegory transformed into a genetic theory of religion; we may leave it to rhetoric and poetry from whence it sprang." Indeed, Frazer's search for a primitive precursor to the death and resurrection of Christ appears to result in a Victorian illusion rather than an ancient category of divinity. Further study may reveal important links, but there is presently no discernible relation between Baal's role in the Ugaritic material and the myths or cults of Tammuz, Adonis, Attis, or Orisis. There is no evidence that the death and resurrection of Baal or its ritual celebration was an annual occurrence in Ugaritic religion. The interpretation that Baal personifies natural vegetation is itself methodologically flawed in its assumption that Ugaritic gods can be reduced to natural phenomena. Unfortunately, no comprehensive and dependable study of Baal's descent to and return from the Netherworld in Ugaritic myth currently exists. Similarities with the descents of Ishtar and Tammuz in Mesopotamian sources call for fresh comparative analysis but this topic is beyond the scope of the present study.

While Frazer may be forgiven his ethnocentric attitudes towards "primitive" religion, it is quite unreasonable to continue with the assumption that ancient Ugaritic religion is only concerned with fertility magic. In discussing the seasonal and fertility interpretation of Ugaritic myth, Miller (1981:125) wisely remarks that "to interpret the Baal Cycle is to become aware that the mythology is much more complex than this and cannot be reduced to a ... reflection of a basically fertility religion any more than one can do that with Israelite religion (where drought was of equal concern and the deity viewed as a dispenser of fertility, rain, and the like)." Although myth-ritual assumptions and seasonal interpretations still dominate Ugaritic mythography, advances are being made in analyzing the multidimensional and complex character of this ancient mythology.[6] Mark Smith (1986b) has considered the major

6 Such an approach is in stark contrast to Gray's (1965) repeated references to the primitive level of thought of ancient Ugarit religion in one of the most influential studies of Ugaritic mythology. Similarly, Oldenberg (1969) prefaces his study of Ugaritic myth with the following statement:

> That which impelled me to begin the study of Canaanite religion was my desire to investigate its relationship to Hebrew religion, to see whether the faith of Yahweh was a product of the soil of the Canaanite religion. The more I studied pre-Israelite religion, the more I was amazed with its utter depravity and wickedness. Indeed there is *nothing* in it to inspire the sublime faith of Yahweh. His coming is like the rising sun dispelling the darkness of Canaanite superstition.

interpretational approaches to the Baal Cycle as a prolegomenon to a forthcoming critical commentary. He concludes that while the seasonal, ritual, and cosmogonic themes all play important roles in the mythic imagery of the Baal Cycle, the central focus of the narrative is on divine kingship. The imagery of natural and seasonal fertility pervades the Ugaritic myths in association with Baal's role in fixing the seasons and sending his luxuriant rains to fertilize the earth, but these images do not dominate the narrative. The description of Baal's battles with Yamm and Mot as battles between Life and Death, Fertility and Sterility, or Order and Chaos are merely modern interpretations of ancient myth. Although these themes may be discerned within the texts through mythic analysis, the literal narrative of the Baal Cycle concerns the power struggles between discrete divine beings of the Ugaritic pantheon. M. Smith (1986b) and Gibson (1984) are surely correct in their conclusion that divine kingship is the central theme of the Baal Cycle.[7]

Interpreting Anat

Completed prior to the discovery of the Ras Shamra tablets, the important study of Albright (1924) placed the study of Anat on a scholarly basis by demonstrating the extent of her cult in the ancient Near East. Vincent's 1937 book on the religion of Elephantine also included a discussion of Anat in the ancient world, with little reference to her role in the Ugaritic texts. While Virolleaud (1938) and Cassuto (1971) presented books naming Anat in their titles, both were more concerned with philological analysis than with presenting a comprehensive analysis of Anat's mythological character. Virolleaud's

---

7 That is, Baal's battles with Yamm and Mot are over the right to be king, *mlk*, in the Ugaritic pantheon. But Baal's title of king does not give him authority over El, as I understand it. Recent studies have emphasized the structural authority relationship between El and Baal (L'Heureux 1978; Mullen 1980), but much remains to be done in interpreting the structure and interrelations of the pantheon. While Pope (1987) and others maintain that Baal replaces El as head of the pantheon in the mythic cycles, I perceive a dynamic balance between the patriachal authority of El and the coercive power of Baal within the pantheon. El determines who will rule as king in the Baal Cycle, and it is he who establishes the dominion of each god. Gibson's (1984:207-10) description of El as the ultimate ruler of the universe who acts through diplomacy and by delegating authority to a "viceroy" to rule the earth on his behalf seems accurate. The divine *mlk* must also be worthy of his position, however, and the Baal Cycle relates the events through which Baal legitimately won his position.

only explicit treatment of Anat (1937) is too early to be of lasting importance. Shorter discussions of Anat can be found in general articles on Syrian deities by Dahood (1958), Pope (1961), Albright (1968:128-32), and Oldenburg (1969:83-90) among others, but the brevity and scope of these works preclude any detailed examination of the mythic function of the Ugaritic goddess. The provocative article by Lipínski (1965) on the sexual characteristics of Anat should also be noted here. The more recent study of the Phoenician goddess Tanit by Hvidberg-Hansen (1979) gives attention to the goddess Anat as well (1979, I:81-105; II:101-46). Unfortunately, this well-documented book recapitulates many earlier opinions and offers few original insights (see Løkkegaard 1982).

The first lengthy study actually devoted to the goddess Anat is a 1964 Yale dissertation by Eaton. While providing much important data, Eaton's study focuses on the history of the cult, mythology, and iconography of Anat throughout the Near East rather than her mythological character. This careful work continues to serve as a useful, if dated, reference for the extent of Anat's presence in the ancient Near East. In 1969 Kapelrud produced his book-length study of Anat, the only such work published to date. Kapelrud provides a comprehensive discussion and analysis of the mythic character of the violent goddess in the Ugaritic texts. Unfortunately, this book appears to be more of a popular summary with many errors and unsupported translations than a scholarly study of Anat. Kapelrud's peculiar ideas occasionally cloud his interpretation and his simplistic approach renders his book untrustworthy.

The third lengthy study of Anat available to scholars is the unpublished Berkeley dissertation of Bowman (1978). Bowman offers an analysis of the mythic character and function of Anat, yet his emphasis on a philological defense of his translations overshadows his discussion of her mythic persona. More importantly, Bowman's analysis is severely limited by his restrictive interpretation of Anat's almost hypostatic relation to Baal. He describes Anat's violence as directly connected to her support of Baal in his yearly struggle to gain supremacy in the pantheon. She only sheds blood to support Baal's fertility function, according to Bowman, and episodes such as Anat's "blood-bath" in *KTU* 1.3 iii are assumed to be ritual in nature. He argues that Anat's self-serving use of violence in *Aqhat* is only a secondary development of her "original" function connected with the fertility cycle of Baal and, therefore, it is not to be taken too seriously in constructing her mythic characterization (Bowman 1978:106-7). Bowman's one-sided analysis of Anat's symbolic function and his apparent interest in fixing her typological character mar the overall use of his study.

These earlier studies provide a firm base for further research into the mythic character of Anat using contemporary tools of myth analysis. Hence, it is unnecessary to present either a survey of the available information concerning Anat in the ancient Near East or a review of twentieth-century scholarship concerning the relevant texts. In order to contribute to the appreciation of Ugaritic mythology, the present study focuses on matters of symbolic interpretation and methodology in analyzing the mythic identity of the goddess Anat. Particular attention is given to the use of feminine sexuality and gender within an androcentric mythological system.

Contemporary discussion of symbols highlights the need for examination of Anat's character in light of the structural relationships within the Ugaritic pantheon. The symbolic identity of Anat will be constructed from all available information, including her age, epithets, social relations, support of and opposition to other characters, and position within the pantheon structure. One important aspect of symbolic interpretation is a character's gender (see Bynum 1986). Gender is the cultural experience of being either male or female, and since no character is without gender, it is necessary to recognize gender as an important category of symbolic communication. Gender has received attention as a useful analytic category only in recent decades under the influence of feminist studies.[8] Discussion of gender in ancient Ugaritic literature is difficult since so little evidence for the roles of female characters, human or divine, has survived. While one cannot adequately reconstruct the cultural gender categories of ancient Ugaritic society, the construction of gender values from the mythological literature may aid in understanding Anat's place within the relational structures of the Ugaritic pantheon. Anat's ambiguous role as nubile

---

[8] On gender and women's studies see Rosaldo and Lamphere (1974), Kessler and McKenna (1978), Hoch-Smith and Springs (1978), Ortner and Whitehead (1981), Sanday (1981), and Lipman-Blumen (1984). Recent scholarly discussions of the relationship between gender and religion note the important function of gender in approaching literary and religious texts (see Bynum, Harrell, and Richman 1986).

maiden and bloody warrior illustrates the importance of gender to her character. The identity of Anat as a gendered character may be informed through the comparative study of categories of gender symbolization in other mythological traditions. Special attention is given to warrior goddesses, divine androgynes, and erotic goddesses in the following chapter.

The hermeneutic process seeks to determine what meanings exist in the text, and how they are communicated through the plot, structure, and symbols of the mythic medium. Meaning is thus an interpretive rather than normative component of myth. As Victor Turner (1967:26-7) points out in his ethnographic study of Ndembu symbolism, there are often implicit meanings of myth and ritual which even native participants do not recognize. Thus, it is up to the mythographer, equipped with a broader perspective and tools of structural and symbolic analysis, to reveal implicit or unconscious meanings through a text-centered study (O'Flaherty 1980:7-9). Analysis of other mythological traditions by specialists in their respective fields demonstrates the available tools and methods of contemporary mythological interpretation which have not been adequately utilized in approaching the Ugaritic myths.[9] The lessons learned from the previous generations of Ugaritic specialists must be borne in mind, but additional approaches to myth must be applied to progress beyond a Frazerian interpretation.

Given the inherent difficulties of analyzing mythological traditions from an archaic society, I advocate a pluralistic approach to myth interpretation. As O'Flaherty (1980:3-14) argues, the complexity of myth requires a complex methodological approach. O'Flaherty (1980:5) provides a candid summation of her approach to interpretation when she writes,

---

9 General theoretical advances in the methodology of myth analysis have been prompted by a greater methodological awareness, discussed in the studies and collections of Middleton (1967), P. Cohen (1969), Kirk (1970), A. Olson (1980), Segal (1980), Dundes (1984), and Doty (1986). The extensive work in symbolic anthropology by Lévi-Strauss (see 1965), Douglas (1966), Geertz (1966), and Turner (1967; 1975) has also affected the contemporary study of myth and symbol through emphasis on the symbolic system at work in cultures. Similarly, psychological approaches have been incorporated in the recent myth analysis. Scholars have applied the theories of Freud (Dundes 1984; Slater 1968) and Jung (Kerenyi 1969, 1978; Neumann 1954, 1956) in approaching ancient myth and symbols.

> Often the explicit content of a myth will give a broad hint as to how it might be interpreted: if it is about castration, try Freud; if it is about heresy, try theology. In the first analysis, it pays to be literal-minded.... This is the toolbox approach to the study of myth: carry about with you as wide a range of tools as possible, and reach for the right one at the right time.

The attempt to apply any universal interpretive method to all mythic texts simply results in reductionism of the complex to the simple, of "spinning gold into straw." By appropriating the best of available methods and models the mythographer is better equipped to treat the ambiguities and subtleties of mythic symbolism. As P. Cohen (1969:338) points out, theories of myth should not be mutually exclusive since the multivalent and multifunctional nature of myth cannot be contained within any one approach. The pluralistic approach to myth interpretation is methodologically conscientious in the realization that different myths call for different methods, and it is the task of the mythographer to determine which approach is most appropriate. While the pluralistic appropach is admittedly subjective, myth analysis has yet to reach the level of objective science.

CHAPTER 2
Comparative Perspectives

The present chapter examines the mythic themes and symbolism associated with Anat in Ugaritic myth in comparison with those of similar goddesses in other mythological traditions. The purpose of this comparison is neither to construct divine typologies nor to reduce divergent goddesses to "feminine archetypes," but soley to aid in elucidating the phenomenological significance of Anat's attributes and symbolic associations. As with most divine images within a mythological system, the symbols and structural relationships of Anat are much more complex than typologies admit. However, analysis of goddesses with similar roles and characteristics in other mythic contexts aids in the development of conceptual categories and structural analogies which prove useful in the interpretation of Anat's character and position within the Ugaritic pantheon.

The wealth of scholarly analysis of goddesses within Classical Greek and Hindu mythology provides important models and methodologies for interpreting feminine images within the context of an androcentric mythological system. Accordingly, this study devotes particular attention to the diverse approaches which recent mythographers have applied to the symbolic analysis of Greek and Hindu goddesses. The myths of the ancient Near East must also play a crucial role in the comparative analysis of the goddess Anat. Although these mythological traditions are more obscure than Greek and Hindu traditions, the geographical proximity and cultural influence of both Mesopotamia and Egypt upon Ugarit are of central importance to the Ugaritic pantheon and mythological tradition. Finally, this chapter gives special emphasis to the analysis of the bloody Hindu goddesses Durga and Kali since previous scholars have consistently, but only superficially, affirmed Anat's similarities to these figures.

The comparative perspective of this chapter concentrates upon the three most obvious and seemingly central features of Anat's character and narrative role within the extant Ugaritic myths:

1) her ambiguous sexual and social role as a "maiden;"
2) her violent temperament and bloody exploits; and
3) her search, burial, and mourning of the slain Baal.

These discrete elements of Anat's narrative character are most amenable to comparative analysis. Hence, this chapter examines the literary character and mythic functions of other goddesses who are prominently depicted as maidens, warriors, and/or mourners. The combination of the traditionally masculine warrior element and the traditionally feminine designation of "maiden" is particularly important to this discussion.

I. FEMININE IMAGES

Myths usually depict goddesses with female sexual characteristics and feminine gender traits. The ascription of these attributes to literary characters provides a fundamental symbolic identity by reference to human sexuality and gender. While sex is an obvious character trait, either male or female, gender is a more subtle component of symbolic identity. Gender roles are "socially created expectations for masculine and feminine behavior" which function as culturally dependent references (Lipman-Blumen 1984:1-2). In other words, gender is a social construction of polarized behavior and attitudes based on sexual identity. Masculine attributes are often described as aggressiveness, rationality, independence, and courage, while feminine qualities are identified as passivity, irrationality, emotional sensitivity, and nurturance. Thus, a culturally dependent model of gender specification holds that femininity is a descriptive category based on psychological and behavioral traits traditionally assigned to females in both Eastern and Western cultures.[1] Utilizing this culturally dependent theory of

1 Dickason (1982) notes that ethnographic studies also support these criteria for masculine and feminine social roles and behaviors, perhaps suggesting some biological connection between sexual identity and traditional gender traits. However, theories of gender differences remain hotly debated. Note Vetterling-Braggin (1982) on the philosophical discussion, Kessler and McKenna (1978) for theoretical discussions of gender as a social category, and Lipman-Blumen (1984) on gender and power. For gender and religious literature see Bynum, Harrell, and Richman (1987).

In contast to culturally dependent models are universalist or "essentialist" theories

gender, myth analysis must consider the symbolic values of gender imagery concerning the "femininity" of goddesses and the "masculinity" of gods within the context of a myth's symbol system in order to appreciate fully a character's identity.

Of central importance to the gendered role of goddesses is their sexual activity. In contrast to the identification of gods with their mythic function, sexual orientation frequently provides the primary metaphor by which mythological traditions define female characters. That is, goddesses are explicitly equated with their sexual role as wife, erotic lover, or virgin while gods have a greater range of mythic activities and identities. Perhaps the androcentric perspective of most mythological traditions explains the emphasis on a goddess's sexual availability. Unfortunately, modern mythographers often portray feminine imagery simply as "female equals fertility" based upon the presupposition that the dominant social role for women in ancient and traditional societies is maternal. The common reduction of all feminine deities to "mother" or "fertility" goddesses illustrates the assumption that all females, including virgins, must have maternal affiliations.[2]

Similarly, mythographers should recognize a greater distinction between goddesses associated with maternal imagery and goddesses associated with sexual activity, but not procreation. Modern interpreters often ignore this ancient differentiation between fertility and eroticism. While the natural metaphors of pregnant females and nursing mothers provide a clear association of femininity with fecundity and nurturance, other symbolic values of feminine images are equally significant. Indeed, the facile interpretation of all ancient Near Eastern goddesses as mother goddesses ignores the diversity of goddesses and their individual qualities. In contrast to maternal imagery, myth often portrays females as aggressive, destructive, and malevolent—traits usually associated with

---

of gender differentiation (see Dickason 1982:19-23). Based on the idea of a universal concept of the "feminine," Jungian theory holds that gender characteristics are innate (see Lauter and Rupprecht 1985; Harding 1972). To Neumann (1954:xxii), the feminine is not a sex-linked characteristic, but a psychological statement, a "symbolic expression" which is archetypal and thus transpersonal.

2 Note the widely used typology of mother goddesses, as seen in Frazer (1911-5), James (1959), Gray (1985), and Neumann (1956), for example. Even many feminist interpretations seem to expect that any one image of the feminine divine should entail all positive attributes associated with feminine gender.

masculine gender. Since maternal characteristics do not form the central metaphors for Anat's character in the Ugaritic myths, symbolic interpretation must pay special attention to her gender, sexuality, and social role in Ugaritic myth.

The sexual identification of feminine characters and their assignment to certain restricted social roles reflects a male perspective in ancient mythological systems. In a widely influential article, Ortner (1974) attempts to explain the logic behind the devaluation of feminine images within androcentric symbol systems. Acknowledging the symbolic polarity of male and female gender roles, she posits the polar relationship of culture and nature. Ortner argues that patriarchal ideologies symbolically associate females with nature while identifying males with culture and that this symbolic association largely rests upon male and female physiological distinctions. Menstruation, pregnancy, childbirth, and lactation associate females with natural, biological processes from which males are excluded. These procreative functions traditionally relegate women to social roles within the domestic sphere while men are free to pursue activities in the public sphere. Thus, men are seen to have a more direct affinity for cultural activity while women are depicted as having a more direct relationship with nature.

Ortner (1974:72) explains the implicit structural dichotomy between culture and nature in human thought:

> Every culture ... is engaged in the process of generating and sustaining systems of meaningful forms (symbols, artifacts, etc.) by means of which humanity transcends the givens of natural existence, bends them to its purposes, controls them in its interests. We may thus broadly equate culture with the notion of human consciousness, or with the products of human consciousness (i.e., systems of thought and technology), by means of which humanity attempts to assert control over nature.

Since feminine attributes symbolically represent the natural, animalistic drives of humanity and masculine attributes represent the rational, ordered qualities of human civilization, an ideological precedent for male dominance and female devaluation is established in androcentric cultures.

Ortner (1974:83-7) emphasizes that while females are symbolically *closer* to nature than males, they are not necessarily *equated* with nature in androcentric symbol systems. Indeed, every culture recognizes women as full and necessary participants. The act of childbirth closely identifies women with nature, yet the primary role of women in childrearing represents their control of the ultimate socialization process. Thus, because of females' equally intimate associations with nature and culture, feminine symbols have the ability to mediate effectively between nature and culture in a manner which masculine symbols cannot. The ambiguity of this mediating position manifests itself in symbols which may either subvert culture (witches, prostitutes, castrating mothers) or support the patriarchal status (submissive wives and mothers). The liminal character of females must thus remain under the control of males in order to alleviate their intrinsic threat to androcentric culture. As Ortner (1974:86) states, "Feminine symbolism, far more often than masculine symbolism, manifests this propensity towards polarized ambiguity—sometimes utterly exalted, sometimes utterly debased, rarely within the normal range of human possibilities." It is this dynamic range which often provides feminine symbols with such mythic potency.

Feminine Social Roles

The anthropomorphic pantheons of ancient Greece and the Near East are largely structured in accordance with human familial and social structures, just as the deities themselves act and react on the analogy of human motivations and responses. The androcentric mythologies of ancient Greece and the Near East present a social ideology in which the primary actors are the male gods, just as the primary actors in the public sphere of human society are males. Based upon either this social subjugation of women or the symbolic polarization of gender roles, goddesses generally have less authority and power than gods in ancient Near Eastern myth. Indeed, the social ideology reflected within Ugaritic literature presents social conventions which emphasize male activity and female passivity (cf. van Selms 1954). While one must not assume that the mythical social organization reflects the actual social environment of the myth's indigenous culture (see Oden 1979:51-5), there is often a recognizable relation between patriarchal social structures and mythic social conventions.

Although femininity is a descriptive category, it may also play a normative function in androcentric ideology by defining and regulating proper feminine behaviors and attitudes. The information and analytical methods currently available for reconstructing the social role and status of women within Ugaritic culture are limited, but enough information exists to support the description of Ugaritic society as patriarchal. Without the intensive familiarity with the myth's indigenous culture that only anthropological fieldwork allows, text-centered myth analysis attempts to discern the values and attitudes associated with the male perspective on the role of goddesses as gendered characters. The best available example of mythic social structure and ideology presenting the male perception of women's proper role in society is the ancient Greek model. The status of women in Classical Athens and its reflection in Greek myth has recently received much scholarly attention.[3] The ancient Greek patriarchal social institutions that restrict social authority to males, limiting females to less powerful domestic roles, embody a social ideology of overt masculine bias often openly misogynous in tone. This androcentric perspective is also clearly exhibited in ancient Greek mythological literature, providing an important context from which to examine feminine symbols of the divine. Thus, the ancient Greek social ideology serves as a model for the present discussion; an examination of Ugaritic social and gender ideology will be pursued below.

As discussed above, Ortner (1974) demonstrates that symbolic systems frequently associate females with nature in contrast to a male equivalence with culture. That is, patriarchal ideology often identifies women with the animalistic and irrational aspects of humanity while portraying men as the guardians of rational, structured civilization. This symbolic association of female with nature and male with culture supports an attitude that women, as animalistic creatures, must be controlled within male boundaries for society to remain properly ordered. Hence, patriarchal domination receives ideological legitimization as the necessary prerequisite for social stability. In fact, the historical process of urbanization in ancient Greece created a strong demarcation between male and female economic roles, with the result

---

3 Ortner (1974), Gould (1980), May (1984), Tyrrell (1984), Walcot (1984), Lefkowitz (1986), including bibliograhies, to name but a few. Gould (1980:55-6) notes the similar conclusions reached by the analytical psychologist Slater (1968) and the French structuralist school of Vernant, Vidal-Naquet, and Detienne (see R. Gordon 1981). Using such different methods, these scholars perceive a profound ambivalence concerning women on the part of ancient Greece.

that women were forced indoors while men were allowed greater opportunities in public circles (Pomeroy 1975:71). Thus, the process of generating and sustaining a Greek symbolic cultural system creates a polarity of gender roles and values in which females are depicted as less civilized than males. King (1983:110-1, 125 n.1) argues that Greek texts generally portray women as undisciplined and licentious because of their lack of self-control (cf. Lefkowitz 1986:112-21). Greek literature metaphorically identifies virginal girls in particular as wild, unbroken, and untamed fillies (King 1983:125 n. 4; Gould 1980:53). In Athenian mythmaking, patriarchal structures channel the negative potential of independent females. Proper marriages transform the untamed girl (*parthenos*) into the controlled and reproductive wife (*gynē*) who supports the institutions of patriarchal society. This transition from girl to wife is central to much Classical Greek myth concerned with the stability of Athenian society (see King 1983; Tyrrell 1984).

Women's perceived threat to social stability results in overt strategies for controlling female power in literature attributed to fifth-century BCE Athens, where control of females was "especially energetic," according to Padel (1983:3). May (1984:107) argues, "Fears of social disruption caused by women's malevolent use of their illegitimate powers were expressed by such figures as Medea and Clytemnestra who could not abide by the rules of the increasingly strident patriarchy." Euripides' *Bacchae* presents another literary scenario wherein women reject urban and domestic confinement and make their escape to the wilderness. The consequence of this symbolic rebellion is the females' reversion to animalistic behavior. These women are out of their minds, just as they are out of their place, and thus constitute a serious threat to patriarchal order (Padel 1983).

Vernant (1981b) analyzes the Greek myth of Pandora, the first and archetypal woman, who brings evil to mankind (cf. Lefkowitz 1986:113-5). Pandora is beautiful and seductive, desired by males who are unable to handle her. Indeed, she is sent by Zeus as a "headlong trap" for man, provided by Hermes with a "bitch's mind and a thieving nature," according to Hesiod (*Works and Days* 60-8). Pandora and her daughters are depicted as consuming everything which men work to produce but contributing nothing in return except sex and offspring. As a result of her introduction into the world, however, this role is now essential to the continuation of humanity. Significantly, it is ultimately not Pandora's sexuality which plagues mankind, but her lack of self-restraint and judgment. This devaluation of the feminine is also entrenched in the cosmogonic myth of Classical Athens, Hesiod's *Theogony*, in which the original feminine creation of Gaia is violent and chaotic. Through its culmination in the structured *polis* under the sovereignty of male Zeus, this mythological text communicates the value of rationality over irrationality, reason over violence, culture over nature, and male over female (Brown 1953:15-35). These examples from Greek literary and non-literary texts illustrate the belief that women may contribute to culture only through male control since unchecked feminine power would destroy the necessary social structures.

The ambivalence towards women as a powerful force which must be contained within patriarchal structures may also reflect the sexual anxiety of Greek males. According to Padel (1983:4), male "fears of carnivorousness in female sexuality" are evidenced in popular names for prostitutes like "the Lioness," and "the Panther." Based on their wild nature, females are pictured in Greek literature as more sexual creatures than males, more susceptible to the influence of the goddess Aphrodite. Like the Sirens' song, the erotic attraction of females promises pleasure but often results in evil or death for mortal men. Greek literature frequently depicts women as devious and dangerous figures, as in Euripides' *Hippolytus* where Phaedra's sexual passions destroy the men she desires (see Gould 1980:56-8). Hence, marriage serves within Greek sources as the proper channel for feminine sexual energies which are dangerous and destructive outside of male restraint.

Lefkowitz (1986:112) provides a balanced perspective on Greek androcentrism when she points out that Greek men were not necessarily afraid of feminine sexuality (cf. Walcot 1984) although they were wary of women in general. Lefkowitz (1986:36) summarizes the Greek attitude toward the proper social control of females:

> Since Greek myth glorified the role of mother, it also tended to condemn to infamy those who in some way rebelled against it. A confirmed virgin who resisted the advances of a god might get away simply with metamorphosis into a tree or flower, but women who consciously denied their femininity, like Amazons, or who killed their husbands and fathers ... were regarded as enemies and monsters.

More will be said below concerning the dangers of feminine sexuality and acceptable feminine activities within patriarchal ideologies.

Feminine Liminality

The preceding discussion presents marriage as the proper sphere for female activity according to patriarchal ideology, with examples from Greek literature. In addition to confining females within certain social structures, this ideology imposes severe constraints upon women's sexual activity. Female sexuality is particularly subject to stringent restrictions because it represents the most naturalistic, and therefore most culturally threatening, of human actions: sex and childbirth. The liminal character of these activities must remain under the control of males in order to alleviate the threat to both individual men and male society.

Social expectation requires virginal young girls to develop into mature, reproductive women, filling the role of wife and mother. Male authority is transferred directly from the girl's father to her husband, effectively containing the otherwise destructive energies of the female. The transitional, or liminal, stage between the two categories—daughter and wife—is fraught with the dangers of anti-structure.[4] As King (1983) convincingly argues, females during the transitional stage have no social value except in relation to their future status and they are therefore a dangerous commodity until reintegrated into a recognized social and sexual role. As a wife and mother, a woman occupies an important social position within the androcentric cultures of Greece and other traditional societies. Females who do not complete this transition—who remain independent of male domination—are a threat to the social and ideological structure of patriarchal and androcentric society (see Tyrrell 1984). They are no longer girls who will develop into women, but simply unmarried females marginal to accepted feminine categories and outside of the normal structures for securing social rank.

Furthermore, women who deviate from the social norms of marriage and motherhood are generally limited to two sexual roles: virgin or whore. Because marriage serves to tame her wild sexual passions, a female independent of this patriarchal constraint is doomed to either neglect or overly exploit her sexuality. While an asexual function may be acceptable for older widowed women, nubile young girls are expected

4. See Turner (1967; 1969) on the social importance of rites of passage and the terminology associated with them.

to fulfill their social duty and to channel their sexual energies through marriage and procreation. According to Greek ideology, the repression of feminine sexuality is dangerous to the female just as its exploitation outside of patriarchal control is socially disruptive (Padel 1983). Hence, a woman's sexual identity, based upon her sexual experience and availability, creates a central metaphor for social identification in androcentric ideology (see Pomeroy 1975). This sexual orientation of feminine symbolism is equally applicable to goddesses, who are often described as divine mothers, virgins, and whores.

Lefkowitz (1986:30-1) points out that Greek myths about goddesses and women concentrate on their relations to males and attribute special importance to the first sexual encounter. This emphasis illustrates the importance of sexual experience for the character and symbolic identity of goddesses in contrast to the more general depictions of gods. In fact, the term "virginity" encompasses a category truly applicable only to female deities, since sexual experience is never central to the mythic identity of male deities. "Virgin gods" with prominent mythological roles are virtually nonexistent, and only those human males who adamantly refuse to engage in sex because they are devotees of Athena or Artemis are noted in Classical myth. The English epithet "maiden" does have a masculine reflex in "youth" to designate a deity of adolescent character, but this epithet serves only as a social designation without any connotation of sexual experience. The feminine epithet "maiden," like "virgin," designates an unmarried girl with the implication of sexual inexperience. The application of these terms to divine images thus provides a symbolically important sexual component for the goddess. The symbolic status of maidenhood or virginity may be further separated into two primary categories in ancient Near Eastern and Classical mythology: youthful or perpetual virginity. That is, one must distinguish between those figures who have simply *yet* to engage in sex and those who will consistently abstain from sexual encounters. Examples of the former category include Atalanta and Persephone, while virgin goddesses such as Athena and Hestia represent the latter.

In his analysis of the myth of Persephone and Demeter, Kerényi (1969) discusses the psychological symbolism of virginity as it pertains to Kore, the divine personification of the youthful maiden. Kerényi (1969:120-4) argues that Kore and Demeter actually form a double figure, "the original Mother-Daughter goddess, at root a single entity."

This image represents the feminine cycle of maturation and marriage as the young girl is raped, becomes a mother, and loses her daughter to a male. Kerényi sees a cycle of rebirth in which the Mother mourns for her own loss of virginity as well as her daughter's. The maiden is abducted and carried away from her mother's house in order to become herself the mother within her husband's house. The myth of Persephone, in which Zeus allows the abduction of his daughter, thus relates that the transition from girl to wife is the inevitable conclusion (Kerényi 1969:107-9). The image of the reluctant bride is certainly a common mythic symbol which often conveys this same tension and resolution in favor of patriarchal society.

While a girl (*kore* or *parthenos*) is expected to mature into a woman, the perpetual virgin, such as Athena and Artemis, excludes herself from traditionally feminine categories, preferring a liminal role apart from the androcentric social structures. Given the sexual orientation of feminine symbolism, the rejection of feminine sexuality by the perpetual virgin goddess arouses questions concerning her gender identity; this is particularly so in the case of warrior virgin goddesses, addressed below. Of course, the symbolic nature of virginity in mythological literature encompasses more than just the idea of socially liminal characters. Dumézil (1973:123) notes:

> To be a virgin, to remain a virgin, is not simply to remain chaste. Chastity is of the order of purity; virginity is something higher, of the order of plenitude. A woman who remains a virgin conserves in herself, unutilized but not destroyed, intact, and as if reinforced by her will, the creative power that is hers by nature.

This creative power is understood by Dumézil to conserve and assure the various and necessary powers for social stability. The powerful, bud-like potential of females is an important mythic theme, focusing on the innate and wonderous ability of young girls. The metaphor of chastity emphasizes the internal aspect of this power which is not contingent upon any outside force. Indeed, the continued survival of the society rests in the ability of the maidens to become reproductive mothers. Without their consent to marriage, society would collapse. In discussing virgin goddesses in Hindu myth, Shulman (1980:148) adds, "Here we detect an intimation of paradox. Only the virgin has the power to create; but the act of sexual creation destroys the basis of that potential..." (see

Shulman 1980:140-8). Virginity in the realm of the gods thus provides a potent mythic symbol.

In contrast to those females who reject their sexual identity in order to maintain a celibate existence is the liminal female who indulges her sexuality through erotic behavior. Commonly described as love goddesses such as Aphrodite and Ishtar, these feminine deities are generally sexual but not maternal, erotic but not procreative, in their myths. The distinctions between feminine roles of mother, wife, and lover are clear in Greek myth, for example, in which Hera is the divine Wife, Demeter the divine Mother, and Aphrodite the divine Mistress.[5] The sexual exploitation of these erotic goddesses frequently results in their acquisition of titles such as "harlot" or "whore" within their native traditions, again evidencing an androcentric perspective on female sexuality. Although many scholars assume a typology of "goddesses of love and war" from the ancient Near East (e.g. Friedrich 1978:12-23; Gray 1985; de Moor), only some erotic goddesses are warlike. More central to their symbolic identity is their unrestrained power and independence from male dominance.

The ancient Greek embodiment of passionate love and sexual pleasure is Aphrodite, a goddess quite familiar to Western thought.[6] Born from the severed genitals of Uranus according to Hesiod (*Theogony* 188-200), Aphrodite is the patroness of sexual desire in both marital love and illicit sex. The Fifth Homeric Hymn describes the power of Aphrodite over all gods, humans, and animals, with only the virgins Artemis, Athena, and Hestia being immune to her coercive effects (see Friedrich 1978:65-9). Indeed, it is because of her boasting of this power that Zeus contrives for Aphrodite herself to suffer the ravages of passion for a human, the shepherd Anchises. With this exception, it seems that Aphrodite is never bound by love in her search for erotic gratification. The usually positive power of sexual desire may also be destructive, even as an encounter with Aphrodite can be detrimental to human males. Apart from the divine nature of erotic attraction, Aphrodite herself can be a truly malevolent force when angered or spurned (see Friedrich 1978:97-8). Yet this anger is never martial in context, as the weapons of

---

5 For a defense of the strict seperation of these roles in Greek myth, see Kerényi (1975) and especially Friedrich (1978). Note also Pötscher (1987). Jung (1973:21-34) provides a discussion of these archetypal feminine roles from his own perspective.

6 Friedrich (1978); Kinsley (1989:185-214); Downing (1981).

Aphrodite are the same as her enticements; she wounds through desire. Aphrodite's power lies in the feminine wiles or trickery of the socially powerless, and she punishes those who would reject or scorn her. This feminine rage, individual rather than social, perhaps reflects the anger of powerless women in the face of Greek society.

While this goddess of love does have a husband (Hephaestus) and child (Aeneas) in Greek mythology, she actively rejects the roles of wife and mother in order to retain her capricious independence. In fact, her marriage to Hephaestus is important primarily as a context for her wanton, adulterous behavior. She never has any offspring by her legitimate husband, preferring the charms of other males, both human and divine. Her behavior towards her one child, Aeneas, also illustrates the symbolic "denial of the mother." Although Friedrich (1978:61-2, 65-9) argues for a maternal side to Aphrodite, she does not care for her own child, giving him instead to nymphs to raise and then abandoning him again in the Trojan War when her hand is wounded (*Iliad* 5.297-448). Friedrich (1978:149-50) further describes her love for the child Adonis as maternal and analogous to Demeter's longing for Persephone, but I do not share his characterization of Aphrodite's love for Adonis as motherly. While this ubiquitous deity has complex symbolic associations, Aphrodite essentially embodies erotic pleasure and the rejection of maternal responsibilities in Greek myth.

Similarly, the Sumerian goddess Inanna, or Semitic Ishtar, is strongly associated with eroticism and female sexual pleasure (see Jacobsen 1976:23-74, 139-40). She is independent of male authority, childless, and wanton in her behavior. Yet, Inanna/Ishtar also serves an important function as warrior in ancient Mesopotamian myth, so she is analyzed more thoroughly in a later context. As a final example of erotic goddesses who serve little or no function as "mother goddesses," one might mention Radha, the lustful lover of Krishna. Forsaking her husband for nocturnal dalliances with the young god, Radha rejects maternal associations in her adulterous quest (see O'Flaherty 1980:103-4; Kinsley 1986:81-94).

In summary of this section on liminal roles, one sees the distinction in feminine imagery of those sexual and social roles open to females within androcentric myth. Marriage and motherhood define the socially acceptable position available to females, with all other options tending towards the fringes of proper society. Similarly, the mother goddess is a benign and passive figure, while independent goddesses often play more ambivalent and destructive mythic roles. The apparent fear of uncontrolled women in Greek myth betrays a social ideology which devalues the feminine and works to concentrate social authority in male hands. The male psychological fear of the sexually demanding and aggressive woman, discussed further below, is also evident in the attitude towards the wild nature of feminine sexuality. While these ideas are explicit in ancient Greek myth, they also appear in other androcentric mythological traditions, including those of the ancient Near East. The relevance of this subject to the analysis of Anat centers on her ambiguous role as maiden and her structural relationships to the other members of the Ugaritic pantheon, discussed at length below.

II. FEMININE WARRIORS

The comparative analysis of the goddess Anat must give due consideration to her infamous violence and blood-lust. In fact, numerous examples of murderous females and goddesses occur in world mythology, but there is a difference between the expression of anger through violent behavior and the structurally recognized role of warrior. While the rage of feminine characters may express itself through a burst of fury, as in the case of Aphrodite, many mythic warrior women perform martial and militaristic roles normally reserved for males. Thus, this section concentrates not upon the tantrums of otherwise benevolent goddesses but upon the more extreme examples of habitual and savage violence by goddesses, many of whom delight in blood and carnage. The common mythic role of warrior goddess is all the more surprising given the dearth of warrior women in human societies.[7] Few explanations are forthcoming for this most "unfeminine" behavior in the realm of the divine which seems to shatter the common feminine attributes of passivity and nurturance. Yet, fierce and violent goddesses take on many feminine forms ranging from virginal chastity to erotic excess, representative of sexual metaphors for feminine power. This diversity of type and the many social implications of these unrestrained mythic females provide much information concerning feminine social roles and images as presented in androcentric myth.

---

7 See Medicine (1983) for warrior women in Native American societies.

Virgin Warriors

Obvious examples of mythic females in militaristic roles are "virgin warriors," liminal characters who are female but do not perform traditionally feminine social roles. Typically, virgin warriors reject their normal social and sexual position as females, claiming independence from male domination. As discussed above, virginity may refer to an age category—a female who has yet to choose a mate—or the perpetual virgin, a female who makes the conscious decision not to engage in sex or marriage. The participation of youthful virgins in myths usually points to their inevitable integration into society as a wife and mother (e.g. Atalanta). This categorical group also encompasses those female characters who perform an important feat in a liminal occupation prior to their re-integration into their community. That is, certain feminine figures are socially acceptable in their violence because they perform some necessary function to restabilize society, as in avenging a blood feud. This temporary status as an asexual female is confined to a liminal period, as in the case of Judith in the apocryphal Jewish work named after her.[8] Indeed, as a widow, Judith is properly celibate and under no male's authority when she dedicates herself to save Israel through the murder of Holophernes. After performing this necessarily bloody role, she returns to her traditionally feminine position of virtuous widow. Even if sexually attractive, the liminal female warrior is frequently celibate, exhibiting gender traits best described as androgynous. Since femininity and warrior status are deemed incompatible in many contexts, the gender of warrior females is of great importance.[9]

---

8 For a discussion of the liminal nature of Judith, see Moore (1985), Craven (1983), and Montley (1978).

9 That is, both youthful and perpetual virgin goddesses often exhibit androgynous gender traits through their rejection of feminine roles. Judith is an interesting case within this context in that she combines attributes of both the virgin warrior and the murderous seductress whose feminine charms and eroticism are used to entice her victim into her fatal trap. This figure is discussed below in the context of Pughat's role in the *Epic of Aqhat.*

A modern literary example of the girl who dons warrior status for a period prior to reverting to her "normal" state and accepting marriage is the character of Éowyn in Tolkien's (1985) *Lord of the Rings* trilogy. Éowyn, princess and sister of the warrior prince Éomer, is able to kill the Nazgûl Lord, whom "no living man may hinder" (Tolkien 1985:140-3) after she lets down her hair and reveals herself as female. Fearless in the face of male opponents, the evil Lord loses his confidence upon

Athena and Artemis. In contrast to youthful virgins, perpetual virgins often play mythic roles pertaining to subjects other than female maturation. The most famous militant maiden in Western civilization is Pallas Athena, the figure many mythographers use as the archetype for the typological category of virgin warrior. The virginal status of Athena within the Greek pantheon is illustrated by her epithets, actions, and birth.[10] In the *Theogony*, Hesiod describes Athena as both "the terrible queen who loves the clash of wars and battles, who stirs up the fury and leads the armies and never retreats" and "the equal of her father in power and prudent understanding" (see Brown 1953:78-9). As the protector of Athens, Athena is a potent mythological symbol combining many aspects into a coherent form to communicate ideas within the ideological context of Classical Greek mythology. Athena represents the *polis* of Athens, for whom men are to live and fight, and her virginity serves as a metaphor for the impenetrable nature of the walls of Athens beginning in the fifth century BCE. Thus, modern mythographers frequently interpret Athena as a political and cultural symbol rather than a divine model of, or for, Greek women. Athena embodies the androcentric values of Athenian civilization in a potent feminine symbol.

In her article on the symbolic function of Athena, May (1984) examines the enigma of Athena in her role as a female who has "risen above her sex" in the Greek tradition. The gender hierarchy of Classical Greece expresses an aversion towards unrestrained women, yet the

---

encountering the female warrior. The virginal Éowyn, the "maiden of the Rohirrim ... fair yet terrible," is able to dispatch him with her sword—a feat unattainable by any male warrior no matter how skilled or brave. Afterwards, she renounces her self-proclaimed role as a "wild shieldmaiden" in order to be "tamed" by a husband (Tolkien 1985:299-300). Here the idea of virginity and warriorhood seem to be closely connected; Éowyn sheds both roles at the same time.

10 The birth of Athena is also important in structural relation to Aphrodite, Athena's polar opposite. Athena and Aphrodite are both described by Hesiod as having no mother, each originating from a male alone. While the militaristic Athena springs forth from the head of Zeus and is equated with rationality, Aphrodite emerges from the severed phallus of Uranus within the foamy sea and embodies carnal lust. The structural relationship of these two goddesses forms a sexual polarity in that each is dependent only upon males for their origin and symbolic function. Athena rejects feminine sexuality in order to associate with males, while Aphrodite revels in her sexuality (see Brown 1953).

independent Athena explicitly demonstrates allegiance to patriarchy.[11] Through the complete rejection of her feminine sexual identity, Athena is free to associate with males in a supportive sisterly role. Friedrich (1978:83) notes that most of the heroes whom she befriends—Heracles, Odysseus, Achilles, Diomedes—are also sons of Zeus, making them actual siblings. Kerényi (1969:107) states that Athena's virginal status frees her from sexuality without forfeiting "the characteristic peculiar to male divinities...., namely, intellectual and spiritual power." In other words, her asexuality allows her access to traditionally male attributes such as restraint, reason, proficiency, and prudence. Athena is always described in Greek myth as calm and thoughtful, never overcome by blind fury or battle frenzy.[12] Taking his characteristic approach to Greek mythology, Kerényi (1978:3-19) unfortunately describes Athena as a "virgin mother."[13] Downing (1981:118-9) is undoubtably more correct in interpreting Athena's "maternal" associations—as guardian of weddings, children and marriage—not as fertility symbolism but as an aspect of her identification with the structures and continuity of Athenian civilization.

The paradox of a feminine symbol for the androcentric society of fifth-century Athens is explained by May (1984:112), with special reference to the Athena Parthenos statue:

> Wearing a warrior's helmet and carrying the spear and shield of the hoplite, she rose above her sex and signaled her intention to enter the male domain. While the masculine talismans served to neutralize her female generative powers, it was nevertheless important that the goddess' female identity remain apparent and not disguised. In a society rent by the extreme sexual

---

11 In his discussion of the independent nature of goddesses in the Greek mythological tradition, Kerényi (1978:20-1) argues that only Aphrodite is truly independent since Athena is under the authority of Zeus. I rather interpret Athena's relation to Zeus not as the daughter of a dominating father, but as the voluntary acquiescence to patriarchal rule. In this way Athena represents the values of androcentric social ideology.

12 The charges of Ares in the *Iliad* (5. 870-80) are certainly slanderous. While Athena may have had a more belligerent side in early Greek myth, she is consistently portrayed as rational and restrained in extant sources.

13 Kerényi (1978:25) states that Athena's "maternal associations are hidden behind the image of *martial maiden*, but they do not contradict it. The inner contraditction of the figure is nonetheless undeniable: it lies in the representation of a *virginal mother*." In his attempt to make Athena more representative of the divine feminine Kerényi (1978:26-7) also argues for the early association of Athena with a male Pallas figure, from an original androgyne.

> dimorphism characteristic of this period, with men and their activities the locus of cultural value, the only possible unifying symbol would be a woman dressed as a man.

While May resorts to an overly emphatic functionalist explanation, she does recognize an important aspect of Athena's symbolic value within the pantheon. Athena represents the dependence of stable Greek society upon the control of the disorderliness and destructive powers of women. Athena's explicit support for the triumph of patriarchy over archaic feminine chaos is displayed in Aeschylus' trilogy, the *Oresteia*, wherein Athena presides over the trial and casts the deciding vote valuing father over mother, male over female. Athena defends her decision by stating that she is always for the male in all things, except in marriage (Aeschylus' *Eumenides*, 736-8). While this self-conscious statement must be understood within the context of the narrative as an attempt to appease the Erinyes, it nevertheless gives insight into the androcentric attitudes associated with this maiden goddess.

Further evidence for the identification of Athena with Greek civilization is furnished by the sculptures and scenes depicted upon and within the Parthenon (May 1984:111-3; DuBois 1982). This civil monument portrays, among other mythological events, the contest of Athena and Poseidon for the city's patronage, Athena's birth from the head of Zeus, and the Athenian Amazonomachy. Inside of the Parthenon stood the statue of Athena Parthenos holding a shield whose inside carried another portrayal of Amazonomachy (see Lefkowitz 1986:20). Concerning the role of Athena and the defeat of the Amazons in these reliefs, Tyrrell (1984:20) concludes, "One warrior-maiden successfully gives her name to the city, while the annihilation of the others affirms that it is under male control." The theme here is obviously that civilization overcomes barbarism, with Athena representing the "enlightened, sophisticated, refined city life; she was the enemy of anything crude, uncivilized, or barbaric" (Kinsley 1989:145). Thus Athena symbolizes the subjection of the feminine characteristics of disorder, typified by the Amazons, to the regulation of patriarchal authority. The consistent symbolic association of Athena with androcentric social ideology in Greek myth supports the conclusions of Tyrrell and other mythographers who apply a "social ideology" method of myth interpretation.

In contrast to the martial and civic character of Athena, the virginal Artemis rejects Greek culture and urban life in favor of the wilderness (see Vernant 1987). While both virgin goddesses refuse marriage and motherhood, Artemis the huntress may represent the denial of the very social ideology and civic values that Athena embodies. Friedrich (1978:82-3, 86-7) analyzes Artemis as a young, unmarried sister figure, symbolizing certain sexual and local anxieties about married life. Artemis identifies closely with her mother, Leto, and kills numerous humans to protect her mother's honor. This attitude contrasts with the necessary separation of mother and daughter in the myth of Persephone. Friedrich argues that Artemis symbolizes virginity and chastity in a manner that sets her apart from others; with the exception of Hippolytus, she is generally an inaccessible and distant character. Similarly, Kerényi (1969:107) explains,

> [Artemis'] world is the wide world of Nature, and the brute realities balanced in her—unsubdued virginity and the terrors of birth—have their dominion in a *purely naturalistic, feminine world.* Athena's maidenhood excluded the very possibility of her succumbing to a man; with Artemis, on the other hand, her maidenhood presupposes this possibility.

According to these psychological interpretations, Artemis, as patron of maidenly rituals and childbirth, represents the fears and tensions of feminine adolescence.

King (1983:118-22) convincingly argues that Greek medical texts closely associate Artemis with the transitions of girls (*parthenoi*) to women (*gynaikes*), especially in relation to the shedding of blood at menarche, defloration, and childbirth. Artemis does not shed her own blood, but sheds others' blood through initiating this feminine maturation process. As Detienne (1979:187-9) points out in his structuralist analysis, only males are supposed to shed blood in war, hunting, and sacrifice, according to Greek values. Thus, Artemis is taking on a male requisite in her relation to females' bleeding, just as she appropriates the masculine role of hunter. King holds that through menarchy, defloration and childbirth, Artemis helps other females to cross the boundaries into social and sexual maturation that she herself refuses to cross. In fact, the association of non-procreative women with childbirth and midwifery is common. By retaining their own sexual energies and creative abilities, celibate females are thought to have a certain power which is helpful to females under their ministrations (see Hoch-Smith and Springs 1978:1-21).

Like King, Vernant (1987) emphasizes the liminal characteristics of Artemis. He offers a structuralist interpretation of the virgin huntress in which she represents the mediation between the natural and cultural realms of human existence. Rather than embodying the complete rejection of culture, Artemis actively symbolizes the necessary interpenetration of the natural and cultural worlds in her myths. Thus, Artemis' patronage of hunting does not represent her exclusive identification with nature, according to Vernant, since hunting was not a savage activity in ancient Greece. The hunt is a strictly regulated component of education and acculturation for Greek youths. Artemis presides over this liminal activity to insure that humans, entering the animal realm as a predator, do not transgress the limits of acceptable human behavior by engaging in unrestrained brutality. Hence, Artemis' association with the wild identifies her with the interpenetration of nature and culture as much as their opposition. That is, she presides over the unavoidable ambiguity of human culture's symbolic boundaries in order to reinforce the proper distinctions between human and animal behaviors. Vernant similarly relates Artemis' association with the birth process to her role as the guardian of liminal situations. She is concerned with birth because this is the time when the animal nature of humanity is most clear. Similarly, as the *kourotrophos*, "rearer of the young," Artemis is the patroness of human and animal babies. She nurtures and guides human children to the threshold of adolescence. Once children accept their proper social role as adults in a segmented society they are abandoned by Artemis. As Ortner proposes, the feminine symbol of Artemis effectively mediates between nature and culture by emphasizing their boundaries as well as their necessary overlap in human existence.

Finally, Artemis is totally ineffectual as a warrior, as portrayed in the *Iliad* (21.460-96) where her arrows are broken and she is thrashed with her own bow by the angry Hera. Friedrich (1978:95) observes that "Artemis' hunting is more probably an aspect of her supervision over the life and death of wild animals; she fosters their young but also slays in the hunt, just as she helps women in labor yet sometimes slays them too." Her androgynous gender is thus important to her role as huntress as well as to her relations with adolescent girls approaching maturity.

Hence, Artemis is not truly a warrior, although she is a virgin who is at times lethal. This maiden is particularly deadly to those males who encounter her in a possibly sexual situation; thus, the figure of Artemis is further discussed below within the conext of the motif of hunter and huntress in the Ugaritic tale of Aqhat. It suffices for the present to note her ambiguous role as an independent maiden who mediates between the natural and cultural components of human existence and whose social liminality is intimately connected to her sexual availability.

Durga. Of less familiarity to most readers is the Indian goddess Durga, a fierce and bloody goddess created by the gods in Hindu mythology for the sole purpose of slaying demons who threaten the stability of the cosmos.[14] Although Hindu texts do not consistently describe Durga as a "virgin warrior," the canonical textual tradition portrays her as a warrior goddess who explicitly claims the status of manhood for herself and abstains from all sexual activity. Indeed, the very males Durga slaughters are those who propose marriage to her. Her rejection of their sexual advances is equated to the rejection of her feminine role in Hindu ideology. Hence, Durga is an asexual or, from the feminine perspective, a virginal character, analogous in form and function to other warrior females who reject their feminine sexual role in order to pursue the masculine role of warrior. This warrior goddess is especially important to the present study because of her relation to the Hindu goddess Kali, analyzed below, whom scholars frequently invoke in studies of Anat.

The history of Durga as a recognizable goddess is verifiable from the early centuries of the Common Era, although scholars date her origins to the pre-Aryan cultures of India rather than to the male-dominated Vedic pantheon. Kinsley (1986:96) reports that iconographic representations of Durga slaying the buffalo-demon Mahiṣa are common throughout India in the fourth century CE, with her cultic worship becoming prominent after the sixth century CE. Durga's mythic exploits are eventually recounted in many Sanskrit texts of the Hindu Great

---

14 On Durga see Kinsley (1986:95-115; slightly revised in 1989:3-24) and Shulman (1976; 1980). The work of these specialists forms the basis for the present discussion of this warrior goddess within the Hindu mythological tradition. Note also Bhattacharyya (1977:57-67) on warrior and bloodthirsty goddesses in Hindu myth.

Tradition (see Kinsley 1986:233 n. 3), where her epithets include *kumārī*, "maiden" (Marglin 1985:55).

The primary mythological narrative concerning the warrior character of Durga is in the *Devī-māhātmya*, dated to approximately the sixth century CE.[15] This text recounts Durga's slaying of Mahiṣa, a buffalo-demon terrorizing the universe. Upon completion of severe austerities, Mahiṣa becomes extremely powerful and is granted a favor by Brahmah. Thinking that no female could ever overpower him, Mahiṣa states that if he must die, he wishes to be killed by a woman. Armed with this apparent invincibility, Mahiṣa attacks the ruling gods and gains control of the cosmos for himself. Frustrated by their inability to expel the usurper, the gods decide to create a warrior capable of defeating this demon who threatens the cosmic order. By emitting their fiery energies, the gods merge their key powers to form the body and weapons of the warrior goddess who emerges impatient for battle. Thus, the beautiful Durga is comprised of the best qualities and strongest powers that each god has to offer.

Explaining that Sanskrit versions usually gloss over or omit entirely the sexual aspect of this scene, O'Flaherty (1980:82-3) translates one Sanskrit expansion of this text from the *Bṛhaddharma Purāṇa* (5.2-11) where the erotic element is clear. When Mahiṣa receives Durga's invitation to battle he responds by sending his messenger to the goddess with his proposal of marriage.

> But she replied that she wanted to kill him, not sleep with him—that she had become a woman in the first place only in order to kill him; that, although she did not appear to be a man, she had a man's nature and was merely assuming a woman's form because he had asked to be killed by a woman. Moreover, she said to Mahiṣa's messenger, "Your master is a great fool, and certainly no hero, to want to be killed by a woman. For to be killed by one's mistress gives sexual pleasure to a man without balls but misery to a hero." The besotted Mahiṣa, however, was persuaded by a counselor, who suggested that this clearly antierotic speech was the amorous love talk of a passionate woman: "She wishes to bring you into her power by frightening you. This is the sort of indirect speech that enamored women use toward the man they love." Mahiṣa then dressed up in his best suit and boasted to the goddess that he was a man who could make a woman very happy. She laughed and killed him by beheading him.

---

15 This separate work constitutes chapters 81-93 of the *Mārkandeya-pūraṇa*. See Kinsley (1975:90-1; 1986:95-100), O'Flaherty (1980:81-2), Beane (1977:175-80), and Shulman (1976) for discussions of this narrative.

Later in the same text (5. 10. 32-4) the counselor's interpretation of Durga's "amorous love talk" is given: "When she said, 'I will cause your master to lie down in a bed that is made of battle', that was an obvious reference to the 'inverted' position. And when she said, 'I will take away your life's breath', she meant (that she would take away) semen, for semen is the life's breath." O'Flaherty (1980:81-7) emphasizes the symbolic equivalence of beheading and castration in her Freudian interpretation of this narrative.

The motif of the underestimation of Durga's warrior prowess and offer of marriage by her opponent appears in other texts as well. Kinsley (1986:97-9) states that in the *Devī-bhāgavata-purāṇa* (5.16.46-65), for example, Mahiṣa insists that Durga, as a female, is too frail and delicate for battle. Rather, she needs a male to protect and care for her; she needs a husband to fulfill her. The assumed helplessness of a woman is common to traditional Hindu attitudes towards females, as presented in the *Dharmaśāstras*. Here, as elsewhere, women are only significant in relation to some dominating male—father, brother, husband—and their social position is defined according to their sexual role. Only rarely, as in the case of Parvati, do females have independent status in Hindu mythological traditions.

In some versions, Durga states that her family has imposed a condition that her prospective husband must defeat her in battle prior to their marriage. The suitor's test is common in other Hindu traditions where the god must first subdue his wife in a contest, but here it appears as a ploy to lure the demon to his death.[16] Durga's manipulation of Mahiṣa's lust in fact weakens him prior to the battle itself (Shulman 1976:122). In addition to the Sanskrit traditions, the erotic aspect of this narrative is explicit in southern versions, where the marriage context is particularly important. Shulman (1976:125) notes a Tamil tradition in which Durga taunts Mahiṣa when he objects to battle because she is female. She questions his virility with the response, "If you are indeed a man, come and show your mettle...." Here Durga actively provokes Mahiṣa using sexual suggestions that he would recognize as an invitation to defeat and marry her. In contrast to his expectations, the female

---

16 Indeed, the motif of having to defeat a women in some contest in order to marry her is also common in Greek literature (see Lefkowitz 1986:43-4), among others.

Durga proves completely competent to care for herself and it is Mahiṣa who loses his head over the woman.

Kinsley (1986:99) make the insighful point that Durga is beautiful, seductive, and "irresistibly powerful," yet her beauty serves not to attract a mate, as expected, but to "entice her victims into fatal battle." Thus, Durga is portrayed here as "possessing untamed sexual energy that is dangerous, indeed, deadly, to any male who dares to approach her" (Kinsley 1986:114-5). Shulman also notes the erotic attraction of the virgin goddess within Hindu tradition, explaining that the source of attraction and power resides in the goddess' undefiled virginity. "For it is the virgin goddess who is the true siren, seductive, powerful, dangerous. The god who desires her must face the threat of death at her hands; in the end, either he dies—as in the myth of Mahiṣa…—or he tames his fearful bride" (Shulman 1976:133). Hindu goddesses are typically presented as fierce and dangerous prior to their marriage and must be subdued and "tamed" by their husbands (see Babb 1975:216-37; Shulman 1980:176-91, 211-23). The theme of "taming" a woman through marriage, common to many myths and folktales concerning the transition of young girls into mature women, is addressed further below.

While Durga's decapitation of Mahiṣa has its erotic elements, the warrrior goddess is herself a completely asexual figure in this episode. The centrality of Durga's celibacy to this myth is reflected in the South Indian tradition's explicit claim that only a virgin goddess is powerful enough to defeat the demon (Shulman 1980:147-8). Apart from her victims, Durga does not associate with males. She fights with only the aid of other female warriors whom she brings forth from herself in parthenogenic fashion. Kinsley (1986:97) comments on the independent stature of Durga in contrast to the typical model of Hindu females:

> She is not submissive, she is not subordinated to a male deity, …and she excels at what is traditionally a male function, fighting in battle.... Unlike the normal female, Durgā does not lend her power or *śakti* to a male consort but rather *takes* power from the male gods in order to perform her own heroic exploits. They give up their inner strength, fire, and heat to create her and in so doing surrender their potency to her.

In contrast to the usual male-female relationship in Hindu mythology, Durga indeed drains male gods of their power for her own benefit (see Shulman 1976:128). The independence from male dominance that Durga enjoys is thus considered dangerous to males. It is significant that

Durga plays roles that are outside of normal social structures, and that she is mythically depicted as dwelling in areas on the fringes of society. Durga's ritual associations further reflect her liminality (Kinsley 1986:97).

While Durga's earliest canonical representation is as an independent warrior goddess, she is eventually identified with the goddess Parvati as the wife of Shiva (see Kinsley 1989:3). According to this historical interpretation, Durga is later assimilated to the Hindu pantheon as but one manifestation of the one Great Goddess, the Mahadevi, and given certain maternal characteristics. The hypostatic explanation of the Hindu deities is treated below within the context of Kali-Durga and Hindu Shakti theology. Yet even after mainstream Hindu theology identifies her with the one Great Goddess, Durga retains her aggressive and virginal character as the guardian of cosmic stability within certain Hindu traditions. Worshipers maintain the independence of Durga through her cultic veneration and the recitation of the ancient myths (see Babb 1975:215-7).

To conclude the discussion of virgin warriors, each of the three mythic figures under consideration has rejected her normal feminine social and sexual roles in order to take on the masculine role of warrior or hunter. While Artemis can be a lethal maiden she does not play the role of warrior in Greek myth. Rather, she exhibits certain associations with adolescent females on the brink of social and sexual maturation. As one who rejects the feminine conventions of society in order to remain untamed and wild, Artemis offers a stark contrast to Athena, who embodies the values of Athenean culture and civilization. This juxtaposition of the two Greek virgin goddesses—along with the domestic spinster Hestia—present alternative reactions to feminine roles within the context of the Greek pantheon. Durga's mythic role as warrior is more bloody and frenzied than Athena, although Marglin (1985:55) points out that Durga's role is "salvific and entirely beneficient." That is, all three virgin warrriors play roles supportive of structured mythic society, even if they do not fit into its feminine categories. Particularly with regard to Athena, this function illustrates the allegiance to patriarchal social institutions upon which society is based.

Finally, all three of these virgin goddesses are sexually attractive young females rather than repulsive hags or bloody gorgons. The power of virginity, or feminine celibacy, is perhaps central to each character's mythic role and function as a violent female. While these goddesses support the structures and values of androcentric ideology, it is noteworthy that each of them threatens individual males who approach them sexually or on the battlefield. The erotic aspect of virginal goddesses and the sexual tension surrounding them in mythological texts are addressed below.

Sexual Warriors

In contrast to the virgin warriors just discussed, certain mythological female warriors retain a feminine sexual role while rejecting traditionally feminine social positions. Exploiting their feminine sexuality outside of the proper constraints of marriage, these mythological females maintain their independence from male authority while engaging in overtly masculine acts of institutionalized violence. The combination of the active eroticism of Aphrodite with the martial function of war gods generates a certain mythic tension to these "goddesses of love and war," making it appear that it is the eroticism of the goddesses which is dangerous to males. The sexual aggressiveness of these goddesses, such as Ishtar, toward whomever they choose worthy of their affections is in direct contrast to the nonthreatening and sexually passive role expected of wives. In direct opposition to virgin warriors, who are lethal if approached sexually, are female warriors who are sexually active but whose eroticism can be equally threatening to males.

Amazons and Valkyries. The Greek pantheon does not encompass a female figure who mediates the passions of sex and war, preferring to contain warrior skill within the bounds of civilized behavior. Ares is presented as a passionate warrior, ruled by his emotions rather than his intellect, but he has no feminine counterpart. Perhaps the idea of a goddess of sex and violence was too much of a threat to Greek androcentric ideology. Indeed, warrior women are employed in Classical myth explicitly to symbolize the complete rejection of Greek culture and all of its values, thus creating the Amazon as the archetypal feminine warrior (see Tyrrell 1984; DuBois 1982; Lefkowitz 1986:15-29).

Renowned for their fierceness in battle, the Amazon queens are reported to have ruled martial societies in which women occupied dominant positions and males are tolerated only for their sexual necessity. Prior to their peremptory defeat by Greek forces, Amazons lived on the edge of the civilized world as a constant threat to the ordered Athenian social ideology, according to legends of the Classical period. In direct opposition to the norms of Athenian society, the gynocentric culture of the Amazons restricts males to domestic duties and child care within the house, while women enjoy the politicial privileges and authority of the greater society (Tyrrell 1984:45-9). Hence, the former matriarchal institutions of these militant females in Classical literature represent the complete antithesis of contemporary Greek patriarchal society.

Amazons embody the Greek fear of unruly women, presented above, in their political legitimation within a gynocentric society. In contrast to the illegitimate use of power by murderous females within Greek society, these warrior women exercise legitimate authority and power, yet in each case the result is utter chaos. From an anthropological perspective, Bamberger (1974:279) explains that myths of ancient matriarchies are frequently social charters offering justification of "male domination through the evocation of a catastrophic alternative—a society dominated by women. The myth, in its reiteration that women did not know how to handle power when in possession of it, reaffirms dogmatically the inferiority of their present condition." The Athenian patriarchal attitude towards gynocracy is certainly similar.

Tyrrell (1984) also stresses the Athenian social context in his thorough discussion of the role and symbolic value of Amazons within Greek mythology. He further argues that the Amazon myth must be seen within the context of individual social maturation and marriage. Tyrrell (1984:64-87) particularly emphasizes the Athenian social imperative that boys develop into warriors and girls become wives and mothers of sons. This transition is essential to social continuity, but the Amazon myth portrays the reversal of this ideal. According to Tyrrell's extensive analysis, Amazons represent the figure of girls who fail to become adults through marriage. Amazons personify the transitional girl who has left social infancy but has not yet been integrated into adulthood. "They are one permutation of the female outside marriage—armed, sexual, and dominant" (Tyrrell 1984:xviii). Women who reject their social postion of wife and mother are equated to Amazons who maintain their sexual and social independence. As I argue below, this is a common mythic theme concerning warrior women.

While they compete with men in manly pursuits of hunting and warfare, Amazon women are certainly sexual creatures. They actively engage in sex, yet threaten their mates with aggressive dominance and, at times, emasculation or death (Tyrrell 1984:86-7). Indeed, men are reportedly captured by Amazons for the sole purpose of sexual services, after which they are executed. Sexual encounters with Amazons are dangerous for males, although the two heroes Theseus and Heracles find the Amazon queen attractive enough to warrant the risk. Marriage to Amazon women must inevitably fail, however, as these two accounts show. Indeed, Amazon society represents the negation of proper marriage (DuBois 1982:40). Tyrrell (1984:65-6) summarizes his interpretation on the sexual role of Amazon warriors:

> They are beautiful women who arouse men sexually, but their erotic appeal cannot be civilized by marriage, its proper sphere, and so is loose, socially unproductive, and dangerous. Like Greek girls, Amazons mate with males and bear children, but they do not leave their mothers for the house of a husband, nor do they become, like Greek women, wives and mothers of sons. They are mothers of daughters who live with mothers.

Again, one sees the theme of independent women serving as a threat to androcentric society. As a group Amazons threaten the Greek social order and patriarchal structure; as individuals they may threaten a man's sexuality and life. In the end, however, the warrior status of these militant women proves no real threat to the superior force of Greek civilization. The Athenian males summarily conquer the foreign women invading the Acropolis and there commemorate forever the defeat of gynocratic ideology (see Lefkowitz 1986:20).

While the ancient Greeks portray the armed and erotic female warrior as a social aberration doomed to failure, other cultures present the feminine warrior as a manifestation of the divine. One obscure source for mythological figures of warrior females is the Old Norse, Germanic and Anglo-Saxon traditions concerning Valkyries and other battlemaids.[17] Indeed, the wealth of literary material concerning divine

---

17 See Davidson (1964:61-6), Damico (1984:41-56, 200 n. 2), and Donahue (1941).

female warriors remains to be exploited by scholars of Indo-European mythology. The lack of available information concerning the mythological role of the valkyries prevents any detailed discussion, but mention should be made of these feminine warriors who choose the slain in battle (Davidson 1964:61-6). Davidson (1964:62) writes, "It seems that from early times the heathen Germans believed in fierce female spirits doing the commands of the war god, stirring up disorder, taking part in battle, seizing and perhaps even devouring the slain."[18] Damico (1984:41-3) describes the figure of the valkyrie:

> For the most part, Old Norse poetic tradition conceives of the valkyries as noble, dignified women; they are generally pictured either astride their horses in full armor, riding through the air over land or sea, or welcoming the *einherjar* to Valhalla with cup or horn outstretched. .... In contrast to this radiant, courtly warrior-figure, Old Norse literature records what is thought to be an earlier conception of the valkyrie as an elemental force, a fierce battle-demon....

While valkyries normally take virginal attributes, the "valkyrie-brides" of the Eddic heroic lays play a more erotic role in their marriage to a human male (see Damico 1984:87-105). The three poems concerning the hero Helgi—the Helgi lays—within the *Poetic Edda* are dominated by the motif of the hero beloved by a valkyrie. The love of a valkyrie leads to death for the hero Helgi, but this conclusion does not have a totally negative value. Similarly, the Norse goddess Freyja, the "chief valkyrie," plays a complex role as a fertility, war, and erotic goddess (Damico 1984:80-1; Davidson 1964:114-24). Damico (1984:48) attributes a perverted eroticism to Freyja, who is portrayed in Eddic poems as "a voluptuous, sexually insatiable creature." While further research on these figures is required for analysis of any depth, it is sufficient for the present discussion to note the appearance of these sexually active warrior goddesses in Norse mythology.

Inanna/Ishtar. The most developed of the independent goddesses of love and war is the Mesopotamian goddess Inanna/Ishtar.[19] A syncretic

---

[18] Davidson (1964:64) continues, "Old Norse literature has left us with a picture of dignified Valkyries riding on horses and armed with spears, but a different, cruder picture of supernatural women connected with blood and slaughter has also survived."

[19] The basic secondary sources on Inanna/Ishtar are Edzard (1965:81-9), Wilke (1976), Seidl (1976), Hallo and van Dijk (1968), Jacobsen (1976:27-63, 135-43), and

fusion of the Sumerian Inanna and the Semitic Ishtar, this composite goddess is of central importance to the discussion of Anat since both play prominent roles in ancient Near Eastern mythology concerning violent females independent of male authority. While Inanna/Ishtar is granted the diverse epithets and attributes of any great deity—"Queen of Heaven," "compassionate protector," "most worthy of praise"—she is consistently identified with warfare and erotic delight. Scholars have emphasized the association of Sumerian Inanna with sex and Akkadian Ishtar with war in the attempt to explain the goddess' bipolar character through syncretistic adaptation (see Heimpel 1982), but such historical explanations avoid the mythic symbolism of the composite goddess in Mesopotamian religion. Indeed, cultic hymns to Inanna/Ishtar frequently praise her as the simultaneous representative of indulgent feminine sexuality and the masculine arts of war. While many Mesopotamian hymns do accentuate one element, Vanstiphout (1984:229-30) argues that this focus is determined by the literary genre rather than by Inanna/Ishtar's consistently diverse character. Thus, the seemingly contradictory aspects of this ancient goddess form a coherent image of the autonomous female in the realm of the divine whose independence from male control contributes to her exploitation of sexuality and violent aggression.

Some of the earliest mythic presentations of Sumerian Inanna clearly attribute martial combativeness to her character (see Bottéro 1987:172-6). Perhaps her bloodiest characterization is given in the still unedited text of *Inanna and Ebih*, which portrays Inanna attacking the rebellious people of the mountainous area (*kur*) of Ebih (Jebel Hamrin) for not adequately honoring her.[20] This motif continues throughout Sumerian literature, as seen below. Kramer (1979:24) explains that the Sumerian word *kur* originally meant "mountain," but since the mountainous regions to the north and east of Sumer were inhabited by people hostile

---

Kramer (1979:71-97). Note also the discussions by Heimpel (1982), Vanstiphout (1984), Groneberg (1986), and Bottéro (1987).

20 Regarding this text see Kramer (1972:82-3, 118 n.77), Limet (1971), and Sjöberg (1975). While a geographical reference is probably intended by Ebih, Jacobsen (1976:53) also points out the common association of these mountains with the Underworld.

to Sumer it came to designate "inimical land." Kramer (1979:76) translates a portion of this hymn:

> Lordly Queen of the awesome *me*, garbed in fear, who rides the great *me*,
> Inanna, you who have perfected the *a-ankara* weapon, who are covered with its blood,
> Who storm about in great battles, who step upon shields,
> Who initiate the flood-storm,
> Great Queen Inanna who are knowledgeable in planning combat,
> Destroyer of *kur*, who have shot the arrow from your arm, who have planted your arm upon the *kur*,
> Like a lion you roared in heaven and earth, you smote the flesh of the people,
> Like a big wild-ox you stood up eager for battle in the inimical *kur*,
> Like an awesome lion you annihilated with your venom the hostile and the disobedient.

Praising Inanna as the "Devastatrix of the lands" (l. 17), the *Exaltation of Inanna* was written by the priestess and poetess Enheduanna in the late third millennium (Hallo and van Dijk 1968; cf. Kramer in Pritchard 1969:579-81). Excerpts from this early hymn include the following lines:

> In the van of battle everything is struck down by you.
> Oh my lady, (propelled) on your own wings, you peck away (at the land).
> In the guise of a charging storm you charge.
> With a roaring storm you roar.
> With Thunder you continually thunder.
> With all the evil winds you snort.
> Your feet are filled with restlessness.
> To (the accompaniment of) the harp of sighs you give vent to a dirge.
> Oh my lady, the Annuna, the great gods,
> Fluttering like bats fly off from before you to the clefts,
> They who dare not walk(?) in your terrible glance,
> Who dare not proceed before your terrible countenance.
> Who can temper your raging heart?
> Your malevolent heart is beyond tempering. (ll. 26-39)
>
> That you devastate the rebellious land—be it known!
> That you roar at the lands—be it known!
> That you smite the heads—be it known!
> That you devour cadavers like a dog—be it known!
> That your glance is terrible—be it known!
> That you lift your terrible glance—be it known!
> That your glance is flashing—be it known!
> That you are ill-disposed toward the…—be it known!
> That you attain victory—be it known! (ll. 125-32)

Kramer (1979:96-7) quotes a self-laudatory chant of Inanna in which she states, "[Enlil] has given me battle, he has given me combat.... I, a warrior am I!" Kramer (1979:88-91) translates additional Sumerian texts glorifying the warrior prowess of Inanna.

As commonly noted, battle is the "dance" of Inanna/Ishtar to the ancient Mesopotamians.[21] As patroness of combat, Inanna proclaims:

> When I stand in the front (line) of battle
> I am the leader of all the lands,
> when I stand at the opening of the battle,
> I am the quiver ready at hand.
> When I stand in the midst of the battle,
> I am the heart of the battle,
> the arm of the warriors,
> when I begin moving at the end of battle,
> I am an evilly rising flood,
> when I follow in the wake of the battle,
> I am the woman (exhorting the stragglers):
> "Get going! Close (with the enemy)!" (Jacobsen 1976:137)

In the Epilogue to the *Code of Hammurapi*, the Babylonian king requests various gods to protect his stela and punish any who would alter it. It is significant that his petition to Inanna, described as "the Lady of battle and conflict," includes the following curse of his enemy:

> May she shatter his weapons on the field of battle and conflict; may she create confusion (and) revolt for him! May she strike down his warriors, (and) water the earth with their blood! May she throw up a heap of his warriors' bodies on the plain; may she show his warriors no mercy! (Pritchard 1969:179-80)

Inanna/Ishtar's bloodlust and eagerness for battle is also evident in a late bilingual text noted by Hallo and van Dijk (1968:51) that depicts her

---

21 One Sumerian reference to battle as the "dance of Inanna" is in Jacobsen (1976:137). On the frequent martial epithets of Inanna/Ishtar, such as *Ištar ša mēlultaša tuquntu*, "Ishtar, whose play is battle," see *CAD* 10/2:15-7 (s.v. *mēlultu*) and 13:12, 14-5 (s.v. *qablum*). *CAD* 1/2:111 (s.v. *anantu*) also records the line "O Ishtar, yours is strife, rebellion, troubles, fighting and carnage" from an Old Babylonian hymn. Most of these references occur in bilingual hymns to Inanna/Ishtar.

Suggested etymologies for the name Inanna also reflect this violent tendency. Roberts (1972:36) has explained the form *Inin* as a *pirs* formation of the Akkadian verb *anānum*, "to skirmish," while Vanstiphout (1984:225) suggests an original Sumerian *IR.NIN, "victoria," which was later traditionally etymologized as *(*n*)*in-an-a*(*k*), "Lady of Heaven."

flying out to battle and heaping up severed human heads like harvested rushes.

Later texts also exhibit the battle fury of the fierce lioness Inanna/Ishtar (Fauth 1981). She serves as the patron for the Neo-Assyrian Empire, granting oracles to Esarhaddon and Ashurbanipal as the overtly militaristic Ishtar of Arbela, fully armed with a bow, two quivers, and sword (Pritchard 1969:449-51, 606). Indeed, this is a common iconographic portrayal of Inanna/Ishtar (see Barrelet 1955). A Neo-Babylonian prayer to Ishtar (Pritchard 1969:384) describes her as "Lady of battle," "supporter of arms, who determines battle," and "the one covered with fighting and clothed with terror." These texts provide evidence for the bloodthirsty and aggressive components of Inanna/Ishtar's mythic character and her uncontrollable nature.

In contrast to her martial manifestations, a consistent tradition dating from early times depicts Sumerian Inanna as a young girl involved in courtship with Dumuzi. Perhaps these courtship texts represent the maturation process of the goddess from virginal maiden to sexual adult. Indeed, the typically lustful Inanna is actually portrayed in one myth (BM 23631) as sexually inexperienced and innocent.[22] But this depiction of Inanna as sexually innocent is certainly overshadowed by the explicit and numerous references to her active sexuality. One particular text (Ni 9602), called the *Herder Wedding Text* by Jacobsen (1976:43-6), includes Inanna's hymn in honor of her vulva. She compares it to the "Boat of Heaven" and the crescent moon before continuing:

As for me, my vulva,
For me the piled high hillock,
Me, the Maid, who will plow it for me?

---

22 In this text the young Inanna says to her brother, Utu the Sun god,

That which pertains to women—copulation—I know not,
That which pertains to women—kissing—I know not,
I know not copulation, I know not kissing (Kramer 1979:95).

Kramer (1979; 1985) argues that Utu wishes to seduce Inanna, but this interpretation is not necessary. Indeed, Utu always seems to play a protective role over his young sister and arranges her betrothal in Sumerian myth. Because this text continues with Inanna's request that she be returned to Ninsun, her mother-in-law, and to Geshtinanna, her sister-in-law, one may assume that she is already engaged to Dumuzi.

My vulva, the watered ground—for me,
Me, the Queen, who will station ox there?

To which the answer comes,

Oh, lovely Lady, the king will plow it for you,
Dumuzi, the king, will plow it for you.

Inanna joyfully responds,

Plow my vulva, man of my heart.
(Kramer 1979:78)

Indeed, Inanna/Ishtar's connection to erotic passion and physical sex is clearly and abundantly attested.[23] Consistently portrayed as voluptuous and beautiful, this nubile goddess incites and partonizes unrestrained sexual desire (see Bottéro 1987:170-2).

Inanna/Ishtar is often defined as a "mother goddess" by modern scholars (e.g. James 1959; Gray 1985), but such a designation is simply incorrect. While Inanna/Ishtar is surrounded by definite fertility connotations, they are based primarily upon her personification of physical desire in both human and animal realms. Inanna/Ishtar never exhibits maternal characteristics in Mesopotamian myth, and her attributes of fertility and fecundity are secondary to her position as an erotic, nonprocreative goddess. That is, sexual activity leads naturally to procreation, but it is only the erotic aspect of this process which is associated with Inanna/Ishtar, not childbirth or nurturance. In addition to her primary role as the patroness of sex, Inanna/Ishtar's association with natural fecundity and abundance is further explained by the secondary relation of all important ancient Mesopotamian deities with fertility (cf. Fauth 1981). That is, the inherent power of the divine encompasses the ability to bestow or withhold the rains and natural fertility necessary for human survival. This divine prerequisite should not be confused with any particular association of Inanna/Ishtar with maternal characteristics.

The natural catastrophe provoked by Inanna/Ishtar's detention in the Underworld in the Akkadian myth concerning her famous descent is portrayed primarily as a languishing of sexual vigor on the part of

---

23 See also Jacobsen (1976:32-47; 1987:88-9, 93-4) and Kramer (1969) on erotic poetry and sacred marriage texts.

humans and animals rather than her inattention to a role as cosmic mother (see Pritchard 1969:106-9). Indeed, the Sumerian version of Inanna/Ishtar's descent to the Netherworld does not mention any response to her "death" on the part of the natural realm. Just as sexual desire ceases when Inanna/Ishtar is detained in the realm of the dead, so she may choose to withhold her patronage when angered. For example, the provocation of Inanna/Ishtar to action by inattention to her worship in a certain land—most probably an allusion to the myth of *Inanna and Ebih* noted above—is depicted in the *Exaltation of Inanna* by Enheduanna. The wrathful goddess brings into play the combination of her powers over nature—the general control of natural fertility and her particular influence over sexual ardor—to punish the recalcitrant people:

> Like a dragon you have deposited venom upon the land
> When you roar at the earth like Thunder, no vegetation can stand up to you. (ll. 9-10)
> In the mountain where homage is withheld from you vegetation is accursed.
> Its grand entrance you have reduced to ashes.
> Blood rises in its rivers for you, its people have nought to drink. (ll. 43-5)
>
> Over the city which has not declared "The land is yours,"
> Which has not declared "It is your father's, your begetter's"
> You have spoken your holy command, have verily turned it back from your path,
> Have verily removed your foot from out of its byre.
> Its woman no longer speaks of love with her husband.
> At night they no longer have intercourse.
> She no longer reveals to him her innermost treasures.
> Impetuous wild cow, great daughter of Suen,
> Lady supreme over An who has (ever) denied (you) homage? (ll. 51-9)
> (Hallo and van Dijk 1968:15-23)

The role played by Inanna/Ishtar within the Mesopotamian pantheon is never maternal or matronly; she is consistently portrayed as a nubile young goddess in Sumerian and Akkadian texts. While Sumerian myth identifies her as a bride to the ill-fated Dumuzi, this erotic goddess is never restrained by matrimonial duties or responsibilities. The social relationship between Inanna and Dumuzi and her role in causing or lamenting his death—as well as the theological purpose of the sacred marriage myth—in Sumerian mythology are confusing and unclear. However, the mythological evidence suggests that Inanna is a bridal rather than a wifely figure. Since she and Dumuzi have no offspring, the widowed Inanna probably maintains the mythic social position as maiden rather than fully mature woman—or she is in a liminal state betwen the two recognized categories. Socially this is certainly true, since she never settles down to monogamy again in Mesopotamian myth.

Virginity and widowhood aside, Inanna mythically represents the role of maiden or bride, not mother/wife. Sumerian texts commonly designate Inanna/Ishtar as a maiden or adolescent female by the epithet *ki sikil* (Sjöberg 1976:200). This epithet appears most commonly in hymns celebrating her erotic and martial roles (see Kramer 1979:76-7). Although Ishtar is not frequently given a similar Akkadian epithet, she is certainly depicted as a nubile young female. In fact, the Akkadian mythological material more clearly identifies Ishtar as an adolescent figure, the overly exuberant daughter of Anu, who takes no spouse and has no children. Bottéro (1987:171-2) emphasizes the independent role of Inanna/Ishtar, arguing that even if she is infrequently given the metaphorical title of the "spouse" of Anu she is never tied to marriage within the larger tradition. The active sexuality of Inanna/Ishtar does not serve marriage and procreation, but is always directed toward her own pleasure. As a sexually mature female, Inanna/Ishtar is marked by her lack of a husband in Mesopotamian myth. This independence is perhaps at the root of her volatile moods and unrestrained behavior.

Arguing that ancient Near Eastern deities, like all others, are constructed on analogies from human personality and society, Bottéro (1987:176) attempts to describe the female type, or "origin," for Inanna/Ishtar in her bipolar aspects of love and aggression, a female who is at the same time desirable and forbidding. According to Bottéro, the human exploitation of erotic sexuality is facilitated by prostitutes, whose paragon and patroness is Inanna/Ishtar. Indeed, this goddess carries the blunt epithet of "prostitute" in both Sumerian (*kar.kid*) and Akkadian (*ḫarimtu*). One bilingual text designates her the "loving prostitute" (*ḫarimtu rāʾimtu*) in Akkadian, while the Sumerian version renders the phrase more crudely as the "prostitute familiar with the penis" (Bottéro 1987:171-2; *CAD* 10:101). Bottéro argues that Inanna's Sumerian title *nu.gig* means "prostitute" and thus *nu.gig.an.na*, usually translated as the "Hierodule of An," is actually the "Heavenly Hierodule."[24]

---

24 While Hallo and van Dijk (1968:87) also hold that Sumerian *nu.gig* is equated with the Akkadian *ḫarimtu* "prostitute," Jacobsen (1987:6 n. 9) more correctly equates

Seizing upon this divine function, Bottéro (1987:177-9) attempts to interpret the bipolar character of Inanna/Ishtar as the Divine Courtesan through analogy to the social role of human prostitutes in ancient Mesopotamia.[25] Confined to the spatial and ideological fringes of society, prostitutes are a disruptive force, generating conflict and discord. Yet all levels of men come to them for their services, seeking erotic titillation apart from matrimonial stability. Bottéro holds that Inanna/Ishtar is not a bellicose deity but is simply emeshed in the discord which her professsion inevitably causes. Bottéro notes the myth of *Enki and the World Order* in which she is given the offices of pestering, insulting, and deriding.[26] Indeed, a Neo-Babylonian prayer to Ishtar (Pritchard 1969:384) describes her as she "who causes peaceable brothers to fight." She embodies the contradictions of love and its inconveniences—erotic charm and social discord. Thus, Bottéro explains Inanna/Ishtar's martial character as only an extension of her originally quarrelsome nature. She is a fractious female, rather than a warrior, whose image is based upon her sexual role as prostitute.

---

nu.gig with Akkadian *qadištu* "holy one," a cultic functionary of some kind (see *CAD* s. v. *qadištu* and *ḫarimtu* for references to bilingual lexical texts). Although she is asociated with feminine sexuality and human prostitutes, Inanna/Ishtar does not play the role of a prostitute among the gods in the available Mesopotamian sources (cf. Sjöberg 1977). Indeed, she appears to prefer human lovers. The modern presumption that sacred prostitutes were active in the temples of Inanna/Ishtar has recently faced serious scholarly challenge (see Oden 1987:131-53). Note Aphrodite's similar association with prostitutes (Friedrich 1978:141-2).

[25] In truth, it appears that Bottéro constructs his analogy based upon modern prostitutes rather than the little we know concerning ancient Mesopotamian women.

[26] Similarly, Vanstiphout (1984:226-8) refers to Inanna/Ishtar's "jealous concupiscence" with reference to her acquisition of the *me*'s from a drunken Enki (see Farber-Flügge 1973; Alster 1976) and the doleful fate of her many lovers listed by Gilgamesh (see Abusch 1986). In her constant struggle for more and greater power, prestige, and lovers, Inanna/Ishtar is never content with what she has gotten. In this regard, Vanstiphout (1984:230-1) notes the text, variously named *Ea and Ṣaltu* or the *Agušaya Hymn*, in which Ea proclaims to the Assembly that Inanna/Ishtar's irritating behavior can no longer be tolerated (see Groneberg 1981; Foster 1977). In order to put an end to her contentiousness, he creates Ṣaltu, whose name means "strife, contention, quarrel," from the dirt under his fingernails. This creature then beseiges Ishtar with her own attributes of battle, loud noise, and unrelenting discord. Although an important part of the tablet is missing, the mythological tale concludes with Ishtar altering her behavior and Ea causing Ṣaltu to disappear.

While Bottéro's interpretation has the benefit of explaining the unity of Inanna/Ishtar's dual association with love and war, his approach is methodologically weak. Yet even if his speculative argument accurately describes the development of Inanna/Ishtar's mythic identity, Bottéro concludes his study without analyzing Ishtar's actual mythic roles where she is clearly depicted as a warrior and not an angry prostitute. Feminine sexuality is probably of central importance to explaining the combination of seemingly antithetical components in Inanna/Ishtar's mythic character. But Bottéro, in reducing a complex divine figure into a simple social metaphor, has not offered an interpretive model with which to approach this analysis.

Of great importance to the analysis of Inanna/Ishtar is also the masculine characteristics attributed to her in Mesopotamian sources. In addition to her role as warrior, with its ambiguous gender position, are overt references to her as male, bearded, or associated with transvestite cultic functionaries. Explanations of these masculine aspects of Ishtar, in particular, suggest an androgynous quality to this mythic character. In his study of ancient Near Eastern Venus deities, Heimpel (1982:14-5) discusses the male aspects of Ishtar with reference to the syncretistic fusion of the Sumerian female evening star (Inanna) and the male morning star of the Semitic world (Athtar). Thus, the "male" and bearded Ishtars are mythic remnants of the earlier Akkadian male morning star deity. Heimpel concludes that Mesopotamian Ishtar is certainly not an androgynous deity, but that she is manifested in male form as the representative of the morning star in northern Babylonian cults as a reflection of the originally separate Semitic deity. For comparative support for bisexual deities, Heimpel refers to the bearded Aphroditos on Cyprus and the Hurrian Shaushka—identified with Ishtar—who appears as male and female on rock reliefs from Yazilikaya. This original gender distinction is also relevant to the combination of the roles of love and war deities into one mythic figure.

In her more recent discussion of divine hermaphroditism and the bearded Ishtar in the Assyrian cult, Groneberg (1986) engages Heimpel's study. Countering his distinction between the male and female Ishtars as Semitic and Sumerian, respectively, Groneberg (1986:31-3) emphasizes the lack of conformity in equating the male Ishtar as a northern representative of the morning star and the female Ishtar as the southern representative of the evening star. Instead, she emphasizes the use of gender and other symbols to distinguish between various cultic manifestations of Ishtar. As a goddess independent of male authority, Inanna/Ishtar takes on certain male epithets, which may be understood not as gendered terms so much as they emphasize her acquisition of roles usually reserved for males. Groneberg notes the holistic portrayal by Mesopotamian texts which attribute the entire spectrum of masculine and feminine powers to this goddess.

Hence, Inanna/Ishtar's bipolar nature combines and mediates many opposites. Groneberg (1987:42-4) notes the mythic theme of the "inverted world" as a context for Ishtar's ability to change right to left, and males to females. The activity of various transvestites and other liminal characters in her cult provides evidence for the non-normative character of the goddess Ishtar. Her associations with such opposite phenomena as the morning and evening stars, heaven and the Underworld, erotic sex and castration of males, and intimacy and conflict further illustrate her antithetical nature. This liminality is especially important since Ishtar is not a mother goddess in Mesopotamian myth. Hence, the seemingly androgynous character of Ishtar must be understood symbolically, spanning the abyss of polarity. Groneberg holds that this diversity further represents Inanna/Ishtar's mythic characterization as an unpredictable, unrestrained goddess.

Groneberg (1986:44-6) concludes that Inanna-Ishtar is a feminine goddess who is only figuratively endowed with masculine power, one symbol of which is a beard. Inanna/Ishtar's equality with the male gods is thus symbolized through her acquisition of the male prerogatives. Rather than an androgynous being, Inanna/Ishtar is a feminine gendered goddess with additional masculine attributes. Indeed, the ambiguous use of gendered epithets is merely one symbolic representation of her liminal mythic character. The common use of sexual imagery to define feminine characters, noted above, is particularly clear and potent in the case of the erotic and martial Inanna/Ishtar. Scholars have often identified Anat as the Western manifestation of Inanna/Ishtar and, in fact, the two goddesses are similar in many respects. Therefore, more attention is given to Inanna/Ishtar below, especially within the context of Anat's relation to the youth Aqhat. We will return to the question of female sexuality as dangerous to masculine virility after analyzing one more example of violent females.

Bloody Mothers

To summarize the previous section, virgin warriors use their independent status to reject feminine sexuality and feminine social roles while erotic warriors manipulate their independence to indulge their sexuality. The final group of violent females to be discussed are maternal figures who engage in bloody violence. This last category is comprised of goddesses who are procreative mothers, thus necessitating some sexual activity, but are generally not erotic in character. Furthermore, the delight taken in bloody carnage by the figures under consideration—Kali and Sekhmet—is antithetical to the generally nurturing role played by divine mothers.[27] Thus, these goddesses reject the traditionally passive maternal role to exercise their bloodlust against enemies of the cosmic order. In contrast to malevolent demons, these divine mothers resort to savage violence in support of universal good. Their actions, however, often threaten to engulf or destroy humanity.

While the psychological archetype of the Devouring Mother has sparked much modern discussion (see Neumann 1956), there is little mythological evidence for mothers who devour their children or husbands. Freudian and Jungian interpretations of certain mythological characters may contribute to the construction of modern images, but actual "mother goddess" figures who turn deadly are rather isolated. Clytemnestra and Medea provide good archetypes for human females who murder their children and husbands as a rejection of their maternal role within the patriarchal order. In Aeschylus' *Agamemnon* (1389-92) Clytemnestra describes her murder of her husband in the following terms:

> Breathing out a spurting slaughter of bloody gore, he hits me with a dark shower of bloody dew. In it I pleasure no less than the new-shorn field in the joy sent by Zeus at the birthing of the buds. (Tyrrell 1984:99)

---

[27] The women in the Dionysian rampages of Euripides' *Bacchae* might be identified as bloody mothers, for example. See also the Hindu *mātrkās* "Mothers," associated with Kali, in Kinsley (1986:151-60). Noted as early as the *Mahābhārata*, these spirits are driven away from their human homes and families, denied motherhood, and take on alternately bloody and maternal roles toward human children. For the neglected concept of a Devouring Father figure, note Kronos' ingestion of his children in Hesiod's *Theogony*.

This exercise of bloody violence is antithetical to maternal nurturance, emphasizing the barbarity of the deeds in Greek literature.[28]

Hathor-Sekhmet. One notable example of the murderous mother is found in the Egyptian goddess Hathor-Sekhmet.[29] In a short myth dating back to at least the fourteenth century BCE which Wilson translates as *Deliverance of Mankind from Destruction* (in Pritchard 1969:10-11), humans revolt against the authoritative rule of the sun god Re. The goddess sets out to diminish the number of rebellious humans in accordance with the wishes of Re, but she becomes intoxicated with bloodlust. Mythically identified as a hypostatic manifestation of Hathor, Sekhmet exults in her victorious slaughter and makes plans to continue her carnage on the following morning. Apparently afraid that Sekhmet's lack of restraint will result in the complete annihilation of humanity, Re floods the battlefield with red-colored beer during the night. Arriving at dawn, Sekhmet happily drinks the blood-red mixture and becomes too drunken to remember her lethal intentions towards the human race. Thus, Re is responsible for the deliverance of humans from utter destruction.

Although she plays a minor role in available Egyptian myth, Hathor is a very complex and versatile goddess whose character combines many diverse attributes (see Bonnet 1952:277-82). She is variously associated with the sun, heavens, trees, dancing, music, royalty, fertility, death, inebriety and joyous revelry. One can distill perhaps two central aspects—maternal and martial—in her relationships with Re, the elder Horus, and other male gods. Hathor is represented iconographically as a mother goddess in bovine form. In addition to fertility and childbirth, she patronizes love and sex, earning the epithet "mistress of the vulva" according to Bleeker (1973:39-40). Hathor's martial character is portrayed by her epithet "Lady of Terror," who is joyful in battle and full of fury for the enemies of Re (Bonnet 1952:282). The combination of joyous revelry and wrathful vengeance in one goddess presents a figure of passion and enthusiasm, to be sure. The most violent manifestation of Hathor, Sekhmet, is a fierce warrior whose

---

28 Note the discussion of Clytemnestra's repudiation of marriage in Aeschylus' *Oresteia* in Tyrrell (1984:33-39, 93-104) and Lefkowitz (1986:119-23).

29 On Hathor see Bonnet (1952:277-82), Bleeker (1973:22-105), and Daumes (1977). On Sekhmet see Bonnet (1952:643-6) and Germond (1981).

theriomorphic form is a lioness (Bonnet 1952:643-6). Although a combative function is central to her character, Sekhmet is not always destructive in her violence; she also protects the universe from enemies of the gods (see Germond 1981). In addition to her martial character in Egyptian mythlogy, Sekhmet has power over epidemics and is thus a goddess to be much feared and placated.

The obscurity of ancient Egyptian mythology, as well as the anomalous structure of the pantheon, prohibits any in-depth analysis of Hathor- Sekhmet. Although she is considered a mother goddess (contra Bleeker 1973:38-9), the range of Hathor's mythic character should preclude any attempt at categorization. Her violence appears to have no connection to her sexual identity. In her manifestation as Sekhmet the goddess exercises no erotic attraction nor does she threaten males in particular. Indeed, Sekhmet acts according to the instructions of Re in her aborted annihilation of humankind; her bloodthirsty violence is not directed against the divine order. While her role in quelling a rebellion among humans may be seen in a positive light, Sekhmet's capricious behavior gives cause to fear her.

Kali. The fearsome Hindu goddess Kali (*Kālī*) is often invoked as a comparison for Anat's violent mythological characterization (e.g. Eaton 1964:76-8; Albright 1968:130-1; Pope 1977:607-10). Scholars describe Kali as a Devouring Mother figure whose symbolism reflects the male psychological perspective of the Mother as both beneficent and destructive (see Neumann 1956). Indeed, the malevolent character and bloodthirsty exploits of Kali are similar to the violent behavior of Anat, who wades in blood up to her knees and fashions a sash of severed hands and a garland of human heads to adorn herself. Analysis of this comparison beyond the point of reference has yet to be presented, however, and a convincing explanation for the similarities is still lacking.[30] While many goddesses perform violent and murderous acts, myth analysis must consider the contextual value of the episode and character.

The function and position of goddesses within Hindu myth are very difficult to assimilate in the present comparative analysis. In the

30 While Albright (1968:130-1) suggests that the similarities are too close for coincidence, his diffusionist theory concerning a prehistoric type from which each goddess developed does little to further discussion.

introduction to his book-length study of Hindu goddesses, Kinsley (1986:1-5) stresses the great diversity of feminine images of the divine within Hindusim. The ubiquitous feminine symbolism, the range of goddess types, and the sheer number of goddesses characterize Hindu myths among the world mythologies. The dynamic interrelations of gods and goddesses within the mythological traditions further hinder the systematic discussion of the Hindu female pantheon. Individual goddesses are frequently difficult to distinguish one from another because of the multiple names, epithets, and forms (*avatāras*) under which they appear. The multiplicity and contradictory nature of the various Hindu mythological traditions over a wide temporal and geographic range further exacerbates the problem of synthesis. This diversity and the uniquely Hindu orientation of many divine symbols greatly complicate comparison with other mythological traditions and pantheons.

One indigenous response to the diversity of the Hindu pantheon is the explanation that all goddesses are actually manifestations of the one Great Goddess (*Mahādevī*), who encompasses the polarities of creation and destruction as the embodiment of the cosmic cycle of life and death (see Kinsley 1986:132-50). This Goddess theology is not simply the result of a monistic tendency but is the systematic identification of all godddesses as aspects of the feminine divine. Although the Mahadevi theologically subsumes all goddesses into herself, many goddesses have maintained their individual character in cultic, iconographic and mythological representation (see Babb 1975:215-29). The mythological and theological depiction of Kali must be understood from within this uniquely Hindu context. Even though Kali originated in Hindu myth as a virginal warrior goddess, the theological development of her persona by later devotees has resulted in a composite deity with maternal attributes. In an attempt to clarify this situation, Kinsley (1975:81-149) traces the historical development of Kali from a hypostatic deity embodying the fury of Durga, to an independent warrior goddess identified as a manifestation of Parvati, and finally into the personification of the Mahadevi (see also Beane 1977).

The goddess Kali is truly a repulsive figure in Hindu mythology and iconography, where she is portrayed wearing severed human arms as a girdle, infants' corpses as earrings, and decapitated heads as a necklace.[31] Either naked or clothed with a tiger skin, Kali has a black complexion, long disheveled hair, clawlike nails, sunken bloodshot eyes, and a gaunt and emaciated body with sagging breasts. Her gaping lips curl to emit a terrifying roar, revealing her long fangs and lolling tongue dripping with blood. Kali's multiple arms menacingly brandish various blood-smeared weapons, a freshly severed head, and a skull from which she imbibes blood. The favorite haunts of this grisly goddess are the battlefield, where she may indulge her craving for blood, and the cremation ground, where she is often pictured sitting on a corpse surrounded by jackals and goblins. When intoxicated by battle, the frenzied Kali howls with insane laughter and dances wildly, shaking the earth and threatening the cosmos with destruction if not subdued. Kali is a most fearsome deity, yet her attitude towards her destructive capacity is one of revelry and light-hearted play. This repulsive representation of the fierce and malevolent goddess with a ravenous appetite for human flesh and blood is consistent throughout her mythological history.

Although Kali appears in earlier texts, Kinsley (1975:90-3) states that she makes her canonical debut into the Great Tradition of Hinduism in the *Devī-māhātmya*, where she aids Durga in defeating the demonic forces assembled against the gods.[32] The dark Kali springs from the furrowed brow of Durga as her personified wrath. Kali eagerly enters the fray against the demons, whom she crushes in her jaws and decapitates with her sword (7.3-22). She truly delights in blood and carnage, sporting with the decapitated heads and limbs of her victims. Indeed, her fondness for drinking blood is instrumental to the defeat of one demon, Raktabīja, whose flowing blood, upon touching the earth, produces replicas of himself. Realizing that her sword and arrows are only worsening the situation, Durga calls upon Kali for aid. The black goddess swallows the blood-born creatures in her gaping maw and sucks all of Raktabīja's blood from his very body, thus killing him (8.49-61). In this text the role and character of Kali is clearly established as the unrestrained and violent aspect of the divine. She is subordinate to

---

31 The basic source is Kinsley (1975: 81-150), summarized in (1986:116-31), with bibliography. On the intrinsically Hindu interpretation of her nature see also Brown (1988).

32 For the prehistory of Kali see Kinsley (1975:86-8) and Beane (1977:61-119).

Durga, personifying the most ferocious and terrifying aspect of the virgin Hindu goddess.

Kinsley (1975:93-6) explains that Kali's minor role as a bloodthirsty and destructive manifestation of Durga remained essentially the same in medieval Hinduism. The acceptance of this seemingly demonic goddess into the maintream Hindu pantheon was slow and largely contingent upon her association with the god Shiva. In the *Devī-māhātmya* Durga maintains an independent status, even though she is understood to have emerged from Parvati. In the *purāṇas,* on the other hand, Kali, Durga, and Parvati are often presented as simply manifestations of the Mahadevi (Kinsley 1975:102-3). It appears that as an independent deity Kali remained peripheral to the mainstream pantheon, but once recognized as a manifestation of Parvati, the traditional spouse of Shiva, she was adopted into the canonical pantheon (see Kinsley 1975:101-8). In the *Vāmana-purāṇa*, for example, *kalī* "the dark one" is an epithet of Parvati, although there is a distinction between her and the violent Kali. Indeed, in one tradition Parvati performs austerities in order to rid herself of a dark, outer sheath, which is transformed into the goddess Kaushki, from whom emerges the warrior Kali. Parvati is henceforth described as Gauri, the "golden one" (Kinsley 1986:119; cf. O'Flaherty 1980:111), in distinction to black Kali.

The mythological presentation of the hypostatic nature of Kali is seen more clearly in the *Linga purāṇa*. Here is also recounted a story concerning a great demoness who usurps the rule of the gods. Since none of the gods wishes to fight a female, they send Shiva to ask his wife Parvati to battle the demoness. She obligingly creates from herself Kali, described in the familiar repulsive form, who eagerly enjoins battle with the usurper. Upon defeating the demoness, however, Kali becomes intoxicated with bloodlust and threatens to destroy the world in her frenzy. In order to save the cosmos from destruction, Shiva intervenes in the form of a crying child lying amongst the corpses on the battlefield. Kali hears his cries, picks him up and begins to nurse him as her madness subsides (Kinsley 1975:104; 1986:118). The maternal characteristics of Kali are thus developed in these texts as she is more clearly identified with the Mahadevi.

Thus, Kali is transformed from an independent warrior goddess into the recognized consort of Shiva, also a liminal deity of macabre and malignant characteristics. Associations such as this aid in consolidating the Hindu pantheon and harmonizing different mythological traditions through assimilation and reinterpretation. This theological development enhances the traditional characters of Durga and Kali, but it also transforms their identities as "virgin warriors" through the acquisition of a male consort. The association with Shiva gives greater prestige to the warrior goddesses, but it also subjugates Durga and Kali to less independent forms of divinity. Indeed, even some of the traditional myths concerning Durga and Kali are reinterpreted to include the presence of Shiva. For example, the myth of Durga's slaying of the buffalo-demon Mahiṣa is reinterpreted in some Indian traditions to equate Shiva with Mahiṣa (see Shulman 1976; O'Flaherty 1980:80-7). In this context the mythological scene takes on different connotations concerning the relationship between the goddess and her consort. In the *Devī-māhātmya* Kali, like Durga, has retained her "virginal" status and concludes her battles once the demons are annihilated. In later developments of Kali's warrior prowess, however, Shiva must intervene to calm his frenzied spouse. That is, the earlier portrait of Kali presents her as a more self-controlled goddess, while later texts describe her as requiring the discipline of her male consort.

The dance of Kali and Shiva is a particularly prominent theme in the mythology and iconography of Kali. When dancing together they may incite one another to wilder and more frenzied behavior, but Shiva is also seen as calming the mad Kali through dance and dance contests. The motif of the dance contest is very similar to the aforementioned "suitor's test" myths of Durga in that Shiva's defeat of the goddess does pacify and subdue her as a prelude to their marriage (Kinsley 1975:104-6; cf. Shulman 1980:211-23). Often Kali is humiliated upon recognizing the superiority of the god. This proof of male supremacy thus "tames" the goddess and prepares her for marriage. Of particular import to this theme is the point that Shiva is said to win the dance contest by performing the *tāṇdava* dance step, thrusting one leg straight up into the air, while the goddess is unwilling to expose herself in this manner. O'Flaherty (1980:140-3) concludes that the goddess is defeated—or, rather, disqualified—because she will not sacrifice her feminine dignity. O'Flaherty states that this is "precisely the point of the myth: by affirming her subservience *as a woman*, she ends the contest." In gaining Shiva as a consort, Kali becomes subservient and more feminine, losing her independence and violent power.

The point of these myths is apparently more sexual than cosmic in nature, focusing on Hindu gender concepts. Indeed, Kinsley (1986:4) argues that Hindu myths about godddesses often express thoughts about sexual roles, relationships, and identities. While Shiva often plays a malevolent role, here he is portrayed as taming the wild Kali in order to save the cosmos from her destructive powers. As noted above in the discussion of Durga's virginity, Hindu goddesses are typically presented as fierce and dangerous prior to their marriage. Their female sexual energies must be controlled and channeled by their husbands to benefit rather than destroy the ordered universe (see Babb 1975:216-37; Shulman 1980:176-91, 211-23). By accepting male dominance the dangerous females are "tamed" and rendered fit for marriage. Pent-up sexual energies provide females with a certain violent power which threatens males, and cosmic order, in Hindu thought.[33] Hence, when Kali is cultically associated with Shiva she plays a secondary role as the dominated and subservient female. But when depicted alone, Kali retains her violent and bloodthirsty power, emphasizing the significance of her independent function (Shulman 1980:218-23).

Even though mythically associated with Shiva, Kali is most frequently depicted as an independent and powerful goddess in her cult and iconography. A most common iconographic depiction of Kali focuses on the myth found in versions of the *Ramayana*, among other texts, in which Kali again engages in a frenzy of drinking blood and unrestrained dancing that will destroy the entire cosmos (Kinsley 1986:236 n. 10). In this myth Shiva intervenes in the form of a corpse lying under her feet. Upon recognizing the corpse as her husband, Kali ceases her dance in embarassment and the world is again saved. Kinsley (1975:107-8) suggests that the more passive role of Shiva in this myth

---

[33] Note Marglin's (1985) criticism and clarification of the position taken by Shulman and Babb on taming female sexuality in Hindu ideology. Marglin argues that it is not female sexuality that constitutes a dangerous power in need of control, but celibacy itself wherein lies danger. Marglin (1985:52-6) holds that female sexuality has a high this-wordly value in association with fertility, while asceticism, although of higher spiritual value, represents drought and sterility. Indeed, many Hindu myths deal with how to control the accumulated power of female ascetics. A goddess' shakti can produce either auspicious or inauspicious power and it is this ambivalence, rather than female sexuality itself, which is malevolent. Feminine power is made auspicious to the world through "conjugal or any sexual relationship." Sex "tames" a male just as much as a female in Hindu literature according to Marglin.

marks the move from Shiva's dominance to the later dominance of Kali in this couple. Indeed, in this mythic scene Kali mounts the erect phallus of her dead consort. This most popular iconographic representation of Kali and Shiva may be variously interpreted. Brown (1988:114) explains that Kali's energy or shakti flows into Shiva, reviving his corpse and producing an erection. Thus, she is the energy sustaining her spouse in the typical Hindu interpretation, rather than draining him of his life. Yet Kali is in the dominant position, receiving his seed into herself in order to fertilize the world. It is noteworthy that she is the active initiator of this scene, rather than the submissive, passive partner.

In later texts, especially the *Devī-bhāgavata*, Kali assumes a dominant position over Shiva, probably evidence for the development of Goddess theology (Kinsley 1975:106). This dominance is further developed in certain Tantric literature (Kinsley 1975:109-14) and in Bengali Shakta devotionalism where Kali is explicitly identified as the personification of the Mahadevi (Kinsley 1975:114-24; Brown 1988; Beane 1977). It is within this context that Kali develops the identity of the great Mother of the universe, emphasizing the cyclical nature of life and death, creation and destruction. Kali, merged with the other virgin warrior goddess Durga, is given maternal attributes and worshiped as the great Mother. As Beane (1977:ix) explains, "Durgā-Kālī is the theistic manifestation of a wide-spread concept in Indian religion called *Śakti*, or the religion of 'Power.' As the 'Goddess' (*Devī*) she is regarded as both Mother of Timelessness and Life and Arbitress of Time and Death." She is the "prototypical image of the worship of Feminine Power" which underlies the entire cosmic cycle (Beane 1977:1).

In contrast to many psychological interpretations of Kali (e.g. Neumann 1956:150-3), the identity of Kali as Mother is less for her maternal characteristics than for her cosmic role as Creatrix and Sustainer. Within the Hindu ontological system the creation and destruction of the universe are but two aspects of one unified cycle. Brown (1988:110, 121) explains,

> It is she, according to her Hindu followers, who creates, governs, and controls the whole of existence. She is the mother of us all, giving us birth from out of her unfathomable depths.... As the good and terrible mother, she represents, or is, the power of the material world—Mother Nature, in her creative, nurturing, and devouring aspects. These really are not separate aspects, for without

> eating her children, how could she sustain them at her breast? Every nursing mother needs food. She eats what she has given birth to, for she has given birth to everything and thus there is nothing else to eat.

Similarly, Kinsley (1986:145-6) explains the prevalence of blood sacrifices—animal and human—to Kali as representative of her need to receive life in the form of blood in order to beget more life.[34]

Thus, it is within this Hindu context which one must understand the bloodthirsty attributes of Kali as Devouring Mother. Though she is addressed as Mother by modern devotees, Kali is mythologically depicted as neither a sexually procreative female nor a nurturing mother within the Hindu Great Tradition. Rather, she retains her virginal role as a martial goddess, performing a positive, structure-supporting function from the divine perspective. Her motherhood, as an intrinsically Hindu soteriological concept, encompasses her modern role as the goddess who creates, sustains, and destroys the universe. Yet, even when she is seen as having "erotic" and motherly characteristics, Kali is a gruesome sight. Only rarely in Tantric literature is she described as attractive, but she is never depicted as such iconographically (Kinsley 1975:113-4). Rather, her terrifying appearance and emaciated body remain consistent in Hindu art.[35]

Eroticism and Danger

The malevolent role of feminine images in mythological traditions requires some explanation on a social, psychological, or symbolic level. Since there is so little information available for the feminine perspective on ancient myth, the interpretational approach of this study concentrates on possible male perspectives of feminine images.[36] In fact, the

---

[34] Note also Kinsley (1986:172-7) and O'Flaherty (1980:86-7) for the discussion of the Tantric goddess Chinnamasta, who cuts off her own head to feed her followers and who thrives on sexual activity. The bloody cult of Durga is described by Kinsley (1986:106-13).

[35] For modern interpretations of Kali's symbolic identity see Kinsley (1975:127-49).

[36] The unsatisfactory results of the attempt to interpret female reaction to violent ancient Near Eastern goddesses is seen in Ochshorn (1981) and Winter (1986). While a feminine message is possible—perhaps expressing a psychological release or reaction against oppression—females could hardly emulate these goddesses in actuality. Even if women did create these mythic images, however, they were accepted by the male population into the canonical, literary traditions and couched in misogynous ideology.

androcentric orientation of much myth compels a male-centered interpretation of the identification of feminine power as dangerous and in need of constraint. In direct opposition to actual patriarchal societies where males dominate females, the powerful role of many goddesses within myth suggests a symbolic meaning based upon either personal or social fears of females. While the social ideology of androcentric and patriarchal societies is discussed above, more attention may be given to the interpretation of mythological symbolism concerning the threat of feminine power to individual males.

The sexual component of many violent goddesses further suggests the appropriateness of a psychological approach to account for issues of masculine sexuality and identity. Myths about goddesses often express concepts and tensions concerning sexual roles and relationships, both personal and social. The fact that these violent warrior deities are cast as feminine characters suggests that gender is a central element of their symbolic identity. The independence of Athena is neither sexual nor dangerous since she, as a daughter, submits to patriarchal ideology. This virginal figure exhibits the superiority of the masculine attibutes of rationality and restraint, and so she is a friendly rather than a threatening figure for males. Durga embodies the great sexual power of feminine virginity—conserving the potential within herself—and is only hostile to those males who would try to approach her sexually.[37] Similarly, Artemis represents the numinous power which cannot be safely encountered by males, emphasizing the distance of the feminine divine from male understanding. Indeed, the innate power and mystery of all feminine images, virginal or sexually active, constitutes a potent force in androcentric myth which must be properly controlled to avoid its destructive effects.

In fact, the greatest threats to individual human males in mythology are the independent, erotic goddesses, such as Aphrodite and Ishtar, whose sexuality, however enticing, is dangerous and occasionally lethal. The male fear of women has been the subject of much psychological research, especially from Freudian (e.g. Lerderer 1968; Slater 1968) and Jungian (e.g. Neumann 1956) perspectives. Since males

37 Shulman (1980:141) comments, "The virgin goddess is a focus of violent eroticisim; she is, indeed, at her most powerful as long as her virginity is intact, so that in marrying her the god exposes himself to an intense, even lethal, danger.... The lustful virgin is really a voracious killer."

traditionally play the dominant and aggressive role in sexual activity, the sexually threatening goddesses take on a greater significance within an androcentric context, perhaps representing psychological fears of sexual dysfunction or castration anxieties. Hence, this section focuses upon images of feminine power and male sexual anxieties concerning the dangers of eroticism in mythology.[38]

The awesome power of females, who hide the secret of life within their very bodies, provides an important symbolic value, exhibited in various ways in different mythological systems. One intriguing example of the use of feminine symbolism is the sheela-na-gigs of the British Isles, dating from at least the twelfth century CE. Andersen (1977) discusses the obscene gestures and iconographic attributes of the female sheelas, including an extensive catalogue (1977:139-53). These grotesque figures, who often appear above doorframes of medieval churches, are typified by the exposure of their exaggerated genitalia. Andersen (1977:131-8) notes the persistent motif of the "power of display" of the female genitalia, citing comparative folkloristic evidence, including a tale of the Devil being frightened from a village he was pestering by a young woman revealing herself to him.[39] Hence, Andersen posits an apotropaic function for the sheelas, who ward off evil spirits through their obscene poses. This evidence for the special abilities of feminine power, perhaps best preserved in virginal figures, suggests the destructive as well as creative aspect of feminine imagery.

The demonic figure of Lilith should also be considered in the discussion of the dangers of divine feminine sexuality since she plays a significant role in Jewish folklore as a succuba, seducing men in their sleep (Patai 1967:207-45; Fauth 1986). In ancient Near Eastern myth Lilith is a night demon, associated with Lamashtu and other terrors of the night (see Fauth 1981). Likewise, the demoness Ardat-lilî is

---

[38] A discussion of Freudian Oedipal anxieties is excluded, since Mother figures are not central to this study. For Freudian analysis of Hindu myth and the eroticism of maternal and violent females see O'Flaherty (1980:105-15).

[39] To be sure, Classical sources include obscure references to the shameless old woman, called variously Iambe and Baubo, making Demeter laugh by exposing herself (see Olender 1987). Hathor similarly shocks Re out of his despondency in Egyptian myth (Pritchard 1969:15). Note also the Lycian women's raising of their skirts in an apotropaic response to Bellerophon mentioned in Plutarch (*Mulierum virtutes* [242e-63d] in the *Morales*). Finally, see the more Freudian discussion of Hertz (1985:161-8) concerning the "power of display" in nineteenth-century France.

associated with human girls whose lives were cut short prior to sexual experience and motherhood (see Lackenbacher 1971:131–41). According to medieval Jewish folklore, Lilith was the first wife of Adam, but abandoned him rather than allow him to lie on top during sex. Her rejection of proper feminine sexuality thus signals the danger she presents to human males. She apparently seeks sexual pleasure and dominance over her human lover. Indeed, she enslaves and sometimes kills those fools whom she, disguised as a prostitute, can seduce while awake (Patai 1967:222). Furthermore, Lilith is procreative, giving birth to thousands of demons from her nocturnal encounters with mortal males. She is most infamous as a killer of human babies, however, since she is jealous of her lovers' human wives and children. This combination of dangerous eroticism, reproductive ability, and rejection of normative feminine roles illustrates her demonic nature. In Jewish tradition Lilith embodies many male fears of sexual impurity and the power of uncontrolled feminine sexuality.

The aggressiveness of goddesses independent of male dominance is a common mythological idea, but it is perhaps clearest in the Hindu tradition discussed above. Gods routinely receive the energy, or shakti, of their consorts into themselves. C. Olson (1988:124-5) explains that this acts to restrain the dangerous sexual power of the goddesses:

> The nonindependent goddesses are able to release their potentially aggressive natures in satisfying sexual relations with their male consorts. This is not possible for the independent goddesses, whose sexual abstinence finds no release except in aggressive and often malevolent behavior towards humans.

The assimilation of the female by her spouse is usually acceptable in androcentric myth, as in the case of Zeus' ingestion of his wife Metis in Hesiod's *Theogony* (see Brown 1953). The consumption of Metis, and her attributes of counsel and cunning, by Zeus is understood as a positive step towards stable patriarchal sovereignty. Since the concept of women being subsumed by their husbands is metaphorically evident on a daily basis in androcentric societies, the idea of a Devouring Male does not have the same impact as the fear of a Devouring Female. That is, it is the normally dominant male who fears the suppressed powers of the female.

Aggressive, sexually active Hindu goddesses are those who have retained their energies, as O'Flaherty (1980:77) explains:

> The dominant woman is dangerous in Hindu mythology, and the dominant goddess expresses this danger in several different but closely related ways. She appears as the killer of her demon lover, beheading him in a symbolic castration; she dances on the corpse of her consort, impaling herself on his still animate phallus. This is the nonmaternal goddess, with whom the worshiper does not dare seek erotic contact for fear of losing his powers.

The sexual power inherent in the female may be seen in the diversity of feminine imagery, such as the black widow, who kills her mate after (or during) sex. Hence, O'Flaherty (1980:80-1) notes that Kali is sometimes represented as a spider who beheads her consort. She has a gaping mouth, bloody fangs, as well as another "mouth" that devours the male (O'Flaherty 1973:186-91). Hindu myths concerning Durga and Kali portray the symbolic association of beheading with castration, as well as suggesting intercourse as the devouring of the penis (the *vagina dentata*) (O'Flaherty 1980:81-7).

The danger of female eroticism—especially of divine females—to males in Hindu ideology is also noted by Shulman (1980:174).

> Sexuality is a dangerous, violent force, and woman an insatiable temptress who drains the male of vitality. Ultimately, in bearing children, woman creates new life; but this life is produced from the violence of sexual union, which clearly is felt to wreak destruction upon the male.

Similarly, O'Flaherty (1980:83-4) notes what she calls "the quintessential metaphor of sexual danger, the draining of life's breath through the draining of semen." She (1980:112) makes the insightful point that erotic women receive (sexual) fluids in contrast to maternal figures who give them (milk). Thus, the erotic power of goddesses drains males of their life, whether in actual death or symbolic unmanning.

A similar fear of castration or impotence caused by sexual contact with the divine feminine is exhibited in the Greek myth concerning Anchises, the human lover of Aphrodite. After discovering the divine nature of his mistress, Anchises pleads not to be made "strengthless," which some interpreters understand as impotence (Friedrich 1978:67; Devereux 1982:33; cf. Lefkowitz 1986:116-7). This fear represents his recognition that the powerful female is dangerous to his masculine sexuality. Similarly, Circe's intent to unman Odysseus after their affair (*Odyssey* 10.301, 341) suggests a Greek anxiety concerning sexually aggressive females (see Friedrich 1978:65-8). The many ill-fated lovers of Inanna/Ishtar, brought to her attention by Gilgamesh (see Pritchard 1969:83-5), also shows the danger of a sexual encounter with the feminine divine. Indeed, if Abusch's (1986) interpretation of Ishtar's attempted seduction of Gilgamesh is correct, then she is deceptively luring the hero to his death through her eroticism. More will be said concerning this mythic episode below. Similarly, Kramer (1979:81-2) argues that Inanna is fully aware of the "law" in Sumerian myth that no human may survive her sexual embrace when she seduces the mortal Dumuzi, sealing his doom. Thus, the erotic encounter of the feminine divine is fatal to the unsuspecting male.

Through her power to change men into women Ishtar also threatens the virility of even those males whom she does not seduce (see Sjöberg 1976:223-6; Hillers 1973 and 1964:66-8; Groneberg 1986:33-41). Various issues are probably involved in Ishtar's transformative ability, and hymns to her give lists of opposites which she is able to reverse, including male and female, right and left, and high and low. Indeed, her ability to transform men into women, and women into men, may be best understood within her cultic context in which transvestites probably served (see Sjöberg 1976:223-6; Groneberg 1986:33-41). However, Ishtar's threat to deprive males of their virility is most poignant in militaristic contexts.

The warrior prowess of Ishtar is so great as to transform male warriors into noncombative women. One curse from Esarhaddon reads, "May Ishtar, mistress of battle and conflict, turn his masculinity into femininity and set him bound at the feet of his enemy" (Hillers 1964:67). Ishtar takes away the warrior's bows and weapons and gives them spindles and mirrors instead (see Hillers 1973:74). Whether Ishtar's threat conveys the actual emasculation of males or symbolic and social transformation, the result is the same. The removal of masculine virility—whether through castration, impotence, or psychological anxiety—is in the power of the erotic and warrior goddess. As Hillers (1973:78) notes in this regard, the prominence of potency rituals in Mesopotamia evidences the ancient interest in male sexual ability (see Biggs 1967; Farber 1977). That Ishtar threatens to change men into women—to take away their masculine virility and place them in feminine social roles—is to unman them sexually.

In conclusion, the lethal intent or effect of sexually active warrior goddesses illustrates the strong connection of these goddesses with unrestrained feminine power and energy. The erotic attraction of goddesses is generally destructive to males, particularly in the case of Inanna/Ishtar, illustrating a male fear of female sexuality as a mysterious and powerful force. Dominant, powerful female images are a threat to masculine identity, which is based upon the subjection of females in androcentric cultures to passive and powerless roles, socially and sexually. The sexually aggressive female thus threatens male sexual identity by the inversion of normal roles, just as the sexually demanding female threatens to drain her lover of his life. Indeed, there is a symbolic equivalence between seduction and castration by dominant females, reflected in the ability of Ishtar to change men into women. In the same way, the armed female warrior inverts the normative expectations of feminine characters. While virgin warriors preserve their powerful potential within themselves in order to play roles normally reserved for males, the sexually active warrior goddess combines masculine and feminine attributes in one potent mythic symbol.

III. MOURNING THE SLAIN GOD

Anat's mourning for Baal is an important element of her character and narrative function in Ugaritic myth. With the aid of Shapsh, Anat searches for Baal's corpse, vigorously mourns him, and provides elaborate sacrificial offerings at his burial. The maiden goddess then avenges her brother's death by exterminating Mot. The return of Baal to earth after these events suggests a causative relationship between her violent acts and his resurrection. However, Anat's precise function within this series of events remains uncertain and enigmatic because of breaks in the Ugaritic texts. Anat's active role in this sequence of events is doubtlessly of mythic importance, but scholars disagree concerning the relative importance of Anat's mourning activities to her mythic character. Kapelrud (1969:82-92) suggests that Anat's mourning for the slain fertility god demonstrates her primary function in Ugaritic religion as the goddess of mourning. He (1969:28) proposes an etymology for her name from the root *ᶜnh*, "to mourn," reflected in BH *ᶜnh*. Essential to Kapelrud's interpretation is his assumption that Anat's mythic role reflects her cultic function; thus, Anat serves as the official mourner in Ugaritic religion according to Kapelrud. While this interpretation is certainly possible, the centrality of Baal's death and its annual dramatization in the Ugaritic cult remain speculative. Regardless, Anat's lamenting of Baal, as one component of her character, provides evidence of her symbolic identity within Ugaritic myth.

As discussed above, the Frazerian category of "dying and rising gods" has largely been discredited and rejected by scholars (see J. Smith 1987). Thus, the present comparative discussion must prescind from an analysis of the slain god himself and note only the roles of mourning goddesses. Similarities to other goddesses who play important roles in lamenting a god may prove useful in analyzing Anat's role in lamenting Baal, but this study can not elaborate upon the motif of a goddess searching and mourning for the slain god. The paucity of evidence restricts the present comparison to two ancient Near Eastern traditions: the search and mourning of Inanna and Geshtinanna for Dumuzi and of Isis and Nephthys for Osiris. Unfortunately, the traditions of these goddesses are also obscure and the scholarly discussions presently available are insufficient for detailed analyses by any other than specialists in the fields of Sumerology and Egyptology. Thus, only a brief summary, with an emphasis on the gender, sexuality, and relationship of the mourning goddesses, is provided in order to note similarities with the tradition of Anat lamenting for Baal.

The passionate mourning activities of Anat are recounted clearly in the Ugaritic texts and we begin with these data. Upon hearing the report of Baal's demise, Anat immediately sets out in search of his corpse.

ap (26) ^{c}nt. ttlk. wtṣd.	Then Anat went to and fro and scoured
kl. ǵr (27) lkbd. arṣ.	every mountain to the heart of the earth,
kl. gb^{c} (28) lkbd. šdm.	every hill to the heart of the fields.
tmǵ. ln^{c}m[y] (29) [arṣ.] dbr.	She reached the pleasant pasture land,
ysmt. šd (30) [šḥl]mmt.	the beautiful fields of *šḥlmmt.*
tm[ǵ.] lb^{c}l. np[l] (31) [la]rṣ	She came upon Baal, fallen to the earth.
[lpš]. tks. miz[rt]	She covered her loins with sackcloth;
KTU 1.6 i	
1) lb^{c}l	(of the Baal Cycle)
2) ^{c}r. bab<n>. td.	she scraped (her) skin with a stone.

psltm[. by^{c}r]	She incised with a razor;
3) thdy. lḥm. wdqn.	she gashed her cheeks and chin.
t[ṯlṯ] (4) qn. ḏr^{c}h.	She raked her arms with a reed;
tḥrṯ. km. gn (5) ap lb.	she plowed her chest like a garden,
l^{c}mq. tṯlṯ. bmt	like a valley she raked her back.
6) b^{c}l. mt. my. lim.	"Baal is dead—what of the peoples;
bn dgn (7) my. hmlt.	Dagan's son—what of the multitudes?
aṯr. b^{c}l. nrd (8) barṣ.	After Baal we will descend into the earth!"
^{c}mh. trd. nrt (9) ilm. špš.	Shapsh, the luminary of the gods, came down to her,
^{c}d. tšb^{c}. bk	as she satiated herself with weeping,
10) tšt. kyn. udm^{c}t.	(as) she drank tears like wine.
gm (11) tṣḥ. lnrt. ilm. špš	She raised her voice to Shapsh, the luminary of the gods,
12) ^{c}ms. m^{c}. ly. aliyn. b^{c}l	"Hoist upon me Almighty Baal!"
13) tšm^{c}. nrt. ilm. špš	Shapsh, the luminary of the gods, obeyed.
14) tšu. aliyn. b^{c}l.	She lifted Almighty Baal;
lktp (15) ^{c}nt. ktšth.	indeed, she placed him on the shoulders of Anat.
tš^{c}lynh (16) bṣrrt. ṣp{^{c}}n.	She carried him up to the heights of Sapon.
tbkynh (17) wtqbrnh.	She wept for him and buried him;
tštnn. bḫrt (18) ilm. arṣ.	she placed him in a grave of the earth gods.
tṭbḫ. šb^{c}m (19) rumm	She slaughtered seventy wild oxen,
kgmn. aliyn (20) b^{c}l	as a funerary sacrifice for Almighty Baal. (1.5 vi 25 - 1.6 i 20)

Anat continues her sacrifices for Baal with seventy bulls, sheep, rams, mountain goats, and asses (see Watson 1989). The text becomes increasingly fragmentary during this sequence and the scene concludes with two obscure lines prior to the recounting of her journey to the divine assembly.

30) [ ]ḥh. tštbm. ^{c}[ ]	… she lifted up (?) …
31) [ ]zrh. ybm. lilm	… his … a brother-in-law of the gods.
32) [id]k. lttn[.] pnm.	Then she set her face
^{c}m (33) [i]l. mbk nhrm.	towards El, at the source of the rivers,
qrb (34) apq. thmtm.	amid the springs of the double Deep.

tgly. ḏd (35) il. w.tbu. qrš. (36) mlk. ab. šnm.	She went into the pavilion of El; she entered the precinct of the King, the Father of Years.
lp^{c}n (37) il. thbr. wtql 38) tštḥwy. wtkbdnh 39) tšu. gh. wtṣḥ. tšmḫ ht (40) aṯrt. w.bnh. ilt. wṣb (41) rt. aryh. kmt. aliyn (42) b^{c}l. kḫlq. zbl. b^{c}l. (43) arṣ	At the feet of El she fell and did homage, she prostrated herself and honored him. She raised her voice and cried, "Let Athirat and her sons rejoice, the goddess and the troops of her kin, for Almighty Baal is dead, for the Prince, Lord of the earth, has perished!" (1.6 i 30-43)

When Anat appears next in the myth she is still wandering about disconsolate at the loss of her brother. The Ugaritic poetry conveys the pathetic quality of Anat's grief: "Like a cow for her calf, like a ewe for her lamb, such was the heart of Anat for Baal" (1.6 ii 5-9 and 28-30). Anat entreats Mot to return Baal to her but Mot denies her request. After an indeterminate length of time, Anat returns and viciously annihilates Mot.

Thus, the central elements of Anat's mourning are her search for her slain brother's corpse, her lamenting and burial of him, and her subsequent avenging of him. Numerous parallels to Anat's behavior may be found in ancient Near Eastern mythology (see also Alster 1983). The mourning of Inanna and Geshtinanna for Dumuzi provides a similar tradition of lamenting goddesses. Kramer (1983) has recently presented a survey of the various Sumerian traditions of the "weeping goddess."

> The 'weeping goddess' image became a recurrent motif in the dirges and laments that abound in the Sumerian literary repertoire. She appears in numerous and diverse guises: as the divine queen bemoaning the destruction of her city and temple, the suppression of her cult, the suffering of the ravaged and dispersed people. Or, she is the spouse, the sister, and above all the mother, of Dumuzi, or a Dumuzi-like figure, who had been carried off into the nether world, a tragic fate that came to symbolize the death of the king and the destruction of her city and temple. (Kramer 1983:76; see also 1982:133-7)

This multiplicity of mourning goddesses in Mesopotamian literature complicates the analysis of the particular goddess lamenting the dead god. Furthermore, the identity of the slain god is neither clear nor consistent in Sumerian tradition (see Kramer 1982:133-7). Jacobsen

(1976:63-73) discusses the motif of Geshtinanna searching for her slain brother, here named Damu, in thirteen often fragmentary and obscure Sumerians texts. Jacobsen also provides numerous examples of a mother and sister, or two sisters, mourning for Dumuzi in the form of Damu. While the relationship of the mourning women is at times confused (see Kramer 1983:76-9), certain texts identify Inanna accompanying Geshtinanna in her search and lament for Dumuzi (Jacobsen 1976:47-55).

The Mesopotamian material is further complicated by the diverse traditions concerning the agent of Dumuzi's death and the initial response of the goddess Inanna. The tradition of Inanna's descent to the Netherworld, found in both Sumerian and Akkadian literary forms, identifies Inanna as the one responsible for Dumuzi's premature death (Jacobsen 1976:55-62). By contrast, the Sumerian *Dumuzi's Dream* clearly describes Dumuzi's death at the hands of demons independent of Inanna (see Alster 1972). Similarly, the Sumerian *Inanna and Bilulu* portrays Inanna as the grieving female who avenges the death of her lover (see Jacobsen 1970; Kramer 1979:83-4). In certain texts Inanna takes part in the search party and laments the slain god (see Kramer 1983:76; Jacobsen 1976:47-55; M. Cohen 1981:71-84). Other texts depict Inanna searching for the living Dumuzi in competition with Geshtinanna in order to make him her replacement in the Netherworld (see M. Cohen 1981:87-9). The evidence of these two contradictory traditions, respresented by *Inanna's Descent* and *Dumuzi's Dream*, can not be explained as simple variations since they are already intertwined in Sumerian tradition. M. Cohen (1981:79, 83) provides evidence that Inanna is ultimately responsible for sending Dumuzi to the Netherworld even in some texts of the *Dumuzi's Dream* type.

The irreconcilable inconsistencies in the Dumuzi myths are noted by Kramer (1983:76-9) and Alster (1972:13-5). Alster (1972) conveniently summarizes earlier approaches to the study of Dumuzi. After rejecting Jacobsen's mythopoeic approach to the Dumuzi myths, Alster (1972:14-5) interprets the figure of Dumuzi as a representative of "the tension between oppositions like man-god, death-life, desert-city.... Thus, Dumuzi is the mediator between life and death, nature and culture.... The contradictions in the Sumerian world were never reconciled, and this is reflected in the different issues of the Dumuzi myths." Thus, the complexity of the Dumuzi traditions excludes a consistent role for

Inanna in mourning for the slain god. While in some traditions she is responsible for his confinement in the Netherworld, in other traditions she clearly mourns his death at the hands of the demons in the sheepfold. Unfortunately, the available Mesopotamian texts never integrate the two traditions in a manner which presents a unified myth. Ultimately, the literary and mythological traditions of Inanna and Dumuzi remain too obscure and contradictory to provide more than a superficial comparison with Anat's role in mourning Baal (cf. Dijkstra 1979). We are left only with literary similarities in females' self-abusive mourning activities and their pathetic grief for a slain god (Kramer 1983:76-7).

Moving away from ancient Mesopotamian mythology, the roles of Isis and Nephthys in the Egyptian myth of Osiris provide another important parallel to Anat's search and mourning for the slain Baal.[40] While the myth of Osiris is not found in a complete form in any ancient Egyptian text, allusions to it are scattered throughout inscriptions dating from the Old Kingdom (see Griffiths 1980:1-40). The primary source for the Egyptian myth is Plutarch's *De Iside et Osiride*. Griffith's (1970) authoritative edition provides the nonspecialist with a valuable source of information concerning this Hellenistic text and its relation to the ancient Egyptian tradition. Indeed, the myth of Osiris and the Ugaritic myth of Baal's conflict with Mot share important themes. These common motifs include the death of a god as a result of conflict over the divine kingship, the search and mourning for the slain god's corpse by two goddesses, and the subsequent return of the god.

According to Plutarch, Isis and Osiris were siblings who "were united in the darkness of the womb" as lovers (Griffith 1970:137). Isis is a multifaceted Egyptian goddess whom even the Greeks had difficulty incorporating into Hellenistic mythology (see Witt 1971). In contrast to the erotic quality of the goddess Hathor, Isis is usually a maternal and nurturing character within Egyptian myth (see Bleeker 1988). Isis and Nephthys together search for the corpse of Osiris after he has been slain by Seth. After recovering the severed parts of his body, Isis and Nephthys energetically lament the fate of their brother. Pyramid Text

---

40 There is a voluminous discussion of the worship of Isis in the ancient Mediterranean world. The more enigmatic goddess Nephthys, however, has received less scholarly attention (see Bleeker 1963; Graefe 1980). See Faulkner (1936) on the *Songs of Isis and Nephthys* and Lichtheim (1980:116-121) for the *Lamentations of Isis and Nephthys*.

1280a-1282a describes this mythological scene: "Isis has come with Nephthys... they have come seeking their brother, Osiris. Hurry, hurry, bewail thy brother, Isis! Bewail thy brother, Nephthys! Bewail thy brother! Isis sits with her hands upon her (i.e. on her head); Nephthys, she has seized for herself the tops of her breasts because of their brother, the King" (Griffiths 1980:26). Indeed, Isis and Nephthys are archetypal wailing women in Egyptian myth and religion (see Bleeker 1983). Isis then revives the dead Osiris and has sexual intercourse with him in order to conceive their son who will avenge his father in the Assembly of the Gods.

Although the function of Isis, as the sister and consort of Osiris, is reminiscent of Anat's search and mourning for Baal, more attention should be given to the second goddess who laments Osiris, the virgin Nephthys (see Bleeker 1963; Graefe 1980). Van Dijk (1986:41-2) points out similarities between Anat and Nephthys as two goddesses who do not play normative feminine roles in ancient myth. Explaining that Nephthys is traditionally childless, te Velde (1984:253) writes, "Nephthys plays those parts in mythology that women without a husband filled in the Egyptian society, i.e. as wailing-woman and nursemaid." While Seth and Nephthys appear as a couple in the Heliopolitan Ennead, their relationship as consorts is abnormal. Te Velde (1977:29-30) concludes that Seth's marriage to Nephthys is one of convenience since she does not have a vagina, a fact related to Seth's deviant sexuality and loss of testicles. Even though she is the nominal spouse of Seth, Nephthys clearly sides with Isis against Seth in lamenting Osiris. It is intriguing that both Anat and Nephthys are virginal wet-nurses who mourn a brother slain by another deity in competition for divine kingship. There is no evidence, however, that the ancients ever explicitly equated Canaanite Anat with Egyptian Nephthys. The lack of such an identification of the virgin goddesses when Baal was readily accepted as the foreign manifestation of Seth is noteworthy. Anat was taken into the Egyptian pantheon as a distinct goddess, perhaps demonstrating her importance as an independent figure. Regardless, the parallels between Anat and Nephthys as maiden goddesses who lament a slain brother are significant in themselves.

In summary, other ancient Near Eastern goddesses play roles similar to Anat in their search and mourning for a brother or lover who is slain by another deity. Unfortunately, none of these examples provides much reliable information for substantative comparative analysis. Baal, Dumuzi, and Osiris are very different mythic figures who play diverse roles in their respective mythological systems. While any typology for mourning goddesses is lacking, there is a similarity in the relationship of the females—often consort and virginal sister—with the slain male. Ugaritic literature also provides descriptions of mourning females which may contribute to our understanding of Anat's role in lamenting Baal. Like Anat, the maiden Pughat mourns and then avenges her slain brother Aqhat in the epic named for him. Of particular significance in this context is Pughat's virginity and sibling relationship to Aqhat. A second Ugaritic example, from the *Epic of Kirta*, depicts the princess Ṯtmnt mourning the impending death of her father. These two cases from Ugaritic literature, like the mythological traditions of Inanna and Geshtinanna and Isis and Nephthys, depict the females of the dead male's family in mourning. If Inanna is Dumuzi's betrothed, then each tradition depicts the mourning of a male by the females of his household. The mother's role in the Dumuzi texts may emphasize the youth of the victim, since the mother would usually have died prior to her son, one might imagine.

Hence, the familial relationship between the slain god and mourning goddesses is significant in approaching the roles of Anat and Shapsh. Unfortunately, the kinship relations of these two Ugaritic goddesses is obscure. The comparative evidence suggests the common role of the wife and unmarried sisters and daughters performing the burial ritual for the males of their family. In fact, these mythological texts of mourning goddesses probably reflect the human traditions of mourning for dead males. In each case, the male is mourned by the women of his immediate household. If this pattern is consistent, then Anat's role as mourner highlights her identity as a young female of Baal's family. It is possible that she is performing these duties as Baal's consort, but it is more plausible that she is his maiden sister, as argued below. As Baal's blood relative, perhaps it falls to her to bury, lament, and avenge the slain god. Although the kinship relations of the Ugaritic pantheon are unclear, this evidence is consistent with the interpretation that Anat is the virgin sister of Baal. We will return to this discussion in the next chapter. For the moment it is sufficient to note the importance of gender and kinship to Anat's role in the mourning and burial of Baal.

IV. CONCLUSION

This chapter has attempted to point out the multivalent potential of feminine symbols within androcentric social and symbolic systems. Particular attention has been given to the central importance of sexual experience and availability of females in androcentric mythologies. The symbolic role of gender and the normative behavior of feminine characters have also been examined within the context of patriarchal social ideology. The relevance of this discussion to the symbolic analysis of the goddess Anat within Ugaritic myth lies in the scholarly neglect of gender symbolism in the Ugartic pantheon and assumptions concerning the sexual activity of all Canaanite goddesses. In fact, Anat is identified as a maiden goddess, *btlt*, within the Ugaritic pantheon. Thus, mythographers should attend to the implications of her adolescent character. As argued below, Anat is never described as sexually active in Ugaritic texts; she is a virginal goddess. The scholarly assumption of her sexual experience thus reveals considerably more about recent mythography than ancient mythology. Anat's independence and role as a female warrior in Ugaritic myth illustrate her liminal position within the Ugaritic pantheon. She rejects the normative feminine roles of wife and mother and thus threatens the patriarchal social ideology in which women are meant to be subordinate to authoritative males. As argued in the next chapter, Anat's identity as an adolescent female further identifies her as a liminal and dangerous force within the Ugaritic mythic cosmos. Indeed, Anat's gender is essential to her mythic identity as the adolescent tomboy. Her violent and unrestrained behavior further reflect her liminal status within the Ugaritic pantheon. The import of these issues will be investigated throughout the following chapters in the attempt to interpret Anat's symbolic identity within the Ugaritic myths.

CHAPTER 3

The Maiden Goddess

In attempting a consistent interpretation of the role and character of Anat within Ugaritic mythology, the literal depiction of Anat within the Ugaritic texts themselves will be noted rather than artificial constructs based upon modern typologies of ancient mythological images. The most basic sources of information concerning Anat are the stock epithets and formulaic descriptions applied to her within Ugaritic poetry. These formal descriptions should contain the most authentic and reliable information concerning Anat's attributes and character within Ugaritic myth and religion. Of course, scholars can assume neither that all of the available texts present a consistent image of the deity nor that all epithets applied to the goddess are necessarily contemporary with the latest tradition recorded in the texts. In addition to historical development within Ugaritic myth, one must take into account the possible existence of divergent traditions based upon geographical, cultic, or hierarchical distinctions. While one assumes a certain homogeneity to the "canonical" corpus, heterodox elements from diverse sources may certainly have been retained. Indeed, inconsistencies in the mythic tradition may provide the most important information concerning the paradoxes and contradictions found in Ugaritic myth. These inconsistencies are particularly relevant to structural analysis, which posits that all details of any given myth fit into the larger mythological structure of that tradition. Hence, a text-centered approach permits the Ugaritic texts to speak with all of their inconsistencies and contradictions in attempting a generally consistent interpretation of the symbolic role and narrative character of Anat within Ugaritic mythology.

I. ANAT'S STATUS

Anat's Age and Gender

The most common epithet or means of reference for Anat within the Ugaritic corpus is *btlt ᶜnt*, "Maiden Anat." Contextually, the term *btlt* occurs in Ugaritic only as an epithet of Anat and thus there is no additional evidence concerning the precise nature of its designation. Ugaritic *btlt* has numerous Semitic cognates, however, and much scholarly discussion surrounds the specific meaning or semantic range of this term. Bowman (1978:170-5) cogently defends the current scholarly consensus that many Semitic cognates for Ugaritic *btlt* do not necessitate physical virginity. Although cognates of *btlt* can designate a virgin in later dialects of Syriac and Arabic, the Akkadian and Biblical Hebrew evidence does not support the precise translation "virgin." *CAD* (2:173-4) translates Akkadian *batultu* as "nubile girl, adolescent" and notes the references to *batulū* as "male adolescents." In a lengthy study, Landsberger (1968) also defines Akkadian *batultu* as an adolescent or pubescent youth, noting the distinction between this term and terms for children (*siḫru* and *siḫirtu*) and sexually mature youths (*eṭlu* and *ardatu*). *CAD* (2:173) concludes that *batultu* primarily denotes an age group although in certain contexts it does appear to specify "virgin."

Similarly, the Hebrew term *bĕtûlâ* generally refers to an age category rather than specifically virginal girls (Wenham 1972). Locher (1986:121-92) has recently presented a thorough survey of scholarship on the meaning of the Hebrew *bĕtûlâ*. He argues that while the Akkadian *batultu* generally does mean "young girl," it is used to designate a virgin in certain Middle Assyrian and Neo-Babylonian legal texts. Locher defends a similar narrowing of the semantic range of BH *bĕtûlâ* within the specialized legal terminology of Deuteronomy 22. In opposition to many scholarly opinions of late, he concludes that female virginity was often highly regarded in the ancient Near East (cf. Patai 1959). The Akkadian usage of this term further supports the argument that *batultu* may signify a recently married woman or a young wife who has yet to give birth to a (male) child (cf. Joel 1:8) (see Gordon 1977:125-6). The similarity of meaning for this term in Akkadian and BH suggests its importance in denoting a particular age and gender category of females eligible for marriage. Thus, while avoiding the later connotations of the Semitic cognates of Ugaritic *btlt*, it is safe to conclude that the use of the term in describing Anat would refer primarily to her age and social category and not necessarily to her sexual experience.

In fact, many scholars have correctly seen that this Ugaritic epithet designates Anat not specifically as a virgin but as a youthful female (see Bowman 1978:174-5 n. 23). I suspect that this consensus is directly related to the widespread opinion that Anat is a goddess of love as well as patroness of war. De Moor retains the translation "virgin" while arguing that Anat is sexually active. He explains that there is no English term equivalent to the proper meaning of *btlt* as "a young woman who did not yet bring forth male offspring" (de Moor 1987:7 n. 33). Following the exemplary lead of Ginsberg, I prefer to translate *btlt* as "maiden" since the primary significance of the term is as an age, social, and gender designation, with the implication of "virgin." Of course, this broad designation does not exclude the possibility of Anat's actual virginity, a matter to which we will return below.

Anat's identification as an "adolescent female," *btlt*, is corroborated by her epithet *rḥm*, understood as a "female" (i.e. "one with a womb") of indeterminate age (*TO* 89-90). The use of the feminine singular and dual of *rḥm* in Judges 5:30 to refer to women as spoils of battle and the term *rḥmt*, "female slaves," in the Mesha inscription (*KAI* 181:17) support this translation. Indeed, the term probably has the connotation of young women. Unfortunately, the orthography *rḥm* in Ugaritic constitutes a homograph, possibly denoting words for "mill-stones," "compassion," as well as "womb" or "girl."[1] Only once (1.6 ii 27) is Anat designated *rḥm* ^{c}*nt*, although the title is reconstructed in the parallel passage in line 5 of the same column. Lines 27-30 read:

rḥm. ^{c}nt. tngṯh	The Damsel Anat searches for him.
(28) klb. arḫ. l^{c}glh.	Like the heart of a cow for her calf,
klb (29) ṯat. limrh.	like the heart of a ewe for her lamb,
km. lb (30) ^{c}nt. aṯr. b^{c}l	such is the heart of Anat after Baal.

---

1 BH includes cognate terms meaning "womb" (*reḥem*), "compassion, compassionate" (*raḥămîm, raḥûm*), "mill-stones" (*rēḥayim*), as well as "carrion vulture" (Lev 11:18 *rāḥām* and Deut 14:17 *rāḥāmâ*).

Although the translation "Damsel" is preferred for Anat's epithet *rḥm*, it is significant that this appellation is applied to Anat as she wanders disconsolate at the loss of her brother. This mournful episode might be all the more poignant if the audience understands *rḥm* as "compassionate;" perhaps the epithet is used as a rhetorical device to heighten the sense of pathos. Similarly, the term *rḥm* occurs in *KTU* 1.16 i 33 with the sense of compassion, again within the context of a female lamenting the (impending) death of a male relative. Regarding Ṯtmnt as one who is qualified to engage in mourning, Kirta speaks to his son, "I know how 'compassionate' is your sister" (*aḫtk ydᶜt krḥmt*). However, if Anat's epithet *rḥm* is a feminine adjective, "compassionate," then it should be marked with a final /t/.

The matter of the epithet *rḥm* is further complicated by the existence of what is apparently a divine name, *Rḥmy*, found once in *KTU* 1.15 ii 6 and thrice in *KTU* 1.23 (ll. 13, 16, and 28). Unfortunately, this divine name never appears in any sacrificial or pantheon lists. This fact leads some scholars to conclude that it must be an epithet of a better known deity such as Anat (Bowman 1978:184). In *KTU* 1.15 ii 6 *Rḥmy* is apparently included in a list of gods who come to the feast offered by Kirta. The complete list of deities in attendance is lost in a damaged portion of the tablet, but Bowman (1978:184) points out that *Rḥmy* immediately precedes Prince Resheph (*zbl ršp*). He holds that this datum supports the equation of *Rḥmy* and Anat since Anat and Resheph frequently appear together in offering and pantheon lists from Ugarit. While this is certainly true, Anat does not always precede or follow Resheph nor is she ever explicitly identified as *Rḥmy*.

The divine name *Rḥmy* appears individually (l. 16) and as a component of the name(s) *aṯrt wrḥmy* (l. 28, restored in 13 and 24) in the liturgical section of *KTU* 1.23.[2] This much studied text begins with a ritual liturgy (ll. 1-29), and then continues with a poetic narrative (ll. 30-76) concerning El's seduction of two unnamed goddesses and the subsequent birth of Shahar, Shalim, and the "Gracious Gods." It is unclear whether *aṯrt wrḥmy* is a double name of Athirat or a reference to two separate goddesses. Many scholars accept the latter interpretation

2 On this enigmatic text see the studies of Trujillo (1973), Cutler and Macdonald (1982), and Foley (1987) with bibliography.

based upon the role of two unnamed goddesses in the mythological section of this text. Cutler and Macdonald (1982:34-5) argue that the Ugaritic term *rḥmy* usually designates cultic functionaries and that its occurrence here refers to Athirat's (divine) Lady-in-waiting. This text must remain enigmatic, however, and can contribute little to our discussion of Anat's epithet *rḥm*.

Gibson (1977:90 n. 4, 77) identifies Raḥmay as a probable name or title of Anat meaning "the merciful" even though he translates *rḥm* *ᶜnt* as "the damsel Anat." The application of an epithet of "compassionate" or "merciful" to Anat would be most ironic, given her frequently bellicose character. Indeed, one of Anat's epithets in a sacrificial list (1.39, 17) and a god list (1.102, 11) is *ᶜnt* *ḫbly*, "Anat the Destroyer."[3] As a divine name, *Rḥmy* more plausibly refers to "the one of the womb," signifying a maternal goddess, than to "the compassionate one." The analogy of the feminine divine names Arsay, Tallay, and Pidray, as well as Athirat's helper Daggay, suggests that *Rḥmy* is the hypostatization of a natural element formed by the addition of the adjectival suffix -*ay* (<-*ayyu*) (see Cross 1973:56). The designation "the one of the womb" is remarkably appropriate for Athirat, the mother of the gods. It should also be pointed out that the two contexts in which the name *Rḥmy* occurs (1.15 and 1.23) are both primarily concerned with the birth of offspring. Thus, based upon both contextual and morphological evidence, *Rḥmy* is best interpreted as "the one of the womb." While there is good circumstantial evidence for the equation of *Rḥmy* and Athirat, including the combination *aṯrt wrḥmy*, this matter is unresolved. Again, that *Rḥmy* is a distinct goddess in the Ugaritic pantheon must not be ruled out (contra Bowman 1978:184).

The possibility that Anat has the epithet "the womb" has not escaped the attention of de Moor, who uses this evidence to bolster his argument that Anat gives birth in Ugaritic myth (contra *TO* 89). De Moor (1987:117-20) concludes that *Rḥmy* is Anat and that she and Athirat are involved with El in the Ugaritic sacred marriage in *KTU* 1.23.[4] While translating *rḥm* *ᶜnt* as "the Damsel ᶜAnatu," de Moor (1987:86 n. 419)

---

[3] See *CAD* (6:3-6) for the Akkadian verb *ḫabālu*, "to oppress, ravage."

[4] De Moor (1987:117-8) goes so far as to say that the king and queen played the roles of El and Athirat while "a priestess, probably a princess, played the role of the goddess of love, ᶜAnatu."

explains that this term, derived from "womb," also means "available woman" and that it is a "special title of the goddess of love who is also called 'the breast'." Thus, de Moor (1987:7 n. 34) explicitly links the meaning of *rḥm,* "Damsel," in this text to Anat's availability as a widow when Baal is dead, as well as to her role as a fertility goddess (see also de Moor 1980:308-9). The connotation of "available woman" which de Moor posits for *rḥm* is nowhere else attested and is in fact only conjecture based entirely upon his overzealous efforts to systematize the Ugaritic myths.

In summary, I am not convinced that *Rḥmy* should be identified with Anat even though she is (once) given the epithet *rḥm.* Furthermore, the terms *Rḥmy, rḥmt,* and *rḥm* should not necessarily be derived from the same etymological root or linked in their semantic nuance. There is simply not enough evidence to arrive at any firm conclusion since *rḥm* is a homograph for various words in Ugaritic. Anat could conceivably be called the goddess with a womb, although this seems inconsistent with her presentation throughout the mythological material. She might be considered the compassionate goddess, especially in view of her heartfelt mourning for Baal. Finally, the epithet may serve as a parallel term for *btlt* to designate her as a young female. While each position is viable, the grammatical analysis of the phrase *rḥm ᶜnt* suggests that *rḥm* is not a feminine adjective, in which case one would expect either *rḥmn* from Hebrew and Aramaic parallels (see Bowman 1978:185) or the feminine *rḥmt,* as perhaps in *KTU* 1.16 i 33. As a feminine title abstracted from a noun or verb, one would expect the form **ᶜnt rḥmy* as in the extant epithet *ᶜnt ḫbly,* "Anat the Destroyer." Hence, the form and syntax of *rḥm ᶜnt* best support the translation "Damsel Anat" as a parallel to *btlt ᶜnt,* "Maiden Anat."

One should respect the fact that Ugaritic myth consistently applies the particular terms *btlt* and *rḥm* to Anat and to no other female, either divine or human. In both literary and other texts young females, such as Pughat and Huray, are designated by the terms *mṯt, nᶜrt, pǵt,* and, simply, *bt.* Thus, the epithets *btlt* and *rḥm* seem to be reserved for the depiction of the goddess Anat. Consistent with these age and gender designations are the available iconographic representations of the goddess Anat from Egypt and Syria-Palestine.[5] In these traditions the goddess Anat is generally depicted as young and nubile, with small breasts and a thin body. Although the Egyptian inconographic tradition tends to conflate distinct Canaanite goddesses and to assign certain maternal characteristics to Anat, the representations of her as a distinct deity consistently treat her as a youthful goddess.

While the iconographic representation and epithets of the goddess Anat seem to attribute female physical features to her, many commentators nevertheless conclude that Anat is an androgynous, or bisexual, figure. This interpretation suggests that Anat's warrior prowess and aggressive character are inconsistent with female sex. Accordingly, scholars interpret certain Ugaritic texts to depict Anat sporting a beard (1.6 i 3) and being described by El as "like a man" (1.18 i 16). Support for this argument is also sought in the "transvestite" nature of Anat's apparel, as described in the Egyptian text, Chester Beatty Papyrus VII. Given the central function of sexual availability to the symbolic identity of goddesses, discussed above, the role of gender in feminine images is of great importance. Regardless of the difficulty of "goddess biology," physically androgynous characteristics would have important ramifications concerning the symbolic identity of the goddess.

The debate concerning the "bearded Anat" has a long history, documented by Loewenstamm (1982). The crucial passage for this theory, *thdy lḥm wdqn*, is found within the description of Anat's elaborate rite of mourning for the dead Baal in *KTU* 1.6 i 3. This same phrase is applied to El's mourning activities, with the masculine verb

---

5 For a discussion of the possible iconographic representations of Anat see primarily Eaton (1964:104-119, 129-45) and Barnett (1969) with references. Note also the more recent discussion of Wyatt (1984:331-2), although many of his views are peculiar and unwarranted. The famous frontspiece of Cassuto's book (1971) is frequently identified as a representation of Anat. In fact, the feminine subject of this relief is depicted with a slightly protuberant belly, suggestive of pregnancy. Ugaritologists have not remarked on this feature of the stela, however. Eaton (1969:105), for example, remarks that this portrayal of Anat is only slighty different from the other Egyptian iconographic portraits of the youthful goddess (cf. Kapelrud 1969:48). Unfortunately, this relief is from a private Egyptian collection rather than from any archaeological context. There no evidence that it portrays the Ugaritic goddess Anat.

form *yhdy*, in *KTU* 1.5 vi 19. While de Moor (see 1980:307 n. 10) has aggressively defended the translation "(Anat) shaved her side-whiskers and her beard," Loewenstamm has championed the reading "(Anat) gashed her cheeks and her chin." Indeed, the summation by Loewenstamm (1982) makes further discussion of the meaning of three lexemes *hdy*, "to cut," *lḥm*, "cheeks," and *dqn*, "beard, chin," unneccessary, as even de Moor (1987:80) appears recently to have been convinced. While the comparative Semitic evidence concerning the correct connotation of **ḏqn* is ambiguous, the Mishnaic use of *zqn* clearly supports the translation "chin" as well as "beard" (Marcus 1977). Moreover, the context and verbal parallels clearly support the rendering "(Anat) gashed her cheeks and chin." Similarly, the comparative evidence for bearded goddesses is dubious. Although Goldman (1961) attempts to identify numerous examples in ancient Near Eastern iconography and literature, each supposed case of androgynous or bearded goddesses must be considered on its own merits. The examination of the bearded Ishtar by Groneberg (1986), discussed above, illustrates the problems with positing an androgynous goddess in the ancient Near East.

The second important point concerning Anat's gender is found in the opening bi-cola of El's reply to her threats to break open his skull if he does not grant her request (1.18 i 16-7 and 1.3 v 27-8). While these episodes will be discussed below, we must here consider El's statement to the belligerent goddess, *ydᶜtk bt kanšt.* De Moor (1987:17 n. 91) cites this text in support of his argument that Anat is androgynous by translating, "I know you, my daughter, (I know) that you are like a man." Scholars have proposed many divergent interpretations of this phrase.[6] While some commentators take the term to mean "companionable" (cf. Arabic *ʾanīsa*) or "gentle" with a sense of irony in El's reply, many scholars explain *kanšt* as a denominative verb meaning

6 Various etymologies have been proposed for *anš* (see Margalit 1983:93). *TO* (132) suggests a connection to Akkadian *nâšu*, "to tremble," although the passage under discussion is translated as "tu es *irascible*" (*TO* 435). Suggesting either *ʾnš* or *nwš* as the root, del Olmo Lete (1981a:515-6) posits the meaning "inexorable, implacable" for *anš*, compared with BH *ʾānûš*. Note Cassuto's (1971:149-50) rendering of this term as "invincible." Van Zijl (1975) argues that *anš* may be an *ʾaphel* form of the root *nšy* with a semantic range involving destruction, threat and rebellion.

"you are like a man" (see Bowman 1978:48-9). The denominative explanation is difficult, however, since the noun **anš*, "man," is unattested in Ugaritic. While the plural *nšm*, "people," is attested, the relationships between this word and Akkadian *nīšu* and BH terms such as *ᵓănāšîm* are not clear. Moreover, the sense of this translation is enigmatic; is El stating that Anat is behaving as a male, rather than a female, or as a human rather than a deity (see de Moor 1971:132)? Neither explanation is very compelling. Instead, attention should be given to an etymology which links this term to BH *ᵓānûš*, "incurable, desperate," as used in Jeremiah 15:18; 17:9, 16 and 30:12, 15. This sense is apparently adopted by *TO* (436), Gordon (1977:18) and del Olmo Lete (1981a:516), who read, respectively, "irascible," "impetuous" and "inexorable." Hence, I understand El's remark to be that Anat is "incorrigible, uncontrollable." Regardless, this phrase clearly provides no evidence that Anat is a bisexual deity.

As a third source of evidence for Anat's androgynous character, the Chester Beatty Papyrus VII reports that Anat's wardrobe includes masculine articles of clothing (Bowman 1978:237-8). The relevant line from this Egyptian incantation reads, "ᶜAnat, the Victorious Goddess, the woman who acts like a warrior, who wears a skirt like men and a sash (?) like women" (van Dijk 1986:33-4). This text portrays Anat as combining masculine and feminine attributes in her character and clothing, but this does not necessitate her androgynous or transvestite appearance (van Dijk 1986:37, 41-2). More to the point, Anat is given explicitly feminine epithets and titles—such as Mistress, Queen, Lady—in Egyptian texts; she is clearly a female deity. Unfortunately, no Ugaritic text describes her attire. Perhaps the mixture of masculine and feminine articles in the outfit which Pughat dons as she sets out to avenge the death of her brother (1.19 iv 44-6) suggests something about Anat's traditional costume at Ugarit. However, all available iconographic portrayals of Anat, as far as can be ascertained, consistently depict her in feminine clothing, occasionally with an exposed breast. Margalit (1983:93) certainly oversteps the available information when he assumes that "Anat's manly dress was proverbial, a sort of internationally recognized 'trade-mark'." Based upon certain biblical and Ugaritic restrictions concerning male and female clothes, Margalit reaches the unwarranted conclusion that "Anat's attire is thus a violation of religious code" (1983:93 n. 6). There is no evidence that Anat's combination of feminine and warrior characteristics is considered offensive although she certainly presents a liminal figure within the mythological tradition.

While each of these three arguments for regarding Anat as bisexual is unconvincing, Anat does exhibit ambiguous gender traits in the Ugaritic literature. That is, the goddess Anat is clearly considered a female deity in Ugaritic material although she does have certain masculine components to her character. Her identification as a huntress and warrior, as well as her desire of Aqhat's bow, suggest she does not accept a standard feminine identity in the ancient world. Just as Groneberg (1986) describes Ishtar as a fully feminine character with additional masculine attributes, so Anat appears to be a female deity who is not restrained by normative feminine behavior. Her sex is female, but her gender is ambiguous.

In summary, the accumulated evidence strongly suggests that Anat is a nubile, adolescent female, a girl of marriageable age in the ancient Near East (see Roth 1987; Locher 1986; Wenham 1976). The common epithet *btlt* explicitly signifies a female of adolescent status, an unmarried female who has yet to give birth. The less frequent epithet *rḥm*, "girl, damsel," further corroborates the identification of Anat as a nubile female, consistent with her common iconographic representation. Indeed, the mythic portrayal of Anat also supports her designation as a youthful female independent of a male consort, as I argue below. This gender and age symbolism may be central to the mythic character and status of Anat as a member of a definite social category, in contrast to the other mature goddesses in the Ugaritic pantheon. This status as an independent female of marriageable age is essential to her position within the Ugaritic pantheon in that she is liminal to normal categories of social structure.

Anat's Kinship Relations

The structure of mythic pantheons provides an important native source of information concerning the symbolic system of mythological traditions, which commonly divide the divine realm into various alliances and classificatory groupings.[7] At Ugarit we see various classes of divine beings, such as the *rp'm*, and certain groups following El, Baal, and Anat. Indeed, the conflict between rival coalitions of Ugaritic deities appears to play a central role in the competition for royal status in the Baal Cycle. Unfortunately, the limited information concerning the Ugaritic pantheon structure and kinship system precludes any definite conclusions at the present time. Archaeologists have yet to discover a theogonic text or divine lineage from Ugarit. The "Pantheon Lists" from Ugarit do not provide information of much significance concerning the structure of the Ugaritic pantheon.[8] This lack of information concerning Anat's kinship relations and social position is most regrettable since it would provide evidence for what we may posit as behavioral expectations among the gods in accordance with her status.[9]

The major stumbling block in the discussion of the Ugaritic pantheon structure is the confusion surrounding Baal's relation to El. The organization of the Ugaritic deities into distinct kinship groups has been

7 Obvious examples pointed out by Dumézil, the father of modern comparative mythology, include the Devas and Asuras of India and the Aesir and Vanir of Norse tradition (see Littleton 1982). Similarly, the Greek pantheon exhibits distinctions between different classes of gods (e.g. Olympians) and other divine beings, including the defeated Titans. Less clearly, the Mesopotamian pantheon includes categories of Igigi and Anunnaki, at Deir Allah the *šaddayīn* seems to be a special group within the gods (*'lhn*), and Egyptian myth groups deities into various Enneads.

On the possible groups and subgroups of Ugaritic deities, see the discussions of Herrmann (1982) and Cunchillos (1985), and the structural analysis of Petersen and Woodward (1977) followed by Wyatt (1987b). Note Kippenburg (1984) on conflicts among the gods. Kinship terms generally play an important role in the structure of ancient Near Eastern pantheons, but it is difficult to distinguish between primary relationships from within one city pantheon and secondary relationships developed to explain the relations between originally independent mythic pantheons.

8 See de Moor (1970) and Healey (1985) (cf. Lambert 1985). The signficance of these lists eludes modern analysis. While some Ugaritologists attempt to attribute structure to the sequence of male and female deities, the results are artificial and unconvincing.

9 Of course, Anat's social context must be understood not as the Ugaritic social environment, with its customs, institutions and structures, but the Ugaritic myths in which she is an actor. However, there must be some relation between the basic behavioral norms of Ugaritic society and Ugaritic myth, otherwise the myths would be unintelligible to their contemporary audience. Hence, while the interpretation of Anat's social status within the Ugaritic pantheon must remain speculative, it is based upon evidence from the texts themselves as well as from a more general understanding of ancient social practices.

most cogently argued by Oldenburg (1969), who posits blood vengeance between the rival El and Baal families as the primary motivation for divine conflict within the Ugaritic myths. In his analysis of the relative rank of El and Baal, L'Heureux (1979:12-26, 94-108) reviews the work of Oldenburg (1969) and Pope (1955). Following the lead of Cross, L'Heureux (1979:3-108) and Mullen (1980:7-110) support the more plausible conclusion that El and Baal fill complementary roles as the authoritative patriarch and the divine warrior, respectively, within the Ugaritic pantheon. More recent work by Pope (1983; 1987b), however, continues to hold the interpretation, based largely upon comparative evidence, that Baal overthrows the senile El within Ugaritic myth. The complexity of this dispute precludes further analysis in the present context. It must suffice for the present study to point out that much ambiguity remains concerning the kinship relationship between El, Baal, and Dagan, although the argument that El and Baal generally work together to govern the cosmos is persuasive. Given the lack of information concerning the organizational structure of the Ugaritic pantheon, the present section will only consider the explicit kinship titles and epithets applied to Anat. A more synthetic interpretation of Anat's position within the pantheon will be attempted in the conclusion of this study.

Anat is addressed as "daughter," *bt*, by El (1.18 i 16-7 and 1.3 v 27-8). While Anat never addresses El as "father," *ab*, in the extant texts, there appear to be references to him as "her father" (*abh*) in *KTU* 1.3 v 10 and 1.13, 21. Her reference to him as "my father," *aby*, may be restored in 1.3 iv 54. While these passages suggest that Anat is the offspring of El, the formal use of *ab* and *bt* for non-related individuals of different social status obscures the point. It is most probable that the titles "father" and "daughter" signify nothing more than a lack of social equality. Similarly, there is no evidence for the identity of Anat's mother; no kinship terms relate her to Athirat. Indeed, Anat's dealings with the creatress of the gods (*qnyt ilm*) in *KTU* 1.4 ii 23-5 do not present the two goddesses as particularly close, nor does she address Athirat as "mother." On the other hand, no deity ever refers to Athirat as "mother" even though she is clearly the progenitress of the gods.[10] Kapelrud (1969:41) summarizes the issue of Anat's parents by stating that she "seems to have been in line with the other gods so far as descent is concerned, i.e. she was a daughter of El and most probably also of Asherah. If she had not been, the texts would have said so. She was a regular goddess, with the father and the mother she was expected to have." This hasty conclusion betrays Kapelrud's desire to attribute a consistency and completeness to the Ugaritic texts which is not necessarily found in the mythological tradition. Based upon the available information, the identity of Anat's parents remains unclear.

"Sister" of Baal. The importance of Anat's designation as the "sister" of Baal rests primarily upon her alleged sexual relationship to the storm god and their kinship to El. While many scholars accept as fact the interpretation that Anat is Baal's spouse, the relationship between these two deities is ambiguous. The kinship terms *aḫ*, "brother," and *aḫt*, "sister," are frequently applied to them within the Ugaritic texts. Although the sibling status accorded to the terms *aḫ* and *aḫt* is clear, these titles also convey numerous non-filial relationships in the ancient Near East. Bowman (1978:176-82) concisely presents the major arguments concerning the semantic range of Ugaritic *aḫt*, "sister," and its cognates, concluding that the semantic range of this appellation includes both a close female companion and a biological sibling. Such imprecision exacerbates the difficulty of determining the kinship and sexual relations of Anat and Baal in Ugaritic myth.

In his discussion of the use of *ʾḥt* in Canticles, Pope (1977:657) notes the ubiquitous appearance throughout the ancient Near East of brother-sister address in love lyrics and poetry depicting human and divine couples. The term *ʾḥt*, "sister," is paralleled by *klh*, "bride," in Canticles 4:9, 10, 12 and 5:1-2, apparently with the meaning "beloved." Hence, many Ugaritologists assume that Anat's designation as Baal's

10 It is possible that Anat addresses Athirat as "(our) mother" in *KTU* 1.3 iii 34, if one reads [*u*]*m*, but this restoration is certainly not definite. The only goddess explicitly called *um*, "mother," in Ugaritic myth is Shapsh in *KTU* 1.100. This fact should not lead to Wyatt's (1983:273) conclusion, however, that Shapsh and Athirat are one and the same goddess.

"sister" signifies their erotic relationship.[11] A similar ambiguity remains in the use of sibling terms in Anat's proposal to the youth Aqhat, *at aḫ wan a*[*ḫtk*], "You are my brother and I am your sister" (1.18 i 24). While de Moor (1987:242 n. 128) is characteristically emphatic that this is doubtlessly a formal proposal of marriage, the sense of this broken passage remains problematic.[12] Since an actual kinship relation seems impossible here, Anat may be offering either an erotic, conjugal, covenantal, or simply a friendly alliance with the young hunter.

KTU 1.3 iv 39-40 applies another kinship term to Anat and Baal: "Baal saw the coming of his sister, the approach of his father's daughter (-in-law?)," *hlk aḫth b*ᶜ*l y*ᶜ*n tdrq ybnt abh.* Scholars have explained *ybnt* as "sister" based upon its parallelism to *aḫt* (*UT* 408) and a possible Arabic cognate (Ginsberg 1945a:9), as a scribal error or variant for *ybmt* (de Moor 1987:14 n. 70), or as a scribal error for *bnt* influenced by *ybmt* (*TO* 172). Hence, this phrase could identify Anat as either the daughter or daughter-in-law of Baal's father. The translation "daughter" for *ybnt* seems more plausible based upon the parallelism with *aḫt*, but neither reading is definite.

While the relationship of Anat and Baal must be considered within the context of all relevant information, the termt *aḫt*, "sister," certainly does not in itself necessitate any sexual or marital relationship. References to Anat as Baal's "sister" may simply denote their similar natures as aggressive warriors. The term may also serve as a general appellation for deities of equal rank, just as members of the younger generation of Ugaritic deities are called the "son" or "daughter" of the

---

11 Other issues raised by the application of this epithet to Anat are incest and the concept of brother-sister marriages in the ancient Near East. Note Eichler (1977) on Nuzi marriage contracts and this long debated matter. However, incest is largely irrelevant to the metaphorical designation of lover as sibling. Furthermore, scholars have yet to seriously consider references to incest as a factor in the interpretation of Ugaritic myth (cf. Starr 1984), although more information concerning Syrian pantheons might alter the present situation. Albright (1968:128) surely goes too far in stating that "the notion of incest scarcely existed" in ancient Egypt and Canaan.

12 Dressler (1979) argues that the initial /a/ of *aḫtk* is not visible on the tablet. Refuting the existence of parallel formulas of proposal, Dressler prefers to translate, "Come, O brother, and I myself will...." While Dressler is correct in emphasizing the conjectural nature of Anat's message, it is not inappropriate to provide a parallel term for *aḫ* in this context. Regardless, even the reading "You are my brother and I am [your sister]" does not necessitate a formal proposal of marriage.

patriarch El. Within this context note the use of these terms in *KTU* 1.10 ii 13-25.

13) wyšu. ^{c}nh. aliyn. b^{c}l	And Almighty Baal lifted his eyes;
wyšu. ^{c}nh. wy^{c}n	he lifted his eyes and saw.
15) wy^{c}n. btlt. ^{c}nt	He saw Maiden Anat,
n^{c}mt. bn. aḫt. b^{c}l	the loveliest among the sisters of Baal.
lpnnh. ydd. wyqm	He quickly rose before her;
lp^{c}nh. ykr^{c}. wyql	he knelt and fell at her feet.
wyšu. gh. wyṣḥ	He lifted his voice and called,
20) ḥwt. aḫt. wnar[ ]	"Greetings, sister, and ... ![13]
qrn. dbatk. btlt. ^{c}nt	The horns of your strength, Maiden Anat,[14]
qrn. dbatk. b^{c}l. ymšḥ	the horns of your strength Baal will anoint;
b^{c}l. ymšḥ hm. b^{c}p	Baal will anoint them in flight!

---

13 The meaning of *ḥwt* in Baal's greeting remains enigmatic; the missing letter(s) at the end of the line complicates the philological analysis. Marcus (1972) has demonstrated that *ḥwt* must represent a factitive D stem rather than a G stem of *ḥyy*, "to live." However, Dahood (1979:448) and others (e.g. Gordon 1977:119) are not convinced, preferring to understand *ḥwt* as "May you live long!" De Moor (1979:643) argues for reading *ḥwt* as a passive D stem, "May you be revived." If *wnark* is restored, the common pairing of the roots *ḥwy* and *ᵓrk* in Phoenician votive inscriptions quoted in Marcus (1972) suggests some idea of preservation in this salutary formula, but the actual sense still eludes me. *KTU* reads a questionable /k/, while *CTA* sees either a /b/ or a /d/. In fact, the clear photograph of the tablet in *CTA* does not suggest a /k/. Perhaps one should read *wnarb*, "and let us set an ambush," cognate with BH *ᵓrb*, "to lie in ambush," keeping with the martial connotation of the following lines. Ultimately, however, the text is uncertain.

14 Although the context requires the sense of anointing Anat's horns for battle (Pardee 1976:252), the lexeme *dbatk* is difficult. Sanmartín (1980) reviews earlier opinions and advocates an understanding of Ugaritic *dbat* as "head-dress." While Anat is certainly iconographically depicted as a horned goddess, Sanmartín's etymological defense is lacking. Cross (1952:163) defends the older idea of connecting *dbat* with the unique *dobᵓekā*, "your strength," in Deuteronomy 33:25. *TO* (284) first suggested explaining this lexeme through an Arabic verb *dabaᵓa*, "frapper avec une bâton," and Akkadian *daᵓāp/bu*, "écraser (un ennemi)." Similarly, Watson (1978:277) reads, "your butting(?) horns." But, like Sanmartín (1980:342), I can not locate the Arabic verb *dabaᵓa*. The Akkadian is also an implausible cognate (see *AHw* 146). Parsing *qrn* as an imperative of *qry* and *dbatk* from the root *bwᵓ*—an interpretation going back to Virolleaud and Dussaud (see *TO* 284)—Kapelrud (1969:95) offers the peculiar reading, "Come here, so that I may have intercourse with you."

nṭ[c] n. barṣ. iby	Let us thrust my enemies into the earth,
25) wb[c] pr. qm. aḫk	and into the dust the adversaries of your brother!"

Here Anat's designation as "the loveliest of the sisters of Baal" may in fact refer to her beauty among the goddesses in general rather than an explicit comparison to only the females of Baal's family.

Indeed, the precise nature of Baal and Anat's relations would not be particularly important except for the point that Baal is frequently called the son of Dagan, *bn dgn*, in the Ugaritic texts.[15] This evidence for the storm god's lineage complicates the analysis of Anat's role as intermediary between El and Baal in *KTU* 1.3 iv-v. Oldenburg (1969) argues that Baal and Anat are the offspring of Dagan and that this family has its origins in the Mid-Euphrates region. Hence, her support of Baal against El in the Ugaritic myths illustrates a family feud. Other commentators (e.g. Kapelrud 1969:40-2) prefer to take Anat's appellation as the sister of Baal figuratively and her title as the daughter of El literally. Astour (1966:279 n. 27) would remove this difficulty by identifying El with Dagan. Such an equation is supported by Baal's frequent reference to El as *ab*, "father" (e.g. 17 i 23; 1.4 iv 47-52 and parallel passages). While some passages in the Ugaritic mythological texts do suggest that the phrase "brothers of Baal" refers to the gods in general (e.g. 1.4 v 28-9), other passages present a clear demarcation between Baal's kin and the family of Athirat (e.g. 1.6 i 39-43; 1.6 v 1-4). In *KTU* 1.6 v 19-20 Mot demands one of Baal's brothers to eat, but in 1.6 vi 10-1 he realizes that Baal has given him his own relative to consume. Mot identifies these gods as *aḫym*, "my own brothers," and *bnm umy*, "sons of my mother." This evidence, while not conclusive, strongly suggests that Baal and Mot, the beloved son of El, are of different parentage.[16] Similarly, one can explain Baal's overt references to El as his father as the language of diplomacy rather than kinship since

15 On the god Dagan, see Oldenburg (1969:47-57), Gese (1970:107-13), and Roberts (1972:18-9, 74-6), with references.

16 Note Cunchillos (1985:210-7), who argues that this character is actually Mut, "the warrior," rather than Mot, "death." Hence, he is "Mut the son of El," *bn ilm mt*, "the Hero, the beloved of El," *ydd bn il ǵzr*, who defends his family against the attacks of Baal, according to Cunchillos.

the storm god is most solicitous when he has a favor to ask (e.g. 1.17 i 23). Note especially Baal's message to El in *KTU* 1.4 iv 47-8 and parallel passages, *any lyṣḥ ṯr il abh il mlk dyknnh*, "Groaning he [Baal] calls out to Bull El, his father, to El the king who created him" when he desires the royal status associated with his own palace. This appellation emphasizes Baal's subservient status to the elder god and probably signifies their political rather than their familial relationship.

Another attempt at harmonization has been offered by Wyatt (1980), who argues that Dagan and Baal Hadad are but two manifestations of one storm deity. Based upon an Arabic etymology for the name Dagan, Wyatt (1980:377-8) suggests that *bn dgn* does not identify Baal as the son of Dagan but designates him as "the Rainy One" (cf. Roberts 1972:18). In fact, the "daughters" of Baal, called *pdry bt ar* and *ṭly bt rb*, are probably hypostatic manifestations of Baal's own fertilizing attributes whose names identify them as sources of water for the earth. Furthermore, Wyatt (1980:378) explains the reference to Baal as *ḥtk dgn* in *KTU* 1.10 iii 32-6 as "Lord Dagan" rather than "son of Dagan."[17] The lack of information concerning Dagan from the Ugaritic texts precludes a definite conclusion, but it is noteworthy that Dagan does appear as the father of the storm god in cuneiform sources (Roberts 1972:75). Finally, the consistent distinction between El, Baal, and Dagan in Ugaritic god lists and sacrificial texts compels me to distinguish among the three gods until further evidence is available.

Other attempts to harmonize the available information concerning the sibling relation of Anat as the daughter of El and Baal as the son of Dagan by positing Athirat as their common mother are overly rationalist and unsatisfying. Similarly, Pope (1971) has advocated a more serious consideration of the theogony of the Phoenician priest Sanchuniathon found in Philo of Byblos' *Phoenician History*.[18] Here El-Kronos defeats

---

[17] On this term see Healey (1980). He concedes that *ḥtk* may mean "lordship" as in Arabic but concludes that Ugaritic *ḥtk* refers to the father-son relationhsip of Baal and Dagan based upon its derivation from the verbal root "to care for."

[18] See Oden and Attridge (1981) and Baumgartner (1981) for critical editions of the fragments of Philo's *Phoenician History*, recorded in the church father Eusebius' *Praeparatio Evangelica*. The history of Kronos is found in *PE* 1.10.15-30. Attridge and Oden (1981:88 n. 94) demonstrate the identity of Sanchuniathon's Zeus and the Ugaritic Baal Hadad. Similarly, Baal is called *dmrn* at Ugarit (1.4 vii 39), while Philo explicitly equates Zeus, Demarous, and Adodos in *PE* 1.10.31. See L'Heureux

his father Ouranos and gives to his brother, Dagan, Ouranos' pregnant mistress, who then gives birth to Baal-Demarous (*PE* 1.10.18-9). Thus, Baal's complex paternity in this tradition makes him the nominal son of Dagan even though he is the biological brother of El. The reliability of this Hellenistic kinship structure as a reflection of Ugaritic traditions, however, is unsure.

The lack of an Ugaritic theogony apart from Sanchuniathon prohibits any clear resolution of the problems at hand. Moreover, caution must be exercised in attributing consistency to divine lineages given the unsystematic nature of ancient Syrian pantheons (see Lambert 1985). For the present study we can say that Baal appears to be of a different social or familial group than the "sons of Athirat." Oldenburg's demarcation of the pantheon into two familial groups is perhaps accurate, although his study is marred by his inherently flawed social and historical explanation of myth. While Baal does not overthrow El in the Ugaritic texts, kinship relations most probably play a role in the struggle for divine kingship between Baal and Athirat's sons. Anat's position within this structure remains ambiguous as she is described as the daughter of El, sister of Baal, and daughter (-in-law?) of Dagan. If Anat is not the consort of Baal, then her identity as his biological sister is largely irrelevant to her role as his faithful companion. Similarly, it is essentially unimportant whether her subordinate status to El is based upon a biological or merely social relationship as long as her inferior position is recognized. The question of her conjugal relation to Baal is further addressed below.

Anat as ybmt limm. One of the more troublesome aspects of Anat's description in the Ugaritic texts is her frequent appellative *ybmt limm.*[19] Unfortunately, this difficult epithet apparently contains important

---

(1979:31-49) on the relation of Sanchuniathon's tradition to Ugaritic myth. While this Hellenistic source is not reliable as evidence of Ugaritic myth, it is noteworthy that El-Kronos retains ultimate authority as he grants dominion over the earth to Baal and other deities (*PE* 1.10.31). This is the same situation which is evident in the Baal Cycle.

19 Bowman (1978:186-93) provides an overview of various opinions concerning *ybmt limm* (see the bibliography in del Olmo Lete 1981:557). See now the opinion of Hvidberg-Hansen (1979, I:100, with notes) that *ybmt limm* is a "political" title designating Anat as a tutelary goddess. Kutsch (1986b) provides an excellent summary of the discussion of the root *ybm* and related terms in Hebrew.

information concerning her place within the Ugaritic pantheon. That is, *ybmt limm* most probably contains a kinship reference, possibly regarding Baal. The lexeme *ybmt* is usually treated as a cognate of BH **yābāmâ*, "widowed sister-in-law," and **yābām*, "brother of deceased husband," both attested only in suffixed forms (Deut 25:5-9; Ruth 1:15). The verbal root *ybm* only appears twice in the Bible, each time in the D stem (Deut 25:5-7 and Gen 38:8), referring to the practice of marrying one's deceased brother's widow in order to produce an heir for him. With one exception, the term *ybm/ybmt* is unattested in Akkadian.[20] The use of the root *ybm* in later dialects of Hebrew and Aramaic reflects the same semantic limitation to levirate marriages as the biblical usage (see Kutsch 1986b:368). In his explanation of the BH verbal root *ybm*, Albright refers to Arabic *wabama*, "to create," and Akkadian *bamatu*, "loins," and thus translates Anat's epithet as "Progenitress of the Peoples." Albright infers that the West Semitic root *ybm* and its derivatives originally denoted "procreation" but came to refer to "widowed sister-in-law" and "brother-in-law" as procreators within the context of the Hebrew levirate marriage.[21] However, the standard lexica do not cite an Arabic root *wabama* (see Kutsch 1986b:369 n.8), thus seriously weakening Albright's interpretation. As I argue below, the accumulated evidence best supports the etymological explanation that BH *ybm/ybmh* refers primarily to a brother- and sister-in-law relationship and that its application in the levirate marriage custom is a secondary development (Kutsch 1986b:370).

Other attempts to explain the Ugaritic *ybmt* apart from the BH cognate are based explicitly upon contextual rather than etymological

---

20 The term **yabam* is attested in an Old Babylonian letter from Tell al-Rimah, apparently as a West Semitic loanword (Page 1968:94-5). The context concerns a woman, Belassunu, who is to leave her husband's home and live with "her brother-in-law," *yabamīša*, written *ia-ba-mi-ša-ma*. This is not a reference to levirate marriage, since the woman's husband is still living. While the translation "brother-in-law" is logical, there is insufficient evidence to know if this is the precise definition of the term. De Moor (1969:183) speculates that the reference is to Belassunu's step-father, who had to marry her mother since Belassunu's father had sired only daughters. Of course, the Akkadian understanding of the term may be different from the (original?) West Semitic usage.

21 See Albright (1938:19 n. 6; 1953:195) and his opinion quoted by Burrows (1940:6-7).

defenses. Virolleaud (1936:151-2) very early attempted to circumvent this problem by positing the translation "protectress of the peoples" from an "unknown" primary meaning of BH *ybmh*. Gese (1971:157), followed by Craigie (1978:377), has suggested the contextual interpretation of *ybmt* as a reference to the independent status of Anat. That is, as a "widowed sister-in-law," Anat may be attributed a social position in which she is not under the direct authority of any one male. While this is a most attractive explanation based upon Anat's narrative role within the mythological texts, there is no evidence to support such a connotation to the West Semitic term. Indeed, both Hebrew and Akkadian legal codes clearly place the widowed woman under the complete authority of her father-in-law unless she is returned to her father's house (see Saporetti 1979:4-5; Westbrook 1988). The lack of even a possible etymological or historical explanation seriously weakens this hypothesis which is based more upon the mythographer's interpretive presupposition than any ancient evidence.

Usually parsed as a root *lʾm* with enclitic /m/, the Ugaritic lexeme *limm* has also provoked numerous scholarly explanations. The most straightforward translation of *limm* is "peoples," based upon the BH cognate *lĕʾōm* (pl. *lĕʾūmmîm*) as well as the contextual use of the Ugaritic term in parallel to *hmlt*, "multitudes" (e.g. 1.5 vi 23-4).[22] Following Driver, Gray (1965:40 n. 8) defends the relation between Ugaritic *lʾm* and Akkadian *limmu/līmu*. Since a *limmu* is an Assyrian official whose name serves as the eponym for a given year, Gray posits the meaning "prince" for BH and Ugaritic *lʾm*. Gray (1965:40 n. 8, 271) further argues for the translation of certain biblical attestations of *lʾmym* as "princes" based upon its rendering in LXX as *archones*, which he holds must mean "rulers." Hence, the Ugaritic term *limm* may refer to either "(human) princes" or "the Prince (i.e. Baal)."[23] Gray (1965:43) accordingly translates *ybmt limm* as "the Sister of the Prince,"

---

22 See Preuss (1984) for a discussion of the lexeme *lʾm* in BH and other Northwest Semitic languages. The BH term *hmlh*, found only in Ezek 1:24 and Jer 11:16, clearly refers to a crowd of humans.

23 Gray (1979:319 n. 28) has more recently suggested parsing *limm* as the active participle of the verbal root *lʾy*, "to be mighty," with "the plural of majesty" and a final /m/ with "the force of the definite article." Hence, *limm* is a reference to Baal related to his stock epithet *aliyn*. Gray translates *ybmt limm* as "the Sister of the Mighty One." This is an unlikely etymology.

while Driver (1956:85) suggests "sister-in-law of rulers." Similarly, Pope (1965:240) offers "widowed spouse of the Prince." However, the biblical attestations of *lʾmym* in the poetic parallelism of Gray's examples (Gen 27:29; Isa 34:1; 41:1; 43:4, 9 and 55:4) are better understood as "peoples" than "princes."[24] Barr (1987:254-5) points out the lack of etymological evidence for rendering Ugaritic *limm* as "rulers" and notes the uniqueness of the development of the Assyrian *limmu* institution. To be sure, a link between Anat's epithet *ybmt limm* and the Assyrian title *limmu* is difficult to substantiate. While an epithet linking Anat with rulers is certainly an attractive one for this militant goddess with royal connections, the lack of a reliable etymological or historical explanation prohibits its serious consideration.

Along the same interpretive lines, Craigie (1978:377) has proposed translating *limm* as "warriors" based upon the use of *lim* to describe the characters whom Anat battles in *KTU* 1.3 ii. Avoiding a definition of *ybmt*, Craigie (1978:377) suggests that Anat's epithet *ybmt limm* describes her as "a leader or patroness of warriors." Gordon (1966:51; 1977:15) apparently adopts a similar understanding as he tentatively offers "Progenitress of Heroes" as a translation for *ybmt limm.* Such appealing epithets are consistent with descriptions of Anat in both Ugaritic and Egyptian materials but are ultimately lacking in etymological foundation. Craigie's translation rests upon his interpretation of the obscure mythological scene in *KTU* 1.3 ii as a reference to humans raiding Anat's house. While Anat is reported to defeat both *ḏmr*, "guards," and *mhrm*, "warriors" (1.3 ii 14-28), the parallelism of *lim* and *adm*, "humans," in lines 7-8 does not support a martial connotation for *lim.* Although the Akkadian cognate *līmu*, "thousand," makes a wider semantic range for the Ugaritic term possible, the clear and consistent use of BH *lʾm* and *hmlh* to refer only to human multitudes is more convincing. The semantic development from "thousands" to "armies" is certainly not a difficult one to imagine, but

---

[24] Barr (1987:254-5) discusses the etymologizing process behind the LXX translation of BH *lĕʾōm* as "ruler." Driver states that the translation *lʾmym* as "rulers" is proven by the frequency of the LXX reading, even though he argues the examples cited by Gray are incorrect. Instead, he gives Psalms 148:11 and 7:9 as better examples of this meaning of *lʾmym.* Barr (1987:255), however, shows that neither of these two passages provides solid evidence for *lʾmym* as "rulers."

there is no proof of this meaning for Ugaritic *lim*. The common parallelism of *lim* and *hmlt* at Ugarit best supports the translation of Ugaritic *limm* as "peoples, multitudes." Translations other than this must provide more reliable etymological explanations, as well as contextual evidence, than those offered above.

Reference has also been made to the god Lim, the patron deity of the royal family at Mari (see Nakata 1974:344-53), in attempting to explain Ugaritic *limm*. The divine name Lim appears exclusively in personal names written without the determinative for divinity, suggesting that this deity represents the collective "thousand gods" (Akkadian *līmu*, "one thousand") honored at Mari (Huffmon 1965:226). Hence, the epithet Lim may serve as the "personification" of the divine totality similar to the designation of the Israelite god Yahweh with the plural form *ᵓĕlōhîm*. Hadad (Bowman 1978:192), Dagan (Dossin 1950), and even Shamash (Lipínski 1967) have been nominated as serious candidates for the Mesopotamian deity represented by the appellative Lim. If Lim does represent a major deity at Mari, then Ugaritic *limm* may refer to either that deity or his divine kin—i.e. the Liᵓmites (de Moor 1969:183)—to whom Anat is a *ybmt*. The meaning of this frequent epithet within the Ugaritic tradition is not clarified by this explanation, however, since it ultimately rests upon a lost mythological tradition from the Mid-Euphrates region.

Bowman (1978:189) attempts to simplify the complex issue of Anat's epithet *ybmt limm* by distinguishing between the writings *lim* and *limm* in Ugaritic texts. In his attempt to identify *limm* as the divine name Lim at Ugarit, Bowman (1978:189) states that "*limm* is found in Ugaritic only as an epithet of ᶜAnatu. But the noun *lim* ["peoples"] is found as well." However, Bowman neglects to note that the writing *lim* also occurs in the theophorous personal name *yrgb lim* (1.102, 22) as a divine name or epithet.[25] Hence, any distinction between the writing *lim*

25 Similarly, Craigie (1978:377 n. 19) neglects to defend his statement that the use of *lim* as a name for Anat in *KTU* 1.13 probably has nothing to do with "the divine name *lim*" in *KTU* 1.102. Perhaps he understands the latter Ugaritic occurrence as a reference to the foreign Lim of Mari. Nakata (1974:344) also notes two personal names in Akkadian letters from Ugarit which appear to have the divine name Lim, written with the DINGIR-sign. These names may be understood as Itūr-^{d}Lim, written GUR.DINGIR.LIM, and Zimri-Lim, written *zi-im-ri*-DINGIR.LIM (see Nougayrol 1956:69 and 178). Since these names may derive from Marite rather than native

as "people," based upon BH *lĕʾōm*, and *limm* as Lim with enclitic /m/ is unfounded. Given the existence of the theophorous element *lim* in *KTU* 1.102 (and possibly in 1.13), the writing *limm* at Ugarit clearly may signify an independent divine name or epithet other than Lim of Mari (cf. Ginsberg 1945a:8-9). Indeed, the lexeme *limm* in *KTU* 1.13, 20 has been understood as an independent name for Anat herself (Herdner 1963:57 n. 27; Craigie 1978:377). Hence, *ybmt limm* may be "(the) *ybmt* Lim," parallel to *btlt ᶜnt*, "(the) Maiden Anat," and *rḥm ᶜnt*, "(the) Damsel Anat." Unfortunately, the available information does not allow for a definite conclusion concerning the existence of the independent divine name *lim* at Ugarit. While the personal names *yrgb lim* and *yrgb bᶜl* in *KTU* 1.102 suggest that *lim* serves as an independent name, the Ugaritic origin of these personal names is unclear. Similarly, the parallelism of *limm* and *btlt ᶜnt* in *KTU* 1.13, 19-20 can not be confirmed because of the broken condition of the text. Thus, whether *lim(m)* denotes an independent divine name at Ugarit is uncertain, although possible. The relevance of this matter to Anat's epithet also remains unclear.

Given the etymological dead-end at which we have arrived, attention must now be focused on possible interpretations of the epithet *ybmt limm* within the larger mythological context. De Moor incorporates his particular etymology of the epithet *ybmt limm* into his comprehensive presentation of Anat as the patroness of wanton love. He (1987:7 n. 34) describes *ybmt limm* as a "technical term" meaning "Wanton Widow of the Nations." By accepting the identification of the god Lim as Dagan, de Moor (1969:183) has defended the view that Anat is the "widow of the Liʾmites," i.e. the clan of Dagan/Liʾmu. De Moor (1980:309) further supports this position through his unique restoration and translation of a scene within the divine assembly after the death of Baal (1.6 i 30-1):[26]

Ugaritic onomastic traditions the existence of the divine name Lim at Ugarit remains uncertain.

[26] De Moor (1980:309) also reads *lim bn dgn* as "the clan of Dagan" in *KTU* 1.5 vi 23-5 and 1.6 i 6-8, although he has since altered his translation minimally to read as follows (1987:81; cf. Gray 1965:62):

bᶜl. mt. my. lim. bn dgn.	Baᶜlu is dead! What about the people of the son of Daganu?
my. hmlt. aṯr bᶜl.	What about the multitude of the followers of Baᶜlu?

[bšp]ḥh. tštbm ᶜ[nt]	In his [Baal's] tribe ᶜAnatu proclaimed herself a nubile widow,
[k. ǵ]zrh. ybm ll!i!m	so that his fellows would fulfil their *ybm*-duty for the clan.

De Moor parses *tštbm* as a Št stem of the verbal root *ybm* and alters the acceptable *ybm lilm* to read *ybm llim.* Yet even de Moor (1987:11) translates Anat's boast of *lištbm tnn* in *KTU* 1.3 iii 40 by the conventional "Did I not muzzle Tunannu?" While *KTU* 1.6 i 30-1 is a difficult passage and the verbal root of the forms *tštbm* and *lištbm* are disputed, de Moor's ingenious proposal of a Št stem of *ybm*, "to proclaim oneself a *ybm*[*t!*]," lacks support.[27]

De Moor has since slightly modified his view to give Anat's position as a "Wanton Widow" a more cosmic allusion. He (1980:308-9) argues that upon the death of her husband, Baal, Anat assumes the social position as a nubile widow whom the nearest male kin was expected to marry. He explains:

> We know that the men obliged to marry such a widow were often unwilling to fulfill their duty (Gen. 38:9; Deut. 25:7-10; Ruth 4:6). Women in this position had to go pretty far in trying to seduce a suitable partner from the clan of their deceased husband (Gen. 38:14ff.; Ruth 3). As a result the *ybmt* aquired a reputation of lewdness. This is the reason why ᶜAnat was the patroness of wanton love, the harlot of the world who virtually denied her widowhood.... (de Moor 1980:309; cf. 1987:7 n. 34)

---

ard. barṣ	I will descend into the earth!

Other scholars understand the text differently. I translate:

bᶜl. mt. my. lim.	Baal is dead—what of the peoples?
bn dgn. my. hmlt.	The Son of Dagan—what of the multitudes?
aṯr bᶜl. ard. barṣ	After Baal I will descend into the Netherworld!
	(1.5 vi 23-5)

The stichometric division of the latter is clearly superior to that of de Moor and Gray. Similarly, de Moor (1987:14 n.70) explains *ybnt abh*, "Wanton Widow of his father," in *KTU* 1.3 iv 40 as an important variant of *ybmt limm* (see also 1969:183 n. 117).

27 See del Olmo Lete (1982:66) on *KTU* 1.6 i 30-1 for his defense of the more usual reading *tšt bm*, and Barr (1987:387-411) on the lack of reliable evidence for the existence of the Ugaritic root *šbm*.

Note that de Moor's interpretation of these passages and Anat's epithet *ybmt limm* is based explicitly upon the condition that Baal "had died without giving her a son" (de Moor 1987:14 n 70). Hence, de Moor appears to prescribe Anat's status as a non-procreative goddess, at least at the time of Baal's death. We will return to this matter below.

Bowman (1978:186-93) also offers an explanation of Anat's epithet *ybmt limm* consistent with his general interpretive approach. After considering the alternatives, Bowman assumes the identity of the Mesopotamian and Ugaritic Lim as Baal Hadad. He (1978:188) argues that the Hebrew cognate of *ybmt* thus can not be applied literally since "ᶜAnatu must then be a widowed sister-in-law, married to one of Baᶜlu's brothers." Understanding BH *ybmh* as "the one to whom a substitute (husband) is given," Bowman (1978:189) conjectures that Anat "is in fact the substitute" based upon her role in the Baal Cycle. Hence, Bowman (1978:189) understands *ybmt limm* as "the substitute for Lim/Haddu." He argues that Anat's intimate association with Baal encompasses her role as his surrogate or substitute while he is confined to the Netherworld. In this role the goddess fights Baal's enemy Mot in order to restore the fertility god to life. Bowman (1978:189) further suggests that the phrase *ybm lilm* in *KTU* 1.6 i 31 refers to Anat as the "substitute/surrogate for the god" (i.e. Baal, with enclitic /m/) without an explanation of the difference in the term's gender here.[28] While consistent with his interpretation of Anat as a hypostatic manifestation of Baal, Bowman's explanation of *ybmt limm* is unconvincing. The semantic leap from "(widowed) sister-in-law" to "substitute" lacks support. The conclusion that "the Ugaritic *ybmt* is the feminine counterpart of Hebrew *yābām*" (Bowman 1978:189) rather than the semantic equivalent of BH *ybmh* is also unsubstantiated. While Bowman presents a coherent interpretation of Anat's epithet as a component of her larger character, his etymological analysis is ultimately lacking.

Bowman, as well as other scholars, discounts the use of the term *yĕbimtēk*, "your sister-in-law," in Ruth 1:15 to designate two women

---

28 Bowman (1978:189 n. 71) does note *KTU* 1.108, 6 "in which the masculine adjective, *g̱tr* is used to describe ᶜAnatu" in order to defend his interpretation. This broken text may be variously interpreted to avoid the attribution of a masculine adjective to the goddess Anat.

related through their deceased husbands. That is, they are affines of equal status who are part of the same household through marriage. Ruth and Orpah are *ybmh*, "sister-in-law," to each other and *klt*, "daughter-in-law," to Naomi. That Ruth is never called the *ybmh* of Boaz, although he is her "redeeming kinsman," *gōʾēl* (e.g. Ruth 3:9), and "relative," *mdᶜ* (Ruth 2:1; 3:2), shows that the term *ybm* is more strictly reserved for "brother-in-law" rather than simply "one who marries a widowed kinswoman."[29] While the status of *ybmh* clearly requires both widowhood and lack of male offspring in the biblical texts, the primary connotation of the term appears to be referential to the brother- and sister-in-law relationship rather than levirate marriage. Again, the exclusive attestation of *ybmh* in suffixed forms in BH shows the relational function of this term and its contexual use suggests its more specific role as an affinal designation for persons of the same generation. This matter is important for the Ugaritic mythological texts, wherein one must account for the two occurrences of *ybm* as well as Anat's epithet *ybmt*. The sole appearance of *ybm* in the Baal Cycle in the phrase *ybm lilm* (1.6 i 31) seems to identify Baal as the "brother-in-law to the gods" in order to distinguish him from the sons of El and Athirat. Such should be the meaning of the phrase if Ugaritic *ybm* is in fact cognate to BH *ybm*, although one can not rule out the possibilities that *ybm lilm* refers to someone other than Baal or that this *ybm* represents a homographic term of which we are presently ignorant.[30]

The possibility of Baal's appellation as the "*ybm* of the gods" brings us to another possible interpretation of Anat's elusive epithet. References to "the thousand gods," *līm ilāni*, are found in letters from Ugarit written in Akkadian (see Nougayrol 1956:258), suggesting that Anat's epithet *ybmt limm* refers to her position as the *ybmt* of the "thousand (gods)." In fact, *ybm lilm* in *KTU* 1.6 i 31 could simply be a scribal error for *ybm limm*, the masculine form of Anat's epithet, especially since the meaning of the two terms would be equivalent in this context. While there are no references to the divine hosts as *limm*, this term's frequent poetic parallel, *hmlt*, is perhaps used to describe the

29 On the legal implications of Ruth's marriage to Boaz, and possible connection to the levirate marriage practice in ancient Israel, see Sasson (1979) with bibliography.

30 The second attestation of *ybm* in the Ugaritic corpus, in a badly broken section of the *Epic of Kirta* (1.16 ii 94), does not aid in determining its sense in Ugaritic.

assembled deities in *KTU* 1.2 i (Gibson 1977:41). If Baal is in fact the *ybm* of the gods—or at least of the circle of Athirat's family—then his sister Anat would be their *ybmt*. Hence, Anat's description as the "sister-in-law of the gods" could merely specify her position within the Ugaritic pantheon structure with no implications concerning her character. Of course, this suggestion prompts the equally difficult question of how Baal was related to the family of Athirat if not through marriage to Anat herself. The suggestion of other marital ties for Baal and Athirat's offspring—such as Athtart or the trio of Baal's "girls"—are equally speculative and do not aid the interpretation at this point. Thus, the Ugaritic phrase *ybm lilm* provides only a tantalizing hint of a more complete kinship structure to the pantheon without shedding any light upon the meaning of Anat's epithet *ybmt limm*.

While etymologically sound, the translation "sister-in-law of the peoples" has posed a great difficulty for some commentators regarding the sense of the epithet. Do the ancient mythographers intend this appellation to signify Anat as a relative of humans? Indeed, there is onomastic and cultic evidence from Akkadian, Syro-Palestinian, and Amorite sources which suggests that human-divine kinship relations were conceivable, although presumably these were understood as metaphorical rather than biological designations. The common use of kinship appellatives as theophorous elements in personal names provides abundant evidence for the indigenous ancient Near Eastern concept of divine-human relations (see Huffmon 1965:99-101). While common onomastic elements such as *ᵓb*, "father," and *ᵓm*, "mother," may be metaphors for close relations of dependence or love, the application of other kinship terms—especially those denoting affinal rather than consanguineous relationships—to deities proves more difficult to explain.[31]

---

[31] See Hoffmon (1965) for the following examples of kinship terms incorporated into Akkadian and Amorite theophorous names: * *ᵓab*-, "father" (154), * *ᵓaḫ*-, "brother" (160), **dād*-, "favorite" or perhaps "(paternal) uncle" (181-2), **ḫāl*-, "maternal uncle" (194-5), * *ᶜamm*-, "paternal uncle" (196-8). Confusion among the Semitic roots * *ᶜmm* and **ḥm* may result from terms for "father's relatives" or "male in-laws." Compare Arabic *ḥam* (Wehr 1976:203), Akkadian *emu* (*CAD* 4:154-6), and BH * *ᶜm* (Gen 19:38; 25:8) and *ḥām*.

Most pertinent to the present study is the use of Semitic *^{c}*ammu*, "paternal uncle," **ḫālu*, "maternal uncle" (Huffmon 1965:194-6), and *ḫatnu*, "son-in-law, male relative by marriage" (Huffmon 1965:205-6; Kutsch 1986a). The application of these terms to deities in Amorite and Akkadian onomastics presents us with less obvious social metaphors for human-divine relations. In particular, the frequent lexeme *ḫtn* in Amorite names appears to describe gods as the "brother-in-law" or male affinal relative of a human devotee. Huffmon (1965:205-6) provides examples, such as Ḫatni-Dagan, "Dagan is my *ḫtn*," Ḫatni-Samas, "Samsu is my *ḫtn*," as well as examples of its use as a theophorous appellative such as Yamṣi-ḫatnu, with the characteristic appellative writing *ḫa-at-nu-ú* (see Huffmon 1965:101). Clear examples of the theophorous use of the appellative include the names Ḫali-Ḫatnu (written *ḫa-li-ḫa-at-nu-ú*), "(the) *ḫatnu* is my maternal uncle," and the odd ^{c}Ammu-ḫalum. In discussing the Mari onomasticon ^{c}Ammi-^{c}Anat, written *ḫa-mi-*^{d}*Ḫa-na-at*, Huffmon (1965:196-7; 200-1) notes that Amorite *^{c}*ammu*, "paternal uncle," may in fact designate "kindred" in describing the goddess Anat. The evidence suggests that terms for affinal relationships are applied to human-divine relations in order to avoid the implication of consanguineity. Only clearly metaphorical terms for blood relations, such as "mother" and "father," might be applied to the divine-human relationships. Any discussion of the relative status of kinship relations, however, must await more detailed studies of kinship systems and terminology within ancient Mesopotamian and Syrian societies (for now see Wilcke 1986). The general conclusion reached here is simply that references to divine-human relations, particularly described with affinal terms, are not unusual in second millennium sources from the ancient Near East. Thus, Anat's position as "sister-in-law of the peoples (of Ugarit?)" would not be completely unprecendented or exceptional.

Although there are numerous onomastic examples of male deities described as divine kinsmen, the lexeme *ybmt* is unfortunately unattested in any ancient Near Eastern personal name. The scarcity of Amorite names with feminine theophorous elements drastically limits any comparative discussion, and Akkadian onomastics do not generally ascribe kinship terms to goddesses (see Stamm 1939). The idea of a divine *ybmt* gives us pause since the very limited information regarding the term suggests a dependent figure rather than one upon whom the human can depend. That is, the problem with Anat as a *ybmt* of humans concerns the gender of the term. Without recourse to the technical uses of these kinship terms, the present discussion can really suggest no explanation for this choice of kinship appellative. Since it is doubtful that Anat was thought to be dependent upon humans, a different route may prove more rewarding. Perhaps her role as "sister-in-law of the peoples" refers to her relationship with humans through the mediation of Baal. That is, if Baal was cultically "married" to a human priestess at Ugarit, then his sister would be the affinal relative of the priestess' human relations (cf. Gaster 1936:136-7). The concept of cultic functionaries being married to the deity whom they serve is not uncommon in the available material from Mesopotamia. Hallo and van Dijk (1968:7-8; 97) point out Sargon's claim to be the *pa*$_4$-*šeš*-AN, "the older brother/brother-in-law of An," apparently based on his daughter's position as a priestess of Nanna. Hence, he and An were related by their children's marriage. This title was also assumed by later Mesopotamian rulers. Thus, perhaps Anat is related to the humans of Ugarit through the marriage of the human priestess to her brother Baal. Our current lack of information concerning the organization of the cultic functionaries of Baal's Ugaritic temple renders this a most speculative proposal although I would defend its plausibility.

Apart from a possible cultic relationship, however, the Ugaritic mythological texts appear to describe a special relationship between Baal and the "multitudes" of the earth. Whether this is due to Baal's particular role as Ugarit's city god or his function as the bringer of rains in their season is ultimately irrelevant. Some special bond appears to connect Baal with humanity in the Ugaritic texts, and this tie may be a factor in Anat's own relationship to "the peoples." An allusion to the connection between Baal and humanity may be evident in the message Yamm has delivered to the divine assembly demanding Baal's capitulation (1.2 i 18-9 and 34-5).[32]

---

[32] Yamm's instructions may also may also be translated, "Surrender, o gods, the one whom you protect, the one whom you protect, o (divine) multitude!", deriving *dtqyn* from the same root as *dtqh* and understanding *hmlt* as a parallel to *ilm* (Gibson (1977:41). With most commentators I derive *tqh* from Ugaritic **yqy*, "to protect," based upon the Arabic *waqā*, "to guard, protect." The form *tqyn*, however, I parse as a 3 pl. f. form of the root **qwy*, cognate to BH *qwh*, "to wait (upon)." Compare Arabic

tn ilm dtqh	"Surrender the god whom you protect,
dtqyn hmlt	the one whom the (human) multitudes attend(?)!
tn b^{c}l w^{c}nnh	Surrender Baal and his lackeys,
bn dgn arṯm pḏh	the Son of Dagan (that) I may possess his gold!"

Similarly, after the defeat of his presumptuous rival and the construction of his royal mansion, Baal boasts of his qualifications for cosmic dominion:

aḥdy. dym(50)lk. ^{c}l. ilm.	"I alone am he who rules over the gods,
lymru (51) ilm. wnšm.	who indeed fattens gods and humans,
dyšb(52)[^{c}]. hmlt. arṣ.	who satisfies the multitudes of the earth!"
	(1.4 vii 49-52)

The intimate relationship beween Baal and the inhabitants of the earth may also be detected in the lament uttered by El and Anat (1.5 vi 23-4; 1.6 i 6-7) upon hearing of the storm god's demise. Here is voiced the expectation that humans are to suffer most from Baal's absence.

b^{c}l mt my lim	Baal is dead—what of the people?
bn dgn my hmlt	The Son of Dagan—what of the multitudes?

Human existence clearly depends upon Baal's fertilizing rains in the Ugaritic tradition (cf. 1.16 iii 5-16 and 1.6 iii) and the advent of Mot's dominion surely threatens the sustenance of humanity in the mythological texts (e.g. 1.6 ii 17-8). Such an intimate relationship between the inhabitants of Ugarit and the god Baal may be expressed in terms of kinship, especially given the marital overtones to the West Semitic term *b^{c}l*, "lord," even without a formal cultic institution. Hence, Anat's metaphorical position as the "sister-in-law of the peoples" may ultimately refer to her status as the sister of Ugarit's patron deity. To be sure, this a most speculative hypothesis but it is not without precedent in ancient Near Eastern religious and onomastic traditions.

In conclusion, I can offer no definite translation or interpretation of Anat's epithet *ybmt limm* within the Ugaritic mythological context. Of

---

qawiya, "to encourage, strengthen, embolden" in the II conjugation (Wehr 1976:802). Any translation of both *tqh* and *tqyn* is tentative, however.

possible interpretations based upon the available evidence, Albright's explanation of *ybmt* as "procreatress" and the attempts of Driver, Gray and Craigie to understand *lim* as "ruler or warrior" should be rejected on etymological grounds. At present, the kinship connotation of this appellative appears to be the most correct since *ybmt* is most easily associated with the BH cognate *ybmh.* This meaning makes little sense, however, without the larger context of the Ugaritic kinship system and pantheon structure. The combination of this etymological interpretation of *ybmt* with the possible translations of *limm* leads one to conclude that Anat is the sister-in-law of either a particular deity, the gods in general, a particular group of humans, or humanity in general. The evidence for an Ugaritic deity named *lim* is based almost entirely on one attestation in a personal name. If Anat is herself *lim*, then the connotation of her epithet *ybmt,* "the sister-in-law," remains unclear. If her epithet identifies her as the *ybmt* of a particular deity, such as Baal, then the mythic context and importance of this inner-pantheon kinship relation is unknown. Many scholars hold that this appellation refers to her position as the perennial "widow" of the deceased Baal. I find this explanation, addressed at length below, completely inconsistent. Perhaps Anat is the *ybmt* of the "thousand (gods)," just as Baal is apparently described as *ybm lilm* in *KTU* 1.6 i 31. On the other hand, *limm* may refer to human multitudes, either generically, marked by the plural, or some specific group of humans, marked with an enclitic /m/. The ancient Near Eastern evidence for human-divine, affinal relations is clearly attested but poorly understood. Thus, the matter of Anat's epithet *ybmt limm* must remain unresolved until the discovery of additional information.

Anat's Independence

The relative independence of Anat may be inferred from the mythological texts in which she plays an active role. Anat does not appear to be under the direct influence of any god in the Ugaritic texts. She sides with Baal in tablets 4-6 of the Baal Cycle, yet works counter to his goals in the *Epic of Aqhat.* Anat consistently acts upon her own desires and is submissive to no one in the extant literature. Her independent status contrasts with the role of the goddess Athirat as the wife of El. The elder goddess is considered a member of El's household in Baal's complaint that he and his "girls" must suffer the indignity of living in his father's house (1.4 iv 50-7, etc.). Anat, however, is conspicuous in her absence from this tirade. Thus, Anat's interrelations with other deities, especially the patriarch El, may provide clues to her dependence upon others for power and authority to fulfill her desired ends. The epithets of Anat will also be considered in this discussion, despite the recognition that epithets, given their hyperbolic nature, are not always reliable markers of relative prestige.

As previously argued, Anat's relationship with El appears to be one of a hierarchical nature. Whether or not El is recognized as her parent, Anat is subordinate in status to the elder god. Two episodes within the mythological corpus from Ugarit best illustrate the interaction of these two deities. In each instance Anat approaches the patriarch in his dwelling with a request, once for permission to have a palace built for Baal (1.3 v 1-3 and 24-5), and once for permission to punish Aqhat for his impudence (1.18 i 6-14). In each episode Anat begins her speech to El with the apparent warning not to rejoice in his own mansion lest she destroy it before turning to assault him. Anat warns El that she will cause his grey hair to run with blood and his grey beard with gore if he does not grant her request. El's response to his belligerent daughter begins with the formulaic statement *yd^{c}tk bt kanšt kin bilht qlṣk,* "I know you, (my) daughter, that you are incorrigible, (and) that there is no restraining you among the goddesses." He then gives her permission, perhaps grudgingly, to do as she desires (1.3 v 28-9 and 1.18 i 17-9).

Various interpretations of these scenes would present El as either amused, terrified, or indulgent in his response to the belligerent goddess. Unfortunately, the texts are not clear concerning El's disposition towards his divine daughter. In sharing her plan of action, Anat merely tells Baal that El "will attend to me," *yṯb ly* (1.3 iv 54), with no indication of El's actual estimation of the violent goddess. The very lines which might contain the description of El at the hearing of Anat's voice (1.3 v 10-6) are broken. Assuming the continuity of tablets *KTU* 1.3 and 1.4, El obviously does not concede her request in the missing section of 1.3 v-vi, since she and Baal must then importune Athirat to intercede with El on their behalf (1.4 iii). Hence, I conclude that El is not terrified of the impetuous young goddess. Her threats against the patriarch El are perhaps all bluff and bravado, in contrast to her truly murderous behavior elsewhere in the mythological material. Ultimately, however, the extant Ugaritic texts contain no explicit indication of El's opinion of Anat apart from her lack of restraint.

Anat is called the daughter of El explicitly when she is most rebellious against the divine patriarch. Yet even in her rebelliousness Anat must receive El's permission prior to accomplishing her desires. El appears to be the source of authority in the divine realm and important acts can not be executed without his acquiescence. Shapsh's persuasion of Mot to cease hostilities with Baal through her warning that El will disinherit him of his divine office is evidence of this (1.6 vi 22-31; cf. 1.2 iii 17-8). El is always a necessary figure for the authorized use of divine power or important decisions made by the gods. An obvious parallel to Anat's relationship to El is the relation of Ishtar to An in the *Epic of Gilgamesh*, discussed below. In each case the image is perhaps of an overly-indulgent father rather than an older god cowed by the demanding young goddess. Like Ishtar, Anat plays an unrestrained and independent role in this scene, exhibiting her lack of respect for the highest cosmic authority.[33]

In addition to the kinship and gender epithets applied to the goddess discussed above, Anat receives more prestigious appellations concerning her ruling authority. Anat is evoked with the following titles in a short mythological or hymnic text from Ugarit (1.108, 6-9).[34]

(6) wtšt. ^{c}nt. gṯr.	And Anat drinks aged wine,
b^{c}lt mlk	the Mistress of Kingship,
b^{c}(7)lt. drkt.	the Mistress of Dominion,
b^{c}lt. šmm. rmm	the Mistress of the High Heavens,
(8) [b^{c}]lt. kpṯ	the Mistress of the (royal) Headdress.

---

33 The actions of Athtart and Anat in *KTU* 1.114, 9-15 can also be interpreted as scornful of El's status (see Bowman 1978:134-9), but this damaged text is too difficult for treatment in the present context.

34 For a discussion of this text see Bowman (1978:139-42), Wyatt (1988:383), and especially L'Heureux (1979:169-81). On *gṯr* see the discussion of L'Heureux (1979:171), who argues for "wine aged in its lees" based upon the Syriac *getrâ*, "dregs, lees." Based upon the Akkadian *gašru*, "strong" (*CAD* 5:56-7), one might understand *gṯr* here and the phrase *gṯr wyqr* in line 2 as references to the establishment (Ugaritic root *šyt*) of strength and honor rather than a description of the gods imbibing (Ugaritic root *šty*) drink at a divine banquet. This is beside the point of the present discussion, however.

w^{c}nt. di. dit	And Anat sets off in flight,
rḫpt (9) [šmm] rm<m>	she who soars (in) the high [heavens(?)],
aklt. ^{c}gl. i(!)l.	she who devours the "calf of El."

The epithets *b^{c}lt mlk* and *b^{c}lt drkt* obviously parallel Baal's ruling attributes in *KTU* 1.2 iv 10, where Kothar-wa-Hasis proclaims *tqḥ. mlk. ^{c}lmk. drkt. dt drdrk*, "You (Baal) will take your eternal kingship, your dominion forever and ever!" I link Ugaritic *kpṯ* with Akkadian *kubšu* as a reference to a headdress, often a part of royal insignia or divinity (*CAD* 8:485-6). The reference to *^{c}gl il* is corrected in line 9 in accordance with line 11 of the present text as well as Anat's boast in *KTU* 1.3 iii 41 that she defeated this creature. Although Anat is not otherwise explicitly described as a royal figure in the extant myths from Ugarit, these epithets are consistent with her presentation in Egypt as "Queen of Heaven," suggesting a widespread acknowledgement of Anat's ruling prowess (Bowman 1978:141; Pritchard 1946:78-9; cf. Wyatt 1984). While these titles may be hyperbolic, no other Ugaritic goddesses are attributed epithets of ruling ability. Athirat is called the "Creatress of the Gods," *qnyt ilm*, an epithet which emphasizes her role as the progenitress of the gods but does not imply royalty. This is not to say that Anat is the most independent or authoritative of the Ugaritic goddesses; Shapsh also appears to play a role of considerable importance and independence. The lack of information concerning Ugaritic Athtart further clouds Anat's relative position among the goddesses. Anat's role in the distribution of divine authority over the cosmos is thus unclear, but it is sufficient at present to note her association with dominion in *KTU* 1.108.

Further evidence for the independent position of Anat within the divine realm is provided by her possession of her own palace and mountain home of *Inbb* (see Bowman 1978:143). As Anat departs for battle in *KTU* 1.3 ii 4, she closes "the gates of (her) mansion," *ṯǵrt bht*. Upon her return from the slaughter in lines 17-8 of the same column, we read, "Anat proceeds to her house, the goddess heads for her palace," *^{c}nt lbth tmǵyn / tštql ilt lhklh*. The designations *bht* and *hkl* clearly convey the palatial nature of her abode. The narrative of *KTU* 1.3 iii also describes her dwelling, explicitly identified as *Inbb* and *Uǵr* in 1.3 iv (contra Clifford 1972:87), at a distance from Baal's own dwelling on Sapon. In a parallel account (1.1 ii 14), El notes Anat's location as *Inbb* as he dispatches his messengers to her home. Similarly, *KTU* 1.13, 9 refers to Anat's home as *ǵrk inbb*, "your mountain *Inbb*." Finally, there is a reference to *^{c}nt w^{c}ṯtrt inbbh*, "Anat and Athtart at *Inbb*," in the mythological incantation against snakebite (1.100, 20). This text places each deity in his or her traditional location, including El at the "source(s) of rivers, at the confluence of the two deeps" (*mbk nhrm b^{c}dt thmtm*), Baal on "the heights of Sapon" (*mrym ṣpn*), Kothar-wa-hasis at *kptr*, and Dagan at Tuttul. Anat's exclusion from the formulaic reference to the dependents of Baal having to live in the house of El and Athirat (e.g. 1.4 iv 50-7) further attests her traditional possession of an independent abode in the mythological literature from Ugarit.[35]

The importance of a deity's possession of a palace as a mark of status is reflected in Baal's efforts to secure his own palace on Mt. Sapon. In discussing the kingdom of Athtar in the Baal Cycle, Waterston (1988:360) notes the accoutrements of royalty attributed to Athtar, including a throne, scepter, and kingship, in *KTU* 1.2 iii. Yet Athtar is unsatisfied and complains, "I have no house like the (other) gods, nor a court like the sons of Qudshu," *ank. in. bt*[. *l*]*y*[. *km.*] *ilm. wḥẓr*[. *kbn qd*]*š* (1.2 iii 19-20). This difficult scene at the beginning of the Baal

---

[35] Although the mythological corpus consistently describes *Inbb* as Anat's residence (see esp. 1.100, 20), there are three references to *^{c}nt ṣpn* in sacrificial lists from Ugarit (1.109, 13, 14 and 17; 1.46, 17). The most obvious explanation for this reference to "Anat-Sapon" (not "Anat of Sapon") is Anat's common association with Baal and his mountain home. That this designation occurs only in the cultic texts further sugests that Anat's cultic manifestation as *^{c}nt ṣpn* may only refer to her association with the cult of Baal, or the cult of the deified mountain Sapon, rather than her abode within Baal's house. Note the numerous Baals that appears in the Ugaritic god lists, including both *b^{c}l hlb* and *b^{c}l ṣpn*, as well as the multiple Anats, *^{c}ntm*. Baal's association with Mount Sapon is abundantly attested in the mythological corpus, although he is only attributed the title *b^{c}l ṣpn* in the liturgical texts (see Clifford 1972:64-5). The only other divine epithets or references incorporating Sapon in the Ugaritic texts are *il ṣpn* and *ilt ṣpn* (see de Moor 1970:190-1, 196). References to *il ṣpn* clearly support the reading "the divine Sapon" rather than "the god of Sapon" (see Clifford 1972:61-4).

De Moor (1987:4-5) contends that Anat, although the spouse of Baal, does not live with him. He refers to the practice of Ugaritic queens to maintain separate quarters from their royal husbands as evidence for his opinion (1987:5 n. 22). Given the cohabitation of El and Athirat—at least in the formal sense that she is a member of his "household" (e.g. 1.4 iv 50-7)— one may question the relevance of this information, if indeed accurate, to the status and independence of Anat.

Cycle is usually interpreted to reflect Athtar's anger at the impending coronation of Yamm as the king of the gods. The possession of a palace bestowed by El appears to be a necessary mark of legitimization for royal status in the Baal Cycle, which celebrates Baal's own installation into his new home and subsequent dominion (1.4 vi-vii). That every mountain home is not indicative of royal status is clear from Baal's occupation of Mount Sapon in *KTU* 1.3 iv prior to his installation into his palace by El. That is, I infer that Baal's residence upon Sapon is not yet "recognized" by El and that royal status is conferred by the construction of a new palace and its formal dedication. Indeed, the construction and inhabitation of a palace by the triumphant god serves as a common motif in ancient Near Eastern mythology to mark divine kingship. Hence, Anat's possession of an independent home may be seen as an important mark of divine status and independence without any royal connotations.

In summary, Anat appears to play a relatively powerful and independent role in the myths themselves. Furthermore, the accoutrements of divine prestige—epithets of ruling dominion and an independent dwelling—are consistently associated with her in the Ugaritic mythological corpus. These marks of divine prestige suggest her important position within the mythic pantheon and allude to her independence. This evidence is in contrast to the more commonly dependent position of young goddesses in the ancient Near Eastern mythological traditions.

II. ANAT'S SEXUALITY

As analysis of her epithets illustrates, Anat is clearly presented as a youthful goddess in the Ugaritic texts. While the translation "maiden" most closely approximates the connotation of Ugaritic *btlt*, the rendering "virgin" offered by many translators would not be inappropriate if it could be demonstrated that Anat does not in fact engage in sexual intercourse in Ugaritic myth. In addition to the attribution of virginity, however, Anat is readily described as an erotic goddess, the patroness of love, by modern interpreters of her myth. De Moor emphasizes the sexual nature of Anat by defining her as one of "the naughty daughters of El" (1987:135 n. 7) and "the patroness of wanton love, the harlot of the world" (1987:7 n. 34). The common equation of Anat and Ugaritic

Athtart—in function if not in actual characterization—has no doubt supported the attribution of erotic tendencies in the Maiden Anat (see Moor 1987:144 n. 27). These two goddesses coalesce into one Syrian goddess in contemporaneous Egyptian records and later mythological traditions, but there is little evidence to support this association in the period of the Ugaritic texts.[36] The glaring contradiction of Anat's traits of virginity and sexual activity attests the assumptions brought to bear on the interpretation of Ugaritic myth concerning the fertility cult and the essentially sexual function of all Canaanite goddesses.[37] While the combination of bipolar characteristics, such as a goddess of love and war, is not an unusual mythic symbol, the alleged synthesis of a virginal and sexually active goddess is more difficult to substantiate.

The alleged contradiction in Anat's character may be easily avoided through the translation of *btlt* as "maiden," without a clear reference to Anat's sexual experience, or by concluding that the goddess is not depicted as sexually active within the Ugaritic texts (e.g. Gordon 1977:125-6; Ginsberg 1945a:9). Many scholars, however, prefer to interpret the texts such that Anat is both a virginal and sexually exploitative figure. The synthesis of the antithetical attributes of virginity and sexual activity is often coupled with the concept of a "virgin mother" by interpreters of Ugaritic myth (see de Moor 1980; del Olmo Lete 1981a) based upon the analogy of Hera's annual bath in the spring Kanathos that restores her virginity (Pausanias II, 38, 2). Hence, Løkkegaard (1982:132) describes certain goddesses "who are able to renew their virginity, like Hera. The year's cycle can thus be secured renewal and a new beginning." Here a ritual significance is attached to Anat's sexual identity. Albright (1953:74-5) states that Athtart and Anat

---

36 See Herrmann (1969), Leclant (1960), Hvidberg-Hansen (1979: *pace*), and Oden (1977:73-98). The combined divine names *ᶜnt w ᶜṯtrt* and *ᶜṯtrt w ᶜnt* appear a total of five times in the Ugaritic texts (1.100, 20; 1.107, 14; and 1.114, 9, 22-3, and 26). The pronominal and verbal forms in *KTU* 1.114, 9-12 and 22-3 show that this designation represents the pairing of two individual goddesses rather than one goddess with a double name.

37 Albright (1953:74-5), for example, blatantly states that the three major Canaanite goddesses, Athirat, Athtart, and Anat, "were principally concerned with sex and war. Sex was their primary function." Ginsberg (1945a:9) more accurately describes the character of Anat as vigorous and girlish "but not a voluptuous and reproductive one."

are "goddesses who were perennially fruitful without losing virginity. They are therefore both mother-goddesses and divine courtesans." Albright (1968:113) is explicit in his estimation of the "prelogical world of thinking" in which such contradictions are meaningless. Wyatt (1984:331) surpasses all rivals in his defense of Anat as virgin, lover, and mother, however, as he interprets the epithet *btlt* itself as communicating an "allusion to the hierogamy." Wyatt (1984:331) explains,

> When a virgin goddess can also be represented as a fecund mother, we are in the realm of mythological and psychological logic, a poetic dimension in which the normal polarities of language and distinctions of space and time dissolve. The nubile and sexually active ᶜAnat has the title [*btlt*] as a designation of her symbolic role as the bride in the *prima nox*, not simply the archetype of all marital encounters, but more specifically of the primordial encounter which initiated all life, of which the *hieros gamos* is the ritual ... reenactment.

The interpretive bias of these approaches, combining mythopoeic and myth-ritual presuppositions, is obvious.[38] Moreover, this discussion misses the point of the appellation *btlt* of Anat, who is in no case a "virgin mother" or parthenogenic goddess. The matter of debate should focus only upon whether or not Anat should be identified as the sexual partner of Baal in Ugaritic myth.

The alleged sexual aspects of Anat's character have prompted scholars to seek an etymology for her name which means "sexual love." The most articulate exponent of this view is Deem (1978:30), who argues that this etymology "relates the name of Anath to one of her main features as the goddesss of love and fecundity." Deem posits the existence in BH of a G stem verb *ᶜānâ*, "to make love," based upon the more common D stem *ᶜinnâ*, "to humiliate, rape." Rejecting the derivation of this D stem from the G stem *ᶜānâ*, "to be humble," Deem suggests an original connotation "to make love," with the D serving as an intensive form meaning "to make love intensively." Deem (1978:26-7) reasons that since the D stem characteristically denotes an intensive or cohortative aspect of the G stem meaning, perhaps the G stem of "to rape" means "to have sexual intercourse by mutual consent." Deem

38 Indeed, one suspects the influence of the Frazerian quest for antecedents to Hellenistic Christianity rather than concepts indigenous to the ancient mythological tradition in the desire to describe certain pre-Christian goddesses as "virgin mothers."

(1978:29-30) further traces the "original meanings" of the names of the fertility gods Baal and Ashtart to terms for natural fecundity. Included within this fertility rubric is the BH term *maᶜănâ*, "furrow," (1 Sam 14:14; Ps 129:3), also evidenced as *ᶜnt* in Ugaritic (1.6 iv 1-3) and *mᶜnh* in Mishnaic Hebrew. In response to Deem's article, Good (1987) argues that while the D stem *ᶜinnâ* certainly expresses some kind of forced or wrongful sexual activity, the suggested meaning of the G stem "to make love" is completely unfounded in BH. While accepting the etymological explanation of Anat's name from the verb "to copulate" based upon his own assumptions, Good objects to Deem's examples of a G stem meaning "to make love" in the Hebrew Bible on etymological grounds. This dialogue is not aided by the difficulty of the texts under discussion—Exodus 21:10, 32:18 and Hosea 2:23-24—but Good's objections are fundamentally sound.[39] Hence, there is no biblical evidence for the Hebrew root *ᶜny* meaning "to have sex." This conclusion seriously weakens Deem's proposition that Anat's name is also derived from the hypothetical root. While the etymology is possible, Deem's confessed search for an etymology to reflect Anat's assumed sexual function betrays the prejudiced nature of her approach.

In addition to the Ugaritic mythological sources in which Anat is explicitly mentioned, scholars have appealed to the enigmatic *KTU* 1.23 for evidence of Anat's sexuality. This bawdy text celebrating El's sexual potency does not identify the two females whom he seduces and thus it offers no support for Anat's sexual activity. Indeed, the coupling of the patriarchal El and the youthful Anat is nowhere else suggested in any ancient source. A more viable candidate for Anat's sexual partner is the virile fertility god Baal, whose sexual escapades are explicitly recounted in various Ugaritic texts analyzed below.

Many Ugaritic scholars simply assume that Anat and Baal engage in sex—often within the context of a sacred marriage rite (e.g. Winter 1983:319-27; Gray 1965:44-5)—based upon the myth and ritual pattern attributed to ancient Near Eastern religions. The glaring simplifications and assumptions brought to bear upon the interpretation of Ugaritic

39 Good (1987) neglects to offer an alternative explanation for the *hapax* occurrence of *ᶜônātāh*, "her conjugal rights"(?), in Exodus 21:10, although Paul (1969) has previously defended the translation "her oils" for this obscure reference.

myth by the myth-ritual position have already been noted. Indeed, the widespread acceptance of Anat's identification as a goddess of eroticism and fertility necessitates a fresh examination of the Ugaritic texts for evidence concerning her sexual activity. Attention will be focused upon Anat's actual depiction in the mythological literature rather than modern scholars' holistic interpretations of her role within Ugaritic myth. Given the central importance of gender and sexual identity for the symbolic associations of goddesses, discussed above, the matter of Anat's sexuality is of utmost concern in offering an interpretation of her symbolic character within Ugaritic myth.

Baal's "Women"

No Ugaritic goddess is explicitly identified as the wife of Baal. The modern assumption that Anat is Baal's spouse or consort is largely based upon this omission in the city pantheon. Kapelrud (1969:42) exemplifies the reasoning behind much Ugaritic interpretation when he states that since Anat is not the biological sister (*aḫt*) of Baal, she must be his spouse (cf. Pope 1977:657). In contrast to the structured and systematic pantheon of Classical Greece, few of the Ugaritic texts use courtship or matrimonial terms (see 1.23, 30-66; 1.24). Pantheon lists and sacrificial texts from Ugarit apparently do not group deities according to familial relations. The use of *aṯt* for "wife" in divine circles is attested in *KTU* 1.2 iii 22, 1.3 iv 84, and throughout 1.23, 39-65. Courtship and marital terms such as *trḫ*, *mhr*, and *ḫtn* are applied to divine affairs in *KTU* 1.24, 18-33 and 1.23, 64. Similarly, communal residences and offspring, as in the case of El and Athirat, would provide possible evidence for familial groups within the ancient pantheons. Thus, there are hints that the Ugaritic pantheon was structured according to sociomorphic patterns but there is insufficient evidence to conclude the matter.

One context within which Baal might be required to have a recognized spouse concerns his qualification for divine kingship (see Waterston 1988). Gibson (1977:20, 38 n.7) notes that a palace and a wife to bear an heir are necessary accoutrements of a king in Ugaritic royal ideology (cf. 1.14 i). Some scholars have thus suggested that Baal takes El's wife Athirat for his own when he usurps the divine kingship (e.g. Pope 1979:68; Oldenburg 1969:115-9). Olyan (1988:38-61) convincingly refutes this view, however, when he demonstrates that Baal and Athirat/Asherah are never presented as a couple in any reliable source for Canaanite myth. Similarly, the qualifications of Yamm and Athtar for sovereignty (e.g. 1.2 iii) and their possession of palaces and wives remain unclear. Waterston (1988:358) argues that Athtar is given kingship over the "earth" (1.6 i 54-65) even though he may lack a necessary prerequisite for cosmic rule. Baal is apparently proclaimed king with the erection of his palace, yet his marital status is not clarified in the extant texts. Thus, the lack of information prevents any definite conclusion concerning the necessary marital status of Baal and his rivals as they vie for dominion within the Baal Cycle.

If Anat is not the formal spouse of Baal then other candidates may be considered. The common association of Baal and Ashtart/Astarte in Phoenician myth is suggestive but certainly not conclusive given the lack of information concerning the Ugaritic Athtart. There is virtually no evidence for the pairing of Baal and Athtart in Ugaritic sources.[40] There are, however, three other goddesses who are intimately connected with Baal and his fortunes in the Ugaritic mythological texts. This divine trio, composed of Pidray, Tallay, and Arsay, are once designated as Baal's "daughters," *bnth* (1.3 i 23).[41] The reference to Baal's *aṯt*, "women/wives," in *KTU* 1.3 iv 84 is also best understood to refer to this triad of goddesses although the text is not explicit. Indeed, various scholars have identified this trio as the wives of Baal (e.g. Ginsberg 1969:136 n. 2) although others object based upon the identification of

---

40 See Herrmann (1969) and Leclant (1960). The reference to *ᶜṯtrt šm bᶜl* in *KTU* 1.16 vi 56 is most intriguing in light of the attestation of this same appellation in Phoenician sources, but it does not substantiate the conjugal relationship of Baal and Athtart at Ugarit.

41 See Astour (1969), *TO* (77-80), Hvidberg-Hansen (1979, II:132 n. 249), and de Moor (1971:81-2). Pidray, Tallay, and Arsay are not consistently treated as a group in Ugaritic myth. Tallay appears only as a member of the trio within the Baal Cycle while Pidray and Arsay are also invoked separately in sacrificial lists from Ugarit (see de Moor 1970). Note the unexpected exclusion of Arsay in *KTU* 1.5 v 6-11, perhaps explained by her chthonic nature, evidenced by her identification with Allatum and Ereshkigal in the Ugaritic god-lists, *Ug. V*, 18 and 170, and *KTU* 1.47 and 118 (see Nougayrol 1968). That is, if she is an "earth" or Underworld goddess then there is no need for her to descend into the Netherworld (Astour 1969:12). Conversely, de Moor (1987:4 n. 18) posits a seasonal interpretation in which Arsay personifies the summer dew and is thus exempt from Baal's annual sojourn in the Netherworld.

the trio as Baal's children (e.g. Astour 1969:9). Albright (1968:128) does not perceive a problem in the dual status of daughter and consort since "both in Egypt and Canaan the notion of incest scarcely existed. In fact, Phoenicia and Egypt shared a general tendency to use 'sister' and 'wife' synonymously." Of course, the use of the kinship term *bt* to refer to other than biological relationships remains a possibility. Albright (1950:9-11; 1968:126) also concludes that Pidray is the primary consort of Baal, as evidenced by the pairing of the god and goddess in an Aramaic incantation text from the Persian period written in Demotic (the Amherst Papyrus). Furthermore, the masculine divine name *pdr/Pidar*, attested in both alphabetic and syllabic texts from Ugarit, is understood by many scholars as an alternate name or title of Baal (see Gibson 1977:47 n.1; de Moor 1970:203).

The trio of goddesses associated with Baal is also designated as *klt knyt*, "the honored brides," in the Baal Cycle (e.g. 1.3 i 1).[42] While the exact import of this epithet is unknown, Ugaritologists frequently ignore its matrimonial significance. Both BH *klh* and Akkadian *kallatu* specify that a woman is a bride, daughter-in-law, or sister-in-law of the household into which she marries (see *CAD* 8:79-82, 85-6). That is, the term must be understood from the perspective of her affinal relatives. *CAD* (8:82) explains that Akkadian *kallatu* signifies "a young woman who was acquired by the master of a household as a wife for his son living in his household." The secondary connotation of "dependent woman" is derived from this primary connotation. Indeed, *kallūtu* infrequently refers to "conjugal sex" in Akkadian literary texts (*CAD* 8:85). Unfortunately, many commentators apparently interpret the term *klt*, "bride," in the sense of "a young woman available for marriage." Astour (1969:10) accordingly argues that the appellative *klt* refers only to the nubility of the trio (cf. Greek *nymphai*), but he is certainly incorrect. The designation *klt knyt* should refer to the trio as Baal's wives or female affines under his authority. Hence, the dependent status of Pidray, Tallay, and Arsay upon Baal does not necessitate that they are

42 Compare the Akkadian verb *kunnû*, "to treat kindly, honor," and its adjectival use in describing deities (*CAD* 8:540-2), and BH *knh* in the D stem, "to give an honored name" (Isa 45:4; Job 32:21-2). Hence, *knyt* may mean "beloved," "honored," "noble," or even "pampered," depending upon the exact nuance of the Ugaritic phrase.

his wives although this is the most obvious explanation.[43] The interpretation that they are called the "honored brides" simply because they are the spouses of the Ugaritic city god Baal is also plausible.

Given the meaning of *klt* in the cognate languages, then, there is a contradiction in the application of the appellations *bt,* "daughter," and *klt,* "dependent female affine," to these goddesses if each is taken in a narrow, literal sense. If Baal is in fact their father, then they can not be *klt* as long as they dwell within his household. I posit that at least one of these two kinship terms is applied metaphorically. While I am not familiar with the nontechnical use of *klt*, the lexeme *bt* clearly has metaphorical applications for someone other than a biological daughter. Just as the BH lexeme *bn*/*bt* may mean "one of the group of," the application of *bt* in the relationship of the trio to Baal suggests their common mythic nature. That is, Pidray (Chubby?), daughter of Mist, Tallay (Dewy), daughter of Showers, and Arsy (Earthy), daughter of *yᶜbdr*, may be hypostatic manifestations of Baal's fertility function. Regardless, they are intimately associated with his symbolic identity as the bringer of rains and fertility, accompanying him in his palatial residence and in his journey to the Underworld. Hence, their position as his "daughters" is easily seen as a metaphorical relationship.

Again, it should be emphasized that the trio is only once referred to as the daughters of Baal, as a collective (*bnth*), while they are repeatedly designated as the *klt knyt* in relation to Baal. Baal is never designated as their father (*ab*). On the other hand, there is a reference to the *aṯt*, "women, wives," whom Baal dismisses from his presence upon Anat's arrival (1.3 iv 84). The clear contextual choice for the identity of these "women/wives" of Baal are the trio of Pidray, Tallay, and Arsay although the text fails to be specific. That the designation *aṯt* is applied to certain women of Baal's household in the very same passage that identifies Anat as the sister of Baal and the "daughter" (*ybnt*) of his

---

43 To be sure, in the extant texts the title *klt knyt* is applied to the trio only when they are within El's household. Thus, it is possible that Baal's complaint relates that his daughters are in the position of women dependent upon some male other than their father as long as Baal does not have his own house. In at least Akkadian and BH, however, *klt* does not designate just any dependent woman, but specifically one who has been given to the authority of another man as a prospective wife (for himself or one of his male dependents). Thus, the term refers to a marital arrangement, not simply a woman's dependent or independent status.

father is significant. Similarly, the fact that Anat is never called a *klt* in Ugaritic texts implies that she, as a *btlt*, is of a different social category. Indeed, Baal's dismissal of his "women" at the arrival of Anat is a sign that Baal wishes to discuss the serious matter of his desire for a royal palace. Hence, he distinguishes between the women of his house and the goddess Anat. While one may counter that he sends away his female attendants out of respect for his primary wife, the choice of language and particular kinship terms in this passage are too important to ignore.

Additional information concerning the relation of Anat and the trio of Baal's women would certainly aid the present discussion. Unfortunately, only oblique references are attested. *KTU* 1.3 iii 4-8 depicts Anat engaged in singing a "love song" when Baal's messengers enter her dwelling.

[ ]št rimt (5) lirth.	[Anat,] putting the *rimt*-instrument to her breast,[44]
mšr. l.dd. aliyn (6) b^{c}l.	singing concerning the love of Almighty Baal,
yd. pdry. bt. ar	the affection of Pidray (Chubby?), daughter of Mist,
(7) ahbt. ṭly. bt. rb.	the love of Tallay (Dewy), daughter of Showers,
dd. arṣy (8) bt. y^{c}bdr.	the love of Arsay (Earthy), daughter of *y^{c}bdr*.

The subject of Anat's song is unclear to many commentators since it is philologically possible that she is singing of her own love for Baal and his trio of goddesses, Baal's love for the goddesses, or the trio's love for Baal.[45] The subject of Anat's song is most plausibly the mutual attraction between Baal and the three minor goddesses, with the reference to "the love of DN" as morphological equivalents (Løkkegaard 1982:133). The term *ahb* is used to describe Baal's sexual act with the cow (1.5 v) and BH *dōdîm* clearly refers to erotic love in Canticles 1:2, 4 and Ezekiel 16:8. While BH *ɔhbh* is also used to refer to nonsexual affection (e.g. 1Kings 10:9), the context of Anat's song suggests the mutual erotic attraction of Baal and his three attendants rather than just

44 On *rimt* as a harp or lyre, rather than the traditional "corral," see de Moor (1986b:222). The clear parallelism between *rimt* and *knr*, "lyre," in *KTU* 1.101, 16-7 confirms this translation.

45 Note the similar scenes in *KTU* 1.101,14-8 and 1.3 i 20-5. Hvidberg-Hansen's (1979, I:97) translation of the incomplete variant in *KTU* 1.101, 14-8, "elle prend sa cithare dans [sa] main, [met] / des coraux sur la poitrine, elle célèbre son amant, *Al*[*iyn*] Ba^{c}al, (qu')elle aime," is unlikely.

Anat's general affection for Baal and his family. Similarly, to use this text as an example of Anat's own lust for Baal should necessitate the unlikely depiction of her desire for the three goddesses. While Baal's love is here sexual rather than paternal, Gray (1965:45-6) oversteps the evidence in perceiving a reference to the *hieros gamos* of the Near Year festival (cf. Wyatt 1987a:382).

Contributing to the confusion of Baal's marital relations is the myth of the marriage of Nikkal and Yarih (1.24) in which Pidray appears to be described as available for marriage. Upon hearing Yarih's request for the hand of Nikkal, *Ḫrḫb* appears to offer an alternate plan for the moon god:

[l] (25) n^{c}mn. ilm	"[O] most gracious of the gods,
lḫtn(26)m. b^{c}l	O (future) son-in-law of Baal,
trḫ pdry b[th?]	Marry Pidray, [his daugh]ter(?) !
27) aqrbk abh. b^{c}[l]	I will introduce you to her father, Baal,
28) yǵtr. ^{c}ṯtr t(29)rḫ	Athtar will ... the brideprice
lk ybrdmy.	Go/to you ... *Ybrdmy* (?) ....
	(1.24, 25-9)

Proposed restorations and translations of this enigmatic passage remain unsatisfying. Some scholars (e.g. Gray 1965:249) complete line 26 as "Pidray, his daughter," *b*[*th*], while others (e.g. Gordon 1977:66) restore *b*[*t ar*]. Similar questions are raised concerning the role of Athtar in this scene as the son of Baal or as an alternate source for daughters. Regardless, it is plausible to interpret this passage such that Pidray is available for marriage as the daughter of Baal although one can not be certain of this. Other explanations of the kinship structure in this broken text are tentative at best. It could be that this text is influenced by a Hurrian tradition which is inconsistent with the Baal Cycle, but such an explanation simply avoids the issue by positing a speculative alternative. Regardless, this one reconstructed line does not prove that Pidray is the daughter of Baal rather than his consort in the Ugaritic mythological tradition.

In summary, the evidence concerning the relations of Baal and the divine trio of Pidray, Tallay, and Arsay—with the exception of *KTU* 1.24—strongly suggests their marital relationship. The standard application of the term *klt*, "bride," within this context is the most convincing bit of data. Indeed, most scholars might reach this conclusion were it not for the overriding presumption that Anat is the (only) consort of Baal. Ultimately, however, the evidence for Baal's marital arrangements are lacking at the present time. While Anat is intimately associated with Baal and his mythic actions, she is never formally described as anything other than his sister. The traditional pairing of Baal and Athtart/Astarte in Phoenician myth is also suggestive, but not conclusive for the Ugaritic pantheon. Conversely, it would not be inconsistent with ancient Near Eastern practice for an important deity such as Baal to have a spouse of much lesser importance concerning whom we have no information. On the other hand, one must seriously consider the possibility that Baal is presented in Ugaritic myth as a bachelor figure rather than as a patriarchal figure such as El. That is, as a symbolic representative of aggressive male sexuality and fertility, perhaps Baal's role within the pantheon is more closely associated with the metaphor of a young buck yet to have "sown his wild oats." Such suggestions are merely speculative, however. We turn now to the Ugaritic texts which explicitly depict Baal's sexuality in an attempt to determine the extent of Anat's involvement in these episodes.

Anat, Baal, and the Cow

Baal's erotic exploits are the subject of at least two Ugaritic mythological episodes which have survived the millennia (1.5 v and 1.10). Two additional texts, *KTU* 1.11 and 1.13, have also been interpreted as references to Baal's sexuality. That the Canaanite god of natural fertility par excellence is portrayed as a sexually active and virile male should not be surprising. Baal's choice in sexual partner, however, might raise a few modern eyebrows as the available Ugaritic texts consistently depict Baal's preference for bovine rather than human or divine anthropomorphic partners. Such a pairing is all the more intriguing since Baal is never portrayed as a bull in Ugaritic sources, nor is he associated with cows in other Ugaritic contexts.[46] Furthermore, the

46 The Ugaritic evidence is consistent in only applying the epithet *ṯr* to the god El. This fact is in contrast to the Late Bronze and Iron Age associations of Baal Hadad with bull cultic iconography (see Pritchard [1974] nos. 490, 500, 501, 531, 537). Yet it should be noted that here he is always depicted standing upon a bull, rather than necessarily identified with the bull. Similarly, Syrian goddesses are often portrayed

sexual function of Baal is not explicitly evidenced in any extant Ugaritic mythological or iconographic source apart from these episodes of apparent bestiality. The meaning of this sexual motif has largely escaped modern exegetes, although Baal's mythic role as provider of fertility to the herds as well as to the fields provides a suitable symbolic interpretation. The imagery of Baal mating with a cow is an obvious fertility symbol in that it vividly presents his function in bringing fertility to the flocks as well as to natural vegetation.

The lack of a definite consort for Baal among the goddesses only serves to make his sexual dalliances with a member of the animal kingdom more enigmatic. A description of Baal's love interest in *KTU* 1.5 v and 1.10 in terms other than a "cow," *arḫ*, is unfortunately unavailable. The Ugaritic texts provide no definite information concerning her identity, mythic role, or status. Is she a common cow, a divine cow or cow goddess, or a goddess in (temporary) disguise? Baal's heifer does not appear in any other ritual texts, god lists, or sacrificial lists apart from these four mythological fragments, and only in *KTU* 1.13 might there be a reference to her as the "cow of Baal," *arḫ bˁl*. Otherwise, a cow, *arḫ*, is simply introduced without further description. Based on the analogy of Zeus' sexual exploits in Greek myth, many scholars conclude that these episodes reflect not bestiality but Baal and a goddess in bovine form. Thus, scholars have concluded that the cow is actually a theriomorphic manifestation of Anat. The lack of a recognized marital, sexual, or procreative partner for Baal within the mythic pantheon undoubtedly spurs on this hypothesis in an attempt to tie together loose ends. Hence, I suspect that this systematizing effort is the primary motivation for modern scholars to identify Anat as the most likely candidate.

De Moor and Lipínski (1965) have most vocally and consistently defended the identity of Anat with the cow of Baal's affections. Indeed, de Moor (1987:186) states that the enigmatic *KTU* 1.93 is a prayer to Anat in which she is addressed as "Cow!"[47] De Moor's (1980;

mounted upon a lion without receiving the epithet "lion." There is in fact a *ˁgl ilm*, "calf of El," mentioned in *KTU* 1.3 iii 44 and 1.108:11–2, probably as a demonic figure, but this character is not relevant to the present discussion.

47 Other commentators disagree. See Margalit (1984) and Dijkstra (1986) for the diverse opinions regarding the unresolved interpretation of this text.

1987:114) rather all-encompassing interpretation concludes that the Virgin Anat is unable to bear offspring of her own, and so must assume the form of a cow in order to deliver Baal's son. Thus, while a procreative mother in her bovine form, Anat is truly virginal in her anthropomorphic manifestation. Evidence to support the equation of Anat with Baal's heifer can be mustered from Anat's epithet of "(milk) cow of Seth" in Egyptian sources (see Massart 1954:71, 73). Scholars have also appropriated the description of the mourning Anat whose heart is "like the heart of a cow for her calf," *klb arḫ ᶜglh*, in *KTU* 1.6 ii 28 as evidence for Anat's theriomorphic form. Yet this simile is also applied to a city mourning for a departing woman "as the cow lows for her calf" in *KTU* 1.15 i 5. This poetic device should not be confused with the form of the goddess Anat in other than anthropomorphic manifestations. There are no explicit statements identifying Baal's heifer with Anat and no evidence can be found apart from *KTU* 1.5 v and 1.10 concerning the offspring of Baal's cow which will aid in identifying his mother with any certainty. Hence, the argument of de Moor and others is circular and overly ambitious in tying together disparate data which are better left separate for the present time. In fact, careful exegesis of the relevant texts argues against even the possibility that Anat is identified with the cow, as Gordon (1977:120) notes. Hence, Baal's sexual partner in *KTU* 1.5 v and 1.10 is best described as an actual cow whose identity is not at issue in the mythological episode.

The purpose of Baal in copulating with the heifer is not certain, but it is most likely that his intent in each myth is to beget a son or heir. Although the relevant texts are damaged and incomplete, Baal's behavior is not presented as particularly passionate or unrestrained. Indeed, his sexual encounter with the cow in *KTU* 1.5 v appears to be quite rational and purposeful in response to the instructions of Shapsh. Hence, while these episodes may provide the mythic depiction of Baal's insatiable sexual appetite and procreative power, the content and result of each encounter is procreative rather than simply erotic. The question remains, however, of Baal's preference for pastoral settings and bovine partners rather than more traditional romantic arrangements. Perhaps Baal's propensity towards the bovine is evidence of his liminal characterization in Ugaritic myth and religion. Indeed, the "uncivilized" nature of Baal may be related to his unpredictable character as both the bringer of rains and the cosmic warrior within Ugaritic myth. Baal is clearly the force behind storms and rain showers (e.g. 1.4 v 6-9; 1.16 iii 6-12). The seasonal imagery incorporated into the Baal Cycle as well as the still enigmatic text of *KTU* 1.12 attest the erratic quality of Baal's seasonal rains upon which agriculture depends (see Gibson 1984). Baal's character in Ugaritic religion as a warrior deity of the younger generation is also relevant to this matter. He is at times overly exuberant and unrestrained, as in his attack upon the messengers of Yamm (1. 2 i 38-43; cf 1.2 iv 28ff) and his impertinence in inviting Mot to his royal palace for a banquet (1.4 vii–1.5 i).[48] Baal's emotional outburst of despair in his battle with Yamm (1.2 iv 1-7) further attests to his relatively volatile or unstable personality.

This unpredictable behavior combines with other evidence concerning Baal as an "uncivilized" and unrestrained character. The obvious parallel to Baal's bestiality is the assumed bestiality of Enkidu in the *Epic of Gilgamesh*. While the texts do not state that Enkidu actually engages in sex with his animal friends, his clear association, communal life, and identification with the wild herds suggests this detail. Enkidu fully shares in their society as a member. Structurally, then, Enkidu represents nature prior to his initiation into human culture through sex with the prostitute. His association with the wild animals represents his own wildness and lack of cultural attributes. In a similar fashion, Baal's consorting with the heifer may structurally reflect his association with nature and natural drives in contrast to the proper values and expectations of (human) culture. This is not to assume that Baal, as a god, is bound by the same mores as the humans who developed this myth. Rather, the intermixing of divine and animal may be seen as contrary to the normal activities of ancient Near Eastern deities.[49] Since Baal's sexual intercourse with the heifer is not necessarily ascribed a negative value in *KTU* 1.5 v or 1.10—indeed, it may support the stable

[48] The latter action apparently is an insult to the Lord of the Underworld, who recognizes the invitation to dine at Baal's court as a sign of Baal's claim to a superior royal status.

[49] Gordon (1977:117-8) argues that these mythic episodes provide evidence of the actual Canaanite practice of bestiality within the orgaistic cult of Baal (cf. Lev 18:23-4). I can not agree with Gordon's conclusion, based upon this myth and the Israelite polemic, that bestiality is thus "glorified as *imitatio dei*" within the Canaanite cult. Similarly, Gordon (1977:117-8) identifies the offspring of Baal and the heifer as "a bull calf" which is associated with the cult of the Golden Calf at Sinai (Exod 32).

structures of the cosmos—one may interpret his associations with the heifer as representative of his generally liminal status within the mythic pantheon. The important matter of to what extent—if any—the norms of human culture were attributed to the divine realm must be deferred at this point, but it is sufficient to note that here Baal is acting in a manner contrary to "civilized" behavior (cf. Hoffner 1973b).

This ambiguous relationship to cultural norms and socially polite behavior is not an unexpected feature of divine warriors, however. The work of Dumézil in analyzing the structures of mythic pantheons is perhaps instructive in this matter (see Littleton 1982). Dumézil points out that warrior deities often fight to support the institutions of cosmic order against the symbolic forces of chaos, yet their very attributes as virile warriors make them a threat to stable social institutions. While Dumézil develops his theories within the context of Indo-European mythological traditions, examples of this theme are also evident in Mesopotamian myths concerning the warrior god Enlil.[50] Although Baal is supportive of the stability of human society in his city of Ugarit, as attested by his role in *Aqhat*, the Ugaritic divine warrior is also unpredictable and periodically dangerous in his manifestation as the thunderstorm (cf. 1.4 vii). This ambivalence concerning the character of Baal suggests his liminal status among the Ugaritic deities in general. Thus, Baal's sexual encounters with the heifer may also be interpreted from the perspective of his ambiguous associations with culture and nature. The vigorous and occasionally brutal Baal has not been tamed by his association with Ugarit and its human culture, even though he is its patron deity.

The ancient exultation in the heroic conquests of Baal—sexual as well as military—is interesting in itself, but outside of the present scope of inquiry. The pertinence of Baal's sexual exploits to the discussion at hand must rest solely in the role played by the goddess Anat. While Baal clearly has sexual relations with a cow, for whatever reason, the central question is whether or not Anat can be identified with this cow.

---

50 In *Atrahasis* Enlil is openly hostile to human society and works to adversely effect the divine society by indirectly depriving them of sacrifices. His rape of Ninlil in *Enlil and Ninlil* also illustrates the overzealous exercise of his masculine powers.

We begin the discussion of the best preserved and clearest of the four texts.

KTU 1.5 v. Approximately eleven lines are missing from the end of the preceding column, and the first four lines of column v are badly damaged. Unfortunately, the missing lines contain Shapsh's instructions to Baal concerning his journey to the Netherworld. In particular, Shapsh appears to say that she will bury someone. Only the following words are left of the initial six lines.

[ ]aliyn	… … Almighty
[b^{c}l]ip. dprk	Baal] … your torch
[ ]mnk. ššrt	… your […] causing to burn (?)…
[ ]t. npš. ^{c}gl	… the life of a (bull) calf
[a]nk. ašt.n. bḫrt	… I [my]self will place him in a hole
ilm. arṣ. wat. qḥ	of the earth gods. And as for you, take…

The subsequent lines include instructions for Baal's journey to the Netherworld accompanied by his entourage. The importance of this passage for the present discussion rests particularly in lines 4-5, which seem to refer to the son of Baal born in lines 18-25 below. The connotation of burial is clear from the reference to the *ḫrt ilm arṣ*, "hole of the earth gods," as Gordon demonstrates (1956), but the identity of the one to be buried is unclear. The form *ašt. n,* "I will place it/him (in the cemetery)," is inconclusive since Shapsh may be foretelling the burial of either Baal's corpse or Baal's son.

That Shapsh has masterminded what follows is confirmed by line 17, *yšm^{c} aliyn b^{c}l,* "Almighty Baal obeyed." Lines 18 through 25 recount his execution of her instructions.

yšm^{c}. aliyn. b^{c}l	Almighty Baal obeyed.
18) yuhb. ^{c}glt. bdbr.	He loved a heifer in *dbr*,
prt (19) bšd. šḥlmmt.	a cow in the field(s) of *šḥlmmt.*
škb (20) ^{c}mnh. šb^{c}. lšb^{c}m	He lay with her seventy-seven times,
21) tš[^{c}]ly. ṯmn. lṯmnym	she allowed (him) to mount eighty-eight times.
22) w[th]rn. wtldn mṯ	And she conceived and gave birth to a young male (?).

23) al[iyn. bᶜ]l. šlbšn	Almighty Baal clothed him,
24) ip[dh]lh. mᶜẓ	with [his ro]be (?) ... as a gift (?) ...
25) y[ ] lirth	He ... to his breast ....

The location of Baal's encounter with the cow is designated in the text as *bdbr* and *bšd. šḫlmmt* but modern exegetes have yet to decipher these terms convincingly (see M. Smith 1986a; Aartun 1986:31). Longer poetic formulas concerning this location (1.5 vi 3-10 and 1.16 iii 3-4) further describe it as on "the edges of the earth, the limits of the watery regions," *qṣm. arṣ ... lksm. miyt* (cf. Ps 48:11 and 65:6). Hence, the accumulated evidence suggests that the location of Baal's intercourse with the heifer, as well as where Anat recovers his corpse, lies outside of the normal inhabited world, most probably as a buffer zone between the land of the living and the domain of Mot (M. Smith 1986a).[51]

The identity of the cow's offspring remains enigmatic and largely ignored by Ugaritic mythographers. The Ugaritic lexeme *mṯ* is frequently attested in the feminine form *mṯt* (see Whitaker 1972:439) and, although an etymological explanation is lacking, the contextual use of the term identifies *mṯt* as a young female and *mṯ* as a young male.[52] Baal's investiture of his son with his robe (*ip*[*dh*]) would imply the bestowing of an office or official status (see Oden 1987:98-104), but the text is unclear. Unfortunately, one cannot reconstruct Baal's treatment of his newborn child from the broken lines that follow this passage. The lack of any further reference to the son of Baal in the extant Ugaritic and Canaanite materials is a puzzle to modern mythographers since one would think the offspring of the Canaanite god of fertility should merit some attention in the ancient myths, rituals, and sacrificial texts. Indeed, Philo identifies the son of Baal-Demarous as Melqart-Hercules (*PE* 1.10.27) although this may be attributed to the overly systematic

---

51 Based upon the description of this locale as "the pleasant (places) of the land of *dbr*, the delightful fields of *šḫlmmt*," *nᶜmy arṣ dbr ysmt šd šḫlmmt* (1.5 vi 4-7, 28-30, and 1.6 ii 19-20), Margalit (1980:125-8) infers an idyllic setting similar to the Elysian Fields of Greek mythology. Conversely, del Olmo Lete (1981a:535) understands this description as a euphemism for a dreary setting. Wyatt (1987a:385) provides an interesting discussion of the symbolic nature of steppe and pasture as liminal space in Ugaritic and biblical myth.

52 De Moor's attempt to understand the term as "twin" based upon Akkadian *māšu* is contrived to fit his particular exegesis discussed below.

interpretation of Asiatic religions by the Hellenistic commentators.[53] Given his associations with the Netherworld, Horon is also a good hypothetical candidate for the son of Baal (see van Dijk 1989), yet it is hard to imagine that no reference to Horon as Baal's son would be found within the Ugaritic sources if this explanation were accurate.

It remains unclear whether the son born to Baal in *KTU* 1.5 v and in 1.10 iii should be identified as the same character. Are the two texts variants of the same episode or different scenes in the mythology of Baal? While *KTU* 1.5 v portrays Baal's intercourse with the cow, the birth of his son and Baal's journey to the Netherworld, the myth of *KTU* 1.10 states that Baal returns to his home on Mount Sapon after mating with the cow and awaits the news of his son's birth. The differences between the two myths suggests that they represent independent traditions; neither text explains the child's significance to Baal's fate in the Netherworld. Gordon (1977:121) states that the fantastic creatures of *KTU* 1.12 who have a bovine body and "the face of Baal" may be the offspring of Baal and the heifer. The problem, of course, is that the role of these destructive creatures in the enigmatic *KTU* 1.12 is insufficiently understood. How this tablet might fit into the context of the Baal Cycle is also unclear. Additional material might clarify the identity and mythic role of the offspring of Baal and the heifer, but no solution to these vexing questions presents itself as the more plausible alternative based upon the available evidence.

De Moor (1987:77-9) interprets this difficult scene as part of an elaborate ruse concocted by Shapsh in order for Baal to avoid death. By assuming the form of a bull Baal engenders a "twin," rather than a son, who will take his place in the Netherworld. Baal bestows his cloak upon this replacement in order that Mot will unwittingly devour him rather than the storm god. Baal is to hide himself within the herds so that Mot will eat his fill before finding him (de Moor 1987:74 n. 352). Thus, Baal is never actually dead, according to de Moor, and the corpse which Anat discovers and buries is in fact that of Baal's twin (see also Gibson

---

53 See Oden and Attridge (1981:90 n. 118), who also demonstrate the equation of Demarous, Adodos (*PE* 1.10.31) (1981:88 n. 94) and Baal Hadad, called *dmrn* at Ugarit in *KTU* 1.4 vii 39. On the other hand, Astour (1969:15) compares the birth of Baal's son, who is taken immediately into the Netherworld, to the myth of Adonis, who is given by Aphrodite to Persephone for safe-keeping as a child.

1977:15-6). To be sure, the idea that the individual sired by Baal is to serve as his replacement in the Netherworld has various precedents in ancient Near Eastern myth. Most obvious is the myth of *The Descent of Ishtar*, wherein the goddess is allowed to return to the land of the living if she provides a substitute for herself. Here, the hapless Dumuzi is punished for not properly mourning his absent consort by serving as her substitute in the Netherworld. Perhaps a better parallel, the Sumerian myth of *Enlil and Ninlil* emphasizes the motif of a son born during the journey to the Netherworld to serve as his father's replacement (see J. Cooper 1980). The plot of bearing a son for the sole purpose of avenging the father is also evident in the Hittite *Myth of Illuyankas* (see Pritchard 1969:125-6). Indeed, the idea of Baal begetting a (semi-) divine substitute through the cow would be an attractive explanation were it not for the importance attached to the birth of a son for Baal by the heifer in *KTU* 1.10, where the newborn is described as a bull (*ibr*) and an ox (*rum*). Hence, the identity and mythic function of Baal's son appears to carry a significance beyond this one text.

In summary, the relation of Baal's sexual contact with the heifer in the land on the edge of Mot's domain and the subsequent birth of his son to Baal's eventual return from the Netherworld is unclear. Shapsh's statement in *KTU* 1.5 v 4-5 suggests that she would bury either Baal or his son, and in fact she does aid Anat in the burial. That Shapsh instructed Baal to love the cow suggests that she has some purpose in mind concerning his offspring, but what this is has been lost. Wyatt (1987a:385) describes Baal's sexual relations with the cow as an "apotropaic episode to counterbalance the imminent death of Baᶜal" and its effect upon earthly fertility. Contra de Moor, it is most prudent to assume that Baal does descend into the maw of Mot and enters the Netherworld with the resultant waning of natural fertility, as described in the Ugaritic texts. Hence, Anat retrieves the corpse of Baal and gives him a proper burial in *KTU* 1.6 i, as discussed above. The conclusion that Baal's heifer in *KTU* 1.5 v is Anat in theriomorphic disguise is most unlikely given her role in searching for his corpse. Regardless, the primary importance of this issue for the present study concerns neither the identity of Baal's offspring nor the fate of Baal in the Netherworld, but Anat's role in Baal's return to the land of the living, an issue addressed below.

KTU 1.10. Another myth concerning Baal's sexual exploits may be found in *KTU* 1.10. This interesting text is marked by the scribal division of lines according to poetic meter. Many commentators (e.g. Kapelrud 1969:43; de Moor 1987:116) identify this text as the affair of Baal and Anat in bovine form, while Gordon (1977:120) more correctly states that here Anat acts as the procuress rather than partner of Baal. Unfortunately, the highly poetic nature and obscure vocabulary of this text complicate its interpretation. One source of confusion in identifying the participants involved rests in reading *arḫ* as a general term for bovine—bull or cow—rather than as a feminine noun designating the heifer. Hence, Hvidberg-Hansen (1979, I:98, with notes) argues that the *arḫ* which Anat sees is actually Baal in his theriomorphic manifestation as a bull. Løkkegaard (1982:133) is certainly correct in pointing out the error of this reading.

The events of the fragmentary first column are completely lost, but the earliest legible lines concern Anat's questioning of Baal's lackeys at his house. She is told that Baal has taken his bow and gone to the banks of *Šmk*, full of wild oxen, and she flies after him (1.10 ii 1-12). Immediately following Baal's martial greeting (1.10 ii 13-25), discussed above, the text reads:

Col. ii

26) wtšu. ^{c}nh. btlt. ^{c}nt	Maiden Anat lifted her eyes,
wtšu. ^{c}nh. wt^{c}n	she lifted her eyes and saw.
wt^{c}n. arḫ. wtr. blkt	She saw a cow and she led (?) in walking,
tr. blkt. wtr. bḫl	she led in walking and led in dancing (?),
30) [b]n^{c}mm. bysmm. ḥ[ ]kǵrt	in the pleasant (places), in the delightful (places) of …
[ql]. lb^{c}l. ^{c}nt. ttnn	Anat called out to Baal,
[ ]i. b^{c}lm. dipi[ ]	"… Baal, the one of the clouds,
[il.] hd. d^{c}nn[.] n[ ]	[the god] Haddu, the one of clouds …
[ ]aliyn. b[^{c}l]	… Almighty Baal …
35) [btl]t. ^{c}n[t]ph	… Maiden Anat …
(4 broken lines)	…

Col. iii

(… c. 20 damaged lines …)	…
1) [^{c}glm.] arḫt. tld[n]	["…calves] the cows (will?) bear.

a[rḫ]. lbtlt. ^{c}nt	A cow for Maiden Anat,
wypt lybmt. lim[m]	and a heifer for *Ybmt Limm*!"
wy^{c}ny. aliyn[. b^{c}l]	And Almighty Baal answered,
lm. kqnym. ^{c}l[m]	"… as eternal is our creator…
kdrd<r>. dyknn[ ]	as generations he creates …"
b^{c}l. yṣǵd. mli[ ]	Baal stepped, full …
il h(!)d. mla. uṣ[ ]	the divine Haddu, full …
btl[t?]. pbtlt. ^{c}n[t]	… the mouth of Maiden Anat,
wp. n^{c}mt. a(!)ḫt[. b^{c}l]	and the mouth of the loveliest of the sisters [of Baal.]
y^{c}l. b^{c}l. bǵ[r]	Baal ascended to the m[ount …]
wbn. dgn. bš[mm]	the son of Dagan to [the heavens?…]
b^{c}l. yṯb. lks[i. mlkh]	Baal sat upon the throne of [his kingship]
bn dgn. lkḥ[ṯ. drkth]	the son of Dagan upon the seat [of his dominion].
lalp. ql. ẓ[ ]	…
lap ql[.] nd. [ ]	…
tlk. wtr. b[ ]	She walked and she led in …
bn^{c}mm. bys[mm]	in pleasant (places), in the delightful (places)…
arḫ. arḫ. [ ]	a cow … a cow…
ibr. tld[. l b^{c}l]	A bull was born [to Baal]
wrum. l[rkb. ^{c}rpt]	and an ox to [the Rider of the Clouds.]
tḥbq. [ ]	She embraced …,
tḥbq. [ ]	she embraced ….
wtksynn. bṯn [ ]	And she covered him with scarlett (?) …
y[ ]šrh. wšḫph	… and his/her milk (?),
[ ]šḫp ṣǵrth	… milk of his youth (?)
yrk. t^{c}l. b[.]ǵr	… she ascended to Mt.
mslmt. bǵr. tliyt	*Mslmt*, (and) to Mt. Victory.
wt^{c}l. bkm. barr	Then she ascended to *Arr*
bm. arr. wbṣpn	to *Arr* and to Sapon.
bn^{c}m. bǵr. t[l]iyt	to pleasant (places), to Mt. Victory.
ql. lb^{c}l. ttnn	She called to Baal,
bšrt. il. bš[r. b]^{c}l	"Good news! Gladden, O Baal,
wbšr. ḥtk. dgn	and gladden, son of Dagan!

35) k. ibr. lb^{c}l[. yl]d	For a bull is born to Baal,
wrum. lrkb[.] ^{c}rpt	and an ox to the Rider of the Clouds!"
yšmḫ. aliyn. b^{c}l	Almighty Baal rejoiced.

The proper interpretation of the frequent unit *tr* proves to be most difficult. Numerous etymological explanations have been offered (see Margalit 1983:87-8 with references) although most commentators prefer to read "she trembles," based on the root *trr*, or "she turns" or "she seeks out," from *twr*. The form *tr* is incorporated into the sentences *tšu knp wtr b^{c}p*, "She lifts her wing and proceeds (?) in flight" (1.10 iii 11), as well as *wtr. blkt*, "She leads (?) in walking," so it seems that the verb designates some form of motion. Ugaritologists usually treat the verb as an infinitive, but I prefer to read it as a 3 f.s. based upon the sequence of verbs in ii 26-29. Here the poetic pattern results in a chiastic verbal sequence. In order to match the previous verbal forms, I propose parsing the verb as a 3 f.s. from **wry*, "to go, advance," as a cognate of Akkadian (*w*)*arû*, "to lead, to bring (mostly persons and animals)" (*CAD* 1/2:313). Hence, perhaps Anat is acting as the procuress and actually leading the cow to Baal.[54]

The term *ḫl* also offers a dilemma to the translator since the root *ḫyl*/*ḥyl* has a clear reference to the writhing of a woman in labor in BH, Akkadian and Ugaritic. The context here obscures its connotation and I tentatively accept the reading "dance" based on BH *ḥwl* (e.g. Judges 21:21). Many interpreters also reconstruct *KTU* 1.10 ii 30 as [*b*]*n^{c}mm.*

54 While the root may also be *yry*, "to shoot," this verbal root is never attested as an intransitive in BH or Ugaritic (e.g. 1.23, 38). Similarly, the translation, "(Anat) lifts her wing and rises in flight" (*tšu knp wtr b^{c}p*), from **try*, "to rise," is attractive, but the Akkadian cognate *tarû* means only "to elevate." The apparent lack of Semitic cognates for the doubly-weak Akkadian verbs, (*w)âru*, "to go, advance," and (*w)arû*, "to lead," (*CAD* 1/2:318) may help explain the existence of an Ugaritic verb **yry* to denote movement of some kind. Thus, Ugaritic *tr* could refer simply to the movement of Anat as she "proceeds in walking, proceeds in dancing" (cf. Ginsberg 1969:142).

De Moor does not explain the etmology for his translation of *tr* as "she starts," unless one is to understand the root *ntr*, "jump, set off, start" (see de Moor and Spronk 1987:156). Regardless, de Moor's (1987:113) translation of 1.10 ii 29, *tr blkt wtr bḫl*, as "She started to flow [from sexual excitement] and started to convulse" is quite fantastic. While Akkadian *alāku* can refer to the movement of liquid (*CAD* 1/1:306), as de Moor notes, it only does so when the liquid is explicitly mentioned as the subject of this common verb.

bysmm. ḥ[*bl*] *kṯrt*, "in the pleasant (places), in the delightful (places) of the band of Kotharat," to associate the myth's setting with the divine midwives.

The difficult nature of this text with its numerous biconsonantal writings and missing lines does not allow one to draw many firm conclusions. This text could be part of the Baal Cycle as a variant of the *KTU* 1.5 v, although this seems highly unlikely since here Baal retreats to his mountain home to await the good news after his encounter with the heifer. While it would appear that Anat and Baal do not explicitly engage in sex in the extant text, it is possible that they do. Here, as in *KTU* 1.5 v, there is a clear distinction between the goddess Anat and Baal's heifer. Her sighting of the cow in 1.10 ii 28 proves the distinction, unless one agrees with de Moor's (1987:114-6) opinion that Anat and Baal then transform themselves into bovine form for their sexual liaison. De Moor interprets *pbtlt ᶜnt*, "the mouth of the Maiden Anat," in 1.10 iii 9 as a reference to her vagina based on the same euphemism in Akkadian and Modern Hebrew. However, I can find no attestations of Akkadian *pû* ever referring to a woman's vagina. Much less likely is de Moor's reading of *btl* in 1.10 iii 9, *btl pbtlt ᶜn*[*t*], as a passive G stem meaning "deflowered." If, however, Anat is identified with the cow in this episode then she is certainly a hardy mother, rushing off to tell the father herself immediately after bearing and suckling the child. The point of the text, as intimated in the final lines, is that a son is born to Baal by a heifer. Whether the exclusively bovine description of the youth is to be taken literally or metaphorically is unclear (see Miller 1971), as is the identity of his mother.

KTU 1.11. In addition to other scholars, Pope (1987a:460) refers to *KTU* 1.11 as a description of Baal and Anat engaged "in torrid love-making from which ᶜAnat becomes pregnant and gives birth" (cf. Lipínski 1965:62-5; Gordon 1977:225-6). This fragmentary text is frequently indentified as part of the missing third column of *KTU* 1.10, although the differences in the color and thickness of the tablets suggest otherwise (Herdner 1963:51-2). *KTU* 1.11 is apparently inscribed on only one side of the tablet, an uncommon feature it shares with 1.10, which suggests that this is a short text able to fit on the obverse of a tablet. There is insufficient evidence to determine whether or not this text is divided by poetic line like *KTU* 1.10. The scribal hand appears to be the same for *KTU* 1.10 and 1.11, and it is perhaps not too rash to associate these two texts with the central theme of divine sex. Thus, *KTU* 1.11 may come from the same mythological text or tradition as 1.10. The tablet is very poorly preserved and there are some disputed letters. The number of signs in the break is unknown although most commentators expect few based upon the estimated size of a column. The photograph in *CTA* is illegible, and the following transliteration follows *CTA* and *KTU* based upon Virolleaud's (1944-5:14-7) copy.

[ ]. yṯkḥ wyiḫd. bqrb[?]	... He droops (?) and grasps ...
[t]ṯkḥ wtiḫd. buš[ ]	... She] droops (?) and grasps ...
[b]^{c}l. ynbd. lalp	... B]aal ... to a bull/thousand (?)
[bt]lt. ^{c}nt	... Mai]den Anat
[nš]q. hry. wyld	... kis]sing, conception, and birth
[ ]m. ḥbl. kṯ[r]t	... band of Kotharatu
[bt]lt. ^{c}nt	... Mai]den Anat
[ali]yn. b^{c}l	... Almi]ghty Baal
[ ]m^{c}n	...
[ ]	...

Ugaritic philologists have posited various etymologies and explanations of the word *yṯkḥ*, usually from the verbal root *ṯkḥ* (see Dietrich and Loretz 1980b:406).[55] Dietrich and Loretz (1980b:406) argue for the meaning "to be excited" in the G stem and "to excite, rouse" in the D stem for Ugaritic *ṯkḥ*, based upon the alleged cognate in Akkadian *šegû*, "to be wild." This explanation seems rather dubious. Sanmartín (1980c) prefers the meaning "to gaze, stare" based upon the BH root *šgḥ*, "to gaze," found only in the C stem. De Moor (1964) links Ugaritic *ṯkḥ* to Arabic *kaṯaḥa* and the very obscure South Arabian *mṯkḥ*, from which he defends the meaning "to denude, strip." Aistleitner (1967:34) defines the Ugaritic root *ṯkḥ* as "to encounter, meet" and Lipínski (1965:63-4) gives "to seize," both citing Syriac *ɔeškaḥ*, although the Ugaritic etymological /ṯ/ normally appears in Syriac as /t/

55 Løkkegaard (1982:133-4) suggests an Arabic root *nkḥ*, "to marry," noting the theory of /ṯ/ as a causative prefix in Ugaritic. He believes "the sexual meaning of *ṯkḥ* is certain."

rather than /š/. Neither the lexical nor phonetic defenses of these translations are convincing.

There are two other Ugaritic contexts within which the word *yṯkḥ* appears: *KTU* 1.5 i 4 (repeated in 30), and 1.24, 4. The former occurrence is in a very difficult passage in which *šmm* may be the subject of the verb although Margalit (1980:88) and Dietrich and Loretz (1980b:406) prefer a different stichometric division. The context of *KTU* 1.24, 4 is perhaps *yrḫ ṯtkḥ yḥ[bq.] d tld*, with *ṯkḥ* describing what Yarih does before he embraces "the one who will bear." Unfortunately, the reading is uncertain and the plot unclear. Thus, neither context is of much assistance in elucidating the meaning of the root *ṯkḥ* although *KTU* 1.24, 4 may involve a sexual content.

Pope (1966:240) notes the convincing work of Albright and Patton (see Patton 1944:26-7) in establishing the meaning of BH *škḥ* as "to waste away, wither, dry up" in various biblical Psalms (e.g. 137:5; 77:10). While this meaning fits the context of *KTU* 1.5 i, Pope concludes that this sense is "most inappropriate" in the "ardent love scene between Baal and ᶜAnat" in *KTU* 1.11. Instead, Pope states that the sense "suggested by the situation" in *KTU* 1.11 and 1.24, 4 is "be hot, ardent, passionate." Hence, he reads *KTU* 1.5 i 4 as "The heavens parched and withered." Accordingly, Pope (1966:240) suggests lines 1-3 of this text mean, "He waxed warm and grasped [her] vulva; [She] waxed warm and grasped [his] testicles." This sense of *ṯkḥ* is derived from the BH root *škḥ,* meaning "to wither, waste away" (e.g. Ps 102:5), which Pope infers to mean "to wither (from heat), be parched." The semantic leap involved in Pope's defense of the connotation "to be passionate" is unsupported. Pope's etymology is based explicitly upon his understanding of this text as a love scene, yet this interpretation of the scene rests solely upon the understanding of a sexual connotation for the verb *ṯkḥ* (cf. *TO* 239-40, 289). Such blatantly circular reasoning is unacceptable as substantiation for the etymology of this root. Whereas Pope argues that the context of this root in both *KTU* 1.11 and 1.24 is one of sexual intercourse and conception, *ṯkḥ* in *KTU* 1.24, 4 may certainly be translated as the moon's "waning." Likewise, the context of *KTU* 1.5 i appears to be one of death rather than sexual excitement. Hence, the necessary sexual connotation of Ugaritic *ṯkḥ* is unconvincing.

Commentators unanimously consider *qrb* the direct object of the verb *ʾḫd* in line 1 of *KTU* 1.11 even though this is the only example of the direct object of Ugaritic *ʾḫd* being marked with the preposition /b/ (see Pardee 1975:340-1, 376-7). Whether or not there is space for a missing suffix /h/ is also disputed. Virolleaud (1944-5:14-7) first proposed the translation "he grasped her womb" and many scholars have followed his lead. *TO* (289) and others (e.g. Hvidberg-Hansen 1979, II:133 n. 253) argue that the meaning of the term here is "vulva," based upon the similar meaning in Genesis 25:22. The biblical passage, however, reads *wayyitrōṣăṣû habbānîm bĕqirbāh*, "And the children struggled in her womb," clearly without reference to Rebekah's vulva. Indeed, *qereb* is a common BH term for "midst," cognate to Akkadian *qērbū* (always plural), "intestines, bowels" (*CAD* 13:226-7), and *qerbītu*, "womb" (*CAD* 13:214). While *qrb* could denote "womb" in Ugaritic, there is no evidence of the semantic range of this cognate extending to include "vulva." Hence, it is inappropriate to understand *qrb* to refer to a vulva here, especially when the Ugaritic term *ḥl*, "vulva," is elsewhere attested.

Important to this discussion is the meaning of the final word in line 2, also supposedly marked by /b/ as the object of the verb *ʾḫd*. Virolleaud (1944-5) originally read *bušk* although Herdner (1967:52) states that the final /k/ is no longer visible. The editors of *KTU* are able to make out a /k/. The Ugaritic term *ušk* is most probably cognate to BH *ʾāšek* (Lev 21:20) and Akkadian *išku*, "testicle" (*CAD* 7:250-1). Other scholars (e.g. Watson 1977:277; *TO* 289) prefer to restore *ušr*, "penis," cognate to Akkadian *išaru* (*CAD* 7:226-7). Apart from this context both *ušk* and *ušr* appear once in Ugaritic, according to Dietrich and Loretz's edition (1975:134, 139) of an Ugaritic version of an Akkadian *šumma izbu* omen text (1.103). Indeed, the reading of either *ušk*, "testicle," or *ušr*, "penis," as a parallel to *qrb*, "womb" is plausible in *KTU* 1.11, 2. Noting the ridiculous image of one "grasping her womb," Løkkegaard (1982:133-4) reconstructs the ends of lines 1 and 2 with *bqrb*[*nh*] and *buš*[*kr*], cognate, respectively, to BH *qorbān* and *ʾeškār*. He tentatively reads, "He couples with (marries) her, and he takes her gift; she couples with him, and she takes [his] present." This eccentric translation well illustrates the difficulty of this passage.

Unfortunately, the next verb, in line 3, is equally difficult. Herdner (1963:52) holds that the second letter could be either /a/ or /n/. The verbal root is thus either **nbd* or *ʾbd*. The former root is unattested in Ugaritic, while the latter occurs with the same meaning as BH *ʾbd*, "to perish," in the D stem, "to kill, destroy" (e.g. 1.14 i 8 and 24). Scholars (e.g. *TO* 289) have also suggested a link to Arabic *ʾabida*, "to be furious, impassioned," although Wehr (1976:1) explains that this root covers the connotations of "to stray, linger, roam, run wild, be shy" in the G stem, and "to make lasting" in the D stem. Thus, the meaning "to be wild" is but one narrow aspect of this Arabic verbal root. The root **nbd* is unattested in Ugaritic, BH, and Akkadian although scholars have noted possible Arabic cognates in *nabaṭa*, "to spring, gush forth" (Wehr 1976:939), *nabata*, "to grow, sprout, produce" in the G stem, "to sow, plant" in the D stem (Wehr 1976:937), and *nabaḏa*, "to hurl, throw" (Wehr 1976:938). Based upon the observation that Semitic roots beginning with *nb* frequently mean "to come out, come forward," van Selms (1954:46 n.16) suggests the meaning of seminal ejaculation for Ugaritic **nbd* in *KTU* 1.11.[56] Attributing a sexual connotation to this verb is further complicated by the common identification of *lalp* as the direct object of Baal's action. But *alp* is clearly a (male) bull in Ugaritic and never denotes Baal's bovine sexual partner. Pope (1966:240) avoids this difficulty by translating, "Mighty Baal copulated by the thousand." Ginsberg (1969:142) certainly chooses the wisest course in leaving this verb untranslated within such a broken context.[57]

Thus, far from providing incontrovertible proof for the sexual involvement of Baal and Anat (Hvidberg-Hansen 1979, I:97-8), the interpretation of this fragmentary text is based more upon circular argument and assumption than proper philological analysis. While the sexual content attributed to *KTU* 1.11 is possible, the etymological defense is weak, to say the least. The meanings of the terms *ṯkḥ*, *qrb*, and the incomplete *uš*[ ] are unclear and imprecise. This fact should dissuade scholars from using *KTU* 1.11 as evidence for the erotic exploits of the goddess Anat. While the meaning of either "penis" or "testicles" is likely in line 2, this word does not aid in understanding the larger context and scene. That is, the probable reference to male genitals

---

56 Thus, Lipínski (1965:63-4) offers the restoration and translation [*dr*^{c} *b*]^{c}*l ynbd lalp*, "[Les sperme] de Baal crût en veau."

57 Perhaps the most innovative solution to this problem is proposed by de Moor (1987:116), who translates "And Ba^{c}lu transformed himself into an ox" based on his emendation of the text to *ynbd<l>* (de Moor and Spronk 1987:50). He is apparently taking an N stem of the root *bdl* which means "to exchange" in Arabic, although this root only appears as the nominal *mbdl*, "merchant," in Ugaritic texts.

is not a sufficient cause to posit a sexual reference for *qrb* since the stichometric analysis of the text is inconclusive. Indeed, the scholarly identification of this text as mythological literature may be incorrect since it is possible, although speculative, that the fragmentary tablet contains an independent incantation or omen text similar to *KTU* 1.103 in which similar vocabulary is attested.[58] The fragmentary quality of this text should caution scholars about inferring evidence for the sexual activity of Anat when *KTU* 1.5 v and 1.10 provide evidence to the contrary.

KTU 1.13. Recent discussions of this difficult text are provided by Caquot (1978), de Moor (1980), and especially del Olmo Lete (1981b), who provides a full bibliography. The damaged condition of the tablet, together with numerous unattested words, possible mistakes, an odd use of line dividers, and an eccentric scribal hand combine to present a most enigmatic text. Scholars disagree concerning the proper interpretation and genre of *KTU* 1.13. The stichometric analysis of the text into poetic lines, essential to any intelligible reading, is most difficult, as the discrepancies between de Moor (1980) and del Olmo Lete (1981b) attest. Thus, the obscurity of this mythological text hinders any conclusions concerning the role of Anat. However, the restorations and interpretation offered by de Moor (1980) result in the clear image of Anat bearing a bull calf for Baal as part of a fertility incantation. Similarly, del Olmo Lete (1981b) refers to *KTU* 1.13 as the "myth of the virgin-mother Anat." While the reliability of these interpretations are unconvincing, the discussion of this text among Ugaritologists must be reviewed.

No division of lines into poetic cola is proposed in the following presentation. The tablet originally had one line of text, now completely defaced, followed by an unintelligible line which is marked as line one.

---

[58] Following the unintentional lead of Watson (1977:277), one might suggest that *KTU* 1.11 is itself an incantation or omen text like the Akkadian texts to which he compares it. Perhaps the first two lines begin with *hm*, "if," like the Akkadian texts begin with *šumma*. In this case the subject of the verbs could be either humans or, better, a disease which "grasps" parts of the patient's anatomy. Anat and Baal could be playing mythic roles as part of the incantation.

[ ]xx	...
[ ]ḥm. tld	... you/she (?) will bear (?)...
[ ]ḫrm. ṯn. ym	... two days
mš[ṯlṯ]ymm. lk.	... [three ?] days, Go!
hrg. ar[b^c]ymm. bṣr	Slaughter, four days ...
kp. šsk. [ ]. lḥbšk.	Hands of your binding (?) ... to your girdle
^{c}tk. ri[št] lmhrk	Attach heads of (?) your warriors
w^{c}p. lḏr[ ]. nšrk.	and fly to ... your eagles
wrbṣ. lǵrk. inbb.	Rest at your mountain, *Inbb*
ktǵrk. ank. yd^{c}t.	the foundation of your mountain indeed (which) I know (?)
[a]n. atn. at. mṯbk. u/b[	Indeed I give you your abode...

The obverse of *KTU* 1.13 contains sufficient evidence to suggest that someone is addressing Anat, most probably inciting her to violence.[59] Many scholars opt to restore line 1 as [*r*]*ḥm. tld*, "The maiden will bear," with reference to the goddess Anat. The final /m/ of [*r*]*ḥm* is unclear in the excellent photographs in *CTA*, making the restoration very questionable. There is an obvious parallel in lines 6-7 to the description of Anat's bloodbath in *KTU* 1.3 ii 11-3, ^{c}*tk rišt lbmth / šnst kp bḥbš*, "(Anat) attaches heads to her waisṭ; she binds hand(s) to her girdle." The use of the words *kp*, *ḥbš*, and *riš*, and the verb ^{c}*tk*, attests a close relation between the two episodes.[60] The imperative verbs in *KTU* 1.13 suggest that Anat is being instructed to perform the episode recounted in *KTU* 1.3 ii, perhaps by either a deity within a mythic

59 De Moor (1980:306) notes the complementary use of the roots *ḥrm* and *hrg* in Joshua 8:24 and 26 as evidence for their poetic parallelism in lines 3 and 5. The words *ḫrm* and *hrg* are otherwise unattested in Ugaritic, although *ḥrm* and *hrg* are common in BH. The alleged attestation of the root *ḫrm* in Ugaritic noted by de Moor (1980:306) is based upon a polyglot vocabulary in syllabic cuneiform text which may actually reflect Ugaritic *ḫrm* (see Heuhnergard 1987:126, 130). Although the root *ḫrm* is designated as Common Semitic, with some meaning of "separate, prohibit, make sacred," it only takes on a violent connotation in BH as a C stem verb.

60 Perhaps *šsk* in *KTU* 1.13, 6 is derived from the verbal root *šns* as in *KTU* 1.3 ii 12 (cf. I Kings 18:46). In this case the form *šsk* may be a scribal error caused by the variant tradition. If the spelling is correct, perhaps *šsk* is an infinitive construct in which the middle /n/ has assimilated, **šassīka*, "your binding." On the other hand, the *šsk* of *KTU* 1.13 may have no relation to the root *šns* in the parallel account of this tradition in *KTU* 1.3 ii, but simply serves a poetic purpose of aural similarity.

context (del Olmo Lete 1981) or by a human as part of an incantation (de Moor 1980).

Lines 12-15, while unclear, contain references to "stars," *kbkbm*, and "heavens," *šmm*. In line 18 Anat is again washing and grooming herself.

18) n^{c}m. [ ]ṣlm. trṭḥṣ[?]	pleasant … (she) washes herself,
btlt. ^{c}nt. tptr^{c}. ṯb[ ]	Maiden Anat performs her toilet, …
20) limm. wt^{c}l. ^{c}m. il[ ]	*limm* and she ascends to El,
abh. ḥẓr. p^{c}lk. yḥ/ṭ[ ]	her father …
šm^{c}k. larḫ. wbn[ ]	He listens to you, O cow (?), and he understands …
limm. ql. budnk w[	*limm*, voice in your ear and …
	(1.13, 18-23)

In contrast to *KTU*'s *ṯb*[ ], *CTA* (57) reads *ṯd*[*h*?] at the end of line 19, supporting de Moor's (1980:308) interpretation of Anat as the "Breast of the Nations." What is surprising is that de Moor understands this alleged epithet as a reference to Anat as the "harlot of the world," compared to the whore in Revelation 17-8, rather than as the more obvious fertility imagery. One might also propose *y(!)b*[*mt*] *limm* (del Olmo Lete 1981:57). Unfortunately, the damaged tablet does not allow a definite reading of either *ṯb* or *ṯd*. Similarly, the occurrence of *limm* in 20 and 23 eludes our understanding. While it may certainly serve as an independent name in parallel to *btlt ^{c}nt* and *arḫ* in lines 19 and 22, the lack of reliable poetic analysis prevents any conclusion. Both de Moor (1980:306) and del Olmo Lete (1981b:52), however, understand *larḫ* in line 22 as an address to the goddess Anat: "O Cow."

The disputed meaning of lines 24-8 can be avoided in the present discussion. The continued use of first-, second-, and third-person references confuses the sense of *KTU* 1.13 as a whole. The primary relevance of this enigmatic text, however, lies in the last legible section of the tablet, lines 29 through 32.

rkm. agzrt. ^{c}[n]t. arḫ.	… Anat, cow
30) b^{c}l. azrt. ^{c}nt. wld	Baal, … Anat, a child

kbdh. lyd^{c} hrh. [ ]ṯdh	her "womb" did (not) know its conception, ... her breast[61]
tnqt. x[ ]. i(?)nxx. p^{c}r	sucking/suckling (?) ... he gave a name...
ydh. [ ]. ṣǵr. glgl	his hand/beloved ... small (one) ...
a[ ]m. rḫ. ḫḏ ^{c}rpt	... wind ... clouds...
gx[ ]yhpk. m[	... he upsets ...

The interpretive crux of this section rests on the translation of the words *agzrt* (l. 29) and *azrt* (l. 30) (see Bowman 1978:148-9). The apparent parallelism and identification of these terms can be explained through either dittography occurring in the first word or haplography in the second. Based upon the attestation of *agzrym* in *KTU* 1.23, 58, commentators often prefer to read *azrt* as *a<g>zrt*. This term is then derived from the root **gzr* in order to fit the present context as well as *KTU* 1.23.

De Moor (1972, II:21 n. 84) is representative of those scholars who translate *agzrt* as "eager" based upon the BH root *gzr*, "to cut." Bowman (1978:148) argues that the parallelism of *gzr* and *ʾkl* in Isaiah 9:19 indicates a verbal nuance of "to cut meat/food" for BH *gzr*. The meaning of *agzrym* in *KTU* 1.23, 58 can then be related to eating of some kind with the added nuance of "gluttonous." Then, just as the creatures in *KTU* 1.23 are gluttonous, or eager for food, one posits the meaning of "eager" to the term *agzrt* in 1.13. Anat's eagerness to bear is also associated with the Egyptian Harris Papyrus, discussed below, in which Anat is described as a goddess who "conceives but does not bear." Indeed, de Moor (1987:4 n.21) suggests that all of Anat's violence is motivated by frustration over her inability to bear offspring for Baal. Accordingly, de Moor (1987:4) translates:

agzrt. ^{c}[n]t. arḫ. b^{c}l	Anat, the Cow of Baal, was eager,
a<g>zrt. ^{c}nt. [l]ld	Anat was eager to bear.

---

61 I provisionally accept this understanding of lines 31-2, but the vocabulary is not clear. BH *kbd* may denote the "liver" in a specific sense, but it never means "womb." Akkadian *kabattu*, which usually refers to the seat of emotions, may rarely denote "insides (of body)" in poetic passages (*CAD* 8:11). One wonders why *qrb* was not used if "womb" were actually meant. The root *ynq*, "to suck," and *mšnqt*, "wet nurse," are attested at Ugarit, but this is the only known occurrence of *tnqt*.

kbdh. lyd^{c} hrh.	Her womb had not known pregnancy,
[w]ṯdh tnqt.	[nor] her breasts nursing.
b[dq] in d. p^{c}r	(But) there was no [sli]t which he could open,
ydh. [tmǵh?]. ṣǵr.	his member [found it?] too small.[62]
	(1.13, 29-33)

Thus, de Moor understands the extant text to portray Anat as unable to engage in sex. This is only a temporary problem, however, which is overcome elsewhere in Ugaritic myth (de Moor 1980:10). In a similar manner, del Olmo Lete (1981:53, 60) interprets *KTU* 1.13 as a mythic birth proclamation (cf. 1.23, 60-1) which relates Anat's birth of a child.

While *agzrym* is frequently translated as "gluttonous" in *KTU* 1.23, there is no evidence apart from this context that the word should mean "eager." Two other explanations of the term *agzrt* have recently been offered. Dietrich and Loretz (1977:53) suggest the meaning "copy, image," based upon BH *gzr.* These scholars understand the "image of Anat" as a poetic parallel to the "cow of Baal." This interpretation distinguishes between Anat and the cow while affirming a special relationship between the two females. Caquot (1978:18*) proposes the meaning "bovine" based upon Syriac *gĕzārā.* According to his translation, Anat is blessing the cow and its child, rather than being identified with Baal's heifer. Thus, Caqout sees no evidence for Anat's pregnancy in this enigmatic text.

In conclusion, the identity of Anat with the cow of Baal's sexual encounters remains ambiguous, with no clear evidence supporting their equation. Although it is easy enough to postulate this identification and interpret the texts accordingly, the philological defense of this interpretive approach is much too weak to support such a hypothesis. Only in *KTU* 1.13 is there any possible reference to Anat as the "cow of Baal," and this text is certainly not definitive. As Caqout (1978:18*)

62 De Moor's (1980:310) peculiar restoration and reading of the text continues with Baal rolling out hailstones and causing a great storm "in frustration over the physical handicap of his bride" before the text breaks off completely. De Moor (1980:309-10) identifies this text is an incantation for a woman's infertility. He translates lines 24-5: "Because the vulva of the wife is closed up, because the "well" is covered up, let the angels from heaven strengthen the husband, let the angels from heaven send him strength!" De Moor assumes that Anat's barrenness was eventually overcome, thus providing a mythic archetype as the source of the incantation's efficacy.

notes, *KTU* 1.13 may supplement the available information concerning the relationship of Anat and Baal's heifer, but it offers no proof of their identity. Of course, the view of de Moor and others does make for a certain consistency in the Ugaritic mythological corpus. But only through an overly-circular and hypothetical argument can Anat be identified as the sexual partner of Baal. Moreover, there are clearly logical problems with the identification of Anat with the cow in *KTU* 1.5 and 1.10. Similarly, the assumed sexual nature of *KTU* 1.11 should not go unchallenged on etymological grounds. While none of this information necessitates that Anat is not the spouse or consort of Baal, neither does it contribute to the description of Anat as a sexually active goddess in Ugaritic myth.

Egyptian Evidence

Since the obscure and damaged textual evidence precludes a definite conclusion concerning the sexual role of Anat in Ugaritic myth, scholars often take recourse to the portrayal of Anat within Egyptian mythological sources. Until recently many respected scholars assumed that Egypt "unquestionably" incorporated into its mythic repertoire translations of certain Canaanite mythic episodes concerning Canaanite deities (e.g. Albright 1968:129). Indeed, the retention of Semitic names for Anat and Astarte within the Egyptian pantheon—rather than equation with indigenous goddesses—suggests that these traditions provide reliable accounts of their Canaanite originals. However, this assumption is based upon scant evidence concerning the process by which Syrian and Palestinian deities were introduced into the Egyptian pantheon. One can not rule out the possibility of Egyptian misinterpretation and simplification of complex mythic relations and symbolic associations in Canaanite myth. Even if the Egyptian texts are reliable accounts of Canaanite myth, however, they are not necessarily representative of the particular mythological tradition found at Ugarit.

Furthermore, the distinction between "original" Semitic elements and Egyptian development is difficult to substantiate. Although the Egyptians equated Seth, as the god of foreign lands, with Canaanite Baal Hadad, the two gods have diverse histories, relations, and attributes. The assumption that a myth concerning Seth and an Asiatic goddess constitutes a "lost" Canaanite myth disregards the possibility that the text represents an Egyptian tradition into which a foreign goddess has been inserted. The complexities of intercultural borrowing further hampers any attempt to establish "original" myths and later variants. Hence, the value of secondary Egyptian materials in elucidating, or even supplementing, the Ugaritic texts is uncertain at best. Yet scholars rountinely ignore this methodological difficulty and appropriate Egyptian mythic evidence in support of Anat's sexual identity. Regardless, we will see that even the meager Egyptian evidence marshalled for Anat's sexual activity has been previously misinterpreted. Thus, a brief review of the evidence pertinent to Anat's sexual characterization in Egyptian sources is provided here. The thorough job of Bowman (1978:223-49) in presenting the evidence for Anat in Egypt renders unnecessary the repetition of the same information here; remarks will be restricted to the evidence concerning the sexual nature of Anat.

The goddess Anat begins to appear frequently in Egyptian records as a theophoric element in personal names during the Hyksos period, but it is during the 19th Dynasty under the patronage of the Ramesside pharaohs that she is incorporated into the Egyptian pantheon.[63] Consistent with her violent portrayal at Ugarit, Anat is usually associated with martial images in Egyptian materials. In addition to onomastic and iconographic sources, Anat appears in mythological incantations of the New Kingdom in which she plays a role seemingly distinct from her warrior function.[64] Anat is most closely associated with the god Seth, although she is also described as the daughter of Re and, once, the daughter of Ptah (see Redford 1973:44-5). Neith's suggestion that the goddesses Anat and Astarte be given as wives to Seth as compensation for his loss of royal status in *The Contendings of Horus and Seth* is often taken as confirmation of Anat's position as the wife of Seth/Baal. Te Velde (1977:29-30) has criticized this conclusion, however, by noting that Anat is elsewhere never called the consort of Seth, a role

---

[63] See Eaton (1964:24-31), Stadelmann (1967:91-6), Helck (1971b:460-3), Leclant (1975), and especially Bowman (1978:223-49).

[64] Only two texts with Anat in an active narrative role are currently known: Chester Beatty Papyrus VII, discussed here, and an episode in the Leiden Papyrus (Massart 1954) in which she pours out blood of sacrificial donkeys upon the ground.

traditionally reserved for Nephthys.[65] In fact, no Egyptian source identifies Anat with the goddess Nephthys, even though both are considered "virginal" goddesses who support the threatened Seth.

The most important Egyptian source for Anat's sexual activity is the Chester Beatty Papyrus VII, a compilation of magical spells and incantations incorporating mythological episodes. Since Gardiner's (1935) initial treatment of this text, scholars have routinely assumed that this mythological fragment reports Seth's rape of Anat in their theriomorphic manifestations (see Helck 1971b:461; Stadelmann 1967:131-2). Gardiner (1935:61-3) translates the opening of the damaged text:

> [The Goddess ᶜAnat was disporting ?] herself in the (stream of?) Khap and bathing in the (stream of) Ḥemket. Now the great god had gone forth to walk, and he [beheld Seth as he mounted?] upon her back, leaping (her) even as a ram leaps, and covering her even as a ... covers [a] ....

Scholars have often noted this Egyptian myth as confirmation of Anat and Baal's sexual relationship. However, more recent study of the mythological fragment by van Dijk suggests a rather different interpretation.

In his provocative article, van Dijk (1986) compares Chester Beatty Papyrus VII with other textual versions of this mythic episode, particularly an unnumbered Turin papyrus published by Roccati (1972). Based upon his collation of these texts, van Dijk (1986:33-4) presents the following translation, retaining the New Kingdom Egyptian reference to Re as Prēᶜ. Text broken in Chester Beatty VII is restored from the Turin papyrus in brackets, and italics mark phrases absent from both sources.

---

65 See *The Contendings of Horus and Seth* (Pap. Ch. Beatty I, rt. 3, 4-5), translated by Wilson in Pritchard (1969:15). Here the goddess Neith suggests that the gods compensate Seth for granting the kinghip to Horus by giving him Anat and Astarte as wives. Te Velde (1977:30) notes, however, that "the gods do not entertain this proposal" and that "essentially Seth remains lonely." Gardiner (1935:62) states that the obelisk of Tanis also implies that Anat is the wife of Seth. Be this as it may, the infrequent descriptions of Anat as the wife of Seth may simply represent Egyptian misunderstanding or development of the original relationship of Anat and Baal in Canaanite myth. Hence, this information is certainly not conclusive.

[The Seed took a bath] on the shore in order to purify herself in the *Ḥmkt*. Then the Great God went out for a walk and he [perceived her (and saw) her beauty because of (?) the girdle] of her buttocks. Then he mounted her like a ram mounts, he covered her like a [bull] covers. [*Thereupon the seed fl*]ew up to his forehead, to the region of his eyebrows, and he lay down upon his bed in his house [*and was ill.* Hur]ried ᶜAnat, the Victorious Goddess, the woman who acts like a warrior, who wears a skirt like men and a sash (?) like women, to Prēᶜ, her father. He said to her: "What is the matter with you, ᶜAnat, Victorious Goddess, who acts like a warrior, who wears a skirt like men and a sash (?) like women? I have ended (my course) in the evening and I know that you have come to ask that Seth be delivered from the Seed. [*Look*], let (his) stupidity be a lesson (to him). The Seed has been given as a wife to the God Above, that he should copulate with her with fire after deflowering her with a chisel." Said the divine Isis: "I am a Nubian woman. I have descended from heaven and I have come to uncover the Seed which is in the body [*of X son of Y*], and to make him go in health to his mother like Horus went in health to his mother Isis. X son of Y shall be (well), for as Horus lives so shall live X son of Y...."

The composite text thus shows that it is not Anat who has sexual intercourse with Seth, but the hypostatic goddess called simply "the Seed." Van Dijk (1986:40-1) explains the difficult concept of Egyptian *t3 mtwt*, meaning both "seed, semen" and "poison (of a snake or scorpion)," as the mythological personification of the divine Seed in various forms. This hypostatic goddess is attested in other Egyptian contexts. That the term can mean "poison" as well as "seed" provides the symbolic connection between the mythological precedent and the magical incantation against the effects of scorpion stings (van Dijk 1986:43-4).

Van Dijk (1986:39-41) explains that the goddess's bathing may be erotic, as in Egyptian love poetry, and meant to attract Seth. Robins (1988:61-2) also notes that the setting of the marsh or shore itself "probably has erotic connotations," as Hathor is depicted in bovine form emerging from a papyrus marsh in other erotic contexts. Indeed, the aquatic setting of erotic scenes may be a widespread ancient Near Eastern literary motif.[66] According to van Dijk (1986:35), the Semitic

---

66 Similarly, Baal copulates with a cow on the banks of a lake in Ugaritic myth (1.10). Also, as van Dijk points out (1986:39), El seduces his two "wives" on the sea shore in *KTU* 1.23, resulting in the birth of the gods of dawn and dusk, and Enlil rapes, or seduces, the goddess Ninlil in a river in Sumerian myth to engender the moon god

term often thought to imply rape, *ᶜmq*, never has a sexual connotation in Semitic languages, and here it merely serves to emphasize the vigor of Seth's sexual activity. Thus, rather than the violent rape of Anat by Seth in theriomorphic form, this text may actually describe the seduction of Seth by the lascivious goddess, and their (mutually) passionate embrace.[67] The Seed goddess is the intended wife of the God Above, *p3 nṯr ḥry,* whom van Dijk (1986:37, 40) identifies as the moon god ("Osiris Lunus")—who is actually the "nocturnal incarnation" of the sun god Re. Thus, van Dijk describes the Seed as Re's primeval wife, further identified with Hathor, whom Re impregnates "with fire" in order to be recreated each morning as the sun. Since the semen cannot develop without the light or fire provided by sexual intercourse with the sun god, in his nocturnal form, van Dijk (1986:41) understands the purpose of Seth's copulation with the Seed as an attempt to frustrate the resurrection of Re, a motif attested in other Egyptian texts.[68]

In summary, Anat's role in this enigmatic mythic episode is limited to interceding with her father Re on behalf of Seth. In a structural interpretation of this myth, van Dijk (1986:41-2) holds that she is the proper intermediary since, as the wife (or sister) of Seth and the daughter of Re, she is not allied with one against the other. The goddess Isis finally resolves the conflict through her own actions, taking on the maternal characteristics of her Nubian manifestation (van Dijk 1986:38). Van Dijk (1986:44-6) concurs with Roccati's (1972) opinion that this myth reflects a native Egyptian tradition, rather than an adaptation of an originally Canaanite myth. As such, its value in supplementing the Ugaritic material is highly questionable. Prior to Roccati's collation of

---

Nanna (see J. Cooper 1980). Note also Enki's seduction of his daughters in a marshland setting (see Pritchard 1969:37-41).

67 The reference to "deflowering her with a chisel" in Chester Beatty VII remains enigmatic but irrelevant to Anat's sexuality. In his defense of this scene as the rape of Anat, Albright (1968:129) mentions the appearance of "the chisel of Anath" in the Leiden Papyrus. Van Dijk (1986:50 n. 70) corrects this misimpression by noting that the reference to the "lady of the chisel" is not necessarily Anat, and even if it is, the context is clearly militaristic rather than sexual (cf. Massart 1954:55 n. 24).

68 See van Dijk 1986:40-1, with notes. In a different context, te Velde (1977:50, 52) also notes the Egyptian idea that sunlight is required for semen to develop within the womb, although he understands the present passage to mean that Seth's phallus actually emits fire.

texts, scholars unanimously followed Gardiner in assuming that Anat was the subject of the opening line missing in the Beatty Papyrus VII. Indeed, this text is often taken as an Egyptian reflection of the Canaanite myth in *KTU* 1.10 based upon the waterfront setting of each episode.[69] Van Dijk (1986:38) emphasizes the differences in the two myths, noting that Seth's illicit sexuality produces only illness, whereas Baal's copulation engenders an heir. The details of van Dijk's exegesis aside, the Chester Beatty Papyrus VII clearly does not depict sexual intercourse between Anat and Seth. Although the defloration of a virgin goddess is not an unexpected mythic episode, Ugaritic scholars may no longer refer to this text as evidence of the rape of the Maiden Anat.

The goddess Anat also appears in an Egyptian incantation against crocodiles in the Harris Magical Papyrus (Papyrus Harris III, 5-10). Here she is paired with Astarte as "those who conceived but do not bear." The hieroglyphic text is copied and translated into poetic lines by Lange (1927:28-32, 99) (cf. Pritchard 1943:79). In order to provide the context for this enigmatic passage, the entire translation of this incantation is provided here. With the missing line 13 restored from his corrections, Lange (1927:30, 99) translates:

> Heil Euch, Ihr fünf grossen Götter,
> die aus Hermopolis hervorgegangen sind,
> Ihr, die nicht im Himmel sind,
> und die nicht auf der Erde sind,
> Ihr die die Sonne nicht erhellt,
> Kommet zu mir,
> untersuchet für mich den Fluss,
> verschliesset [den Mund] dessen, der darin ist;
> Ihr, die untertauchen, kommet nicht empor!
> Verschliesset euren Mund!
> Sperret euren Mund!
> wie das Fenster in Mendes verschlossen wurde,
> als die Erde in Abydos erhellt wurde,
> wie der Mund der Gebärmutter der Antit und der Astarte verschlossen wurde,
> die beiden grossen Göttinnen,
> die schwanger wurden, aber nicht gebaren.

69 Helck (1971b:461), Albright (1968:129), Pope (1965:236) and Stadelmann (1967:131-3) all consider this Egyptian text as solid evidence for the sexual activity of the Syrian Anat. Albright (1953:197 n. 39) further connects *Ḥmkt* in Chester Beatty VII with *Šmk*, the swampy scene of Baal's copulation with the cow in *KTU* 1.10.

> Sie wurden verschlossen durch Horus,
> und sie wurden geöffnet von Seth.
> Die im Himmel besorgen den Schutz gegen euch.

In a personal communication, Professor Betsy Bryan has suggested reading "shrine" rather than "window" in line 12. Furthermore, the reference to the *ḥm.t*, "womb", in line 14 may be a misreading for *dm.t*, "knife." Hence, the text may actually read "as one closes the mouth for the knife of Anat and Astarte" rather than "as the mouth of the womb was closed." Thus, this reading, while obscure, provides no evidence for the sexual and procreative nature of Anat.

Even if the incantation does refer to the wombs of Anat and Astarte, however, the invocation against the crocodile to keep his mouth shut as the mouth of the womb of Anat and Astarte is shut provides the context within which the pregnancy and delivery of the Canaanite goddesses must be understood. Unfortunately, most scholars treat this reference to the goddesses apart from the Egyptian magical context (e.g. van Dijk 1986:42). Hence, Albright (1968:129-30) quotes this text, "...the mouth of the wombs of Anath and Astarte, the two great goddesses, was closed by the god Horus, so they could become pregnant but could not bear, and was opened by Seth," apparently considering the context irrelevant. Like Albright, Helck (19971b:462) infers that Horus, identified with Canaanite Horon, was keeping the pregnant goddesses from giving birth while Seth is responsible for their delivery. Van Dijk (1986:42) also holds that Anat conceives a child in Papyrus Harris (iii, 8-9) but is unable to give birth to it. Bowman (1978:240-1) compares this episode with *CTA* 13 with possible reference to the eagerness of Anat to bear. However, the assumption that Seth here allows Anat and Astarte to bear children by "opening" their wombs does not fit the context. It is the mythic precedent used in this and other magical spells which make the incantation effective. Thus, it would seem that the closure of the crocodile's mouth is contingent upon the closed nature of the mythic symbols, including the wombs of Anat and Astarte cited in line 14.

Unfortunately, the references to the shrines in the cities of Mendes and Abydos, as well as the myth concerning the gods and goddesses, are unknown, depriving us of vital information. Without these metaphors, the interpretation of the concept concerning Anat and Astarte must remain speculative. It would seem, however, that the incantation suggests that the wombs of the goddesses traditionally remain closed.

While reference is perhaps made here to the unknown myth in which their normally open wombs were (temporarily) closed by Horus, it is more plausible to infer the opposite. The common approach to interpreting this passage is to ignore line 14, as Albright does, and find the mythic precedent in lines 15 through 18. In fact, the emphasis on the closed nature of Anat's and Astarte's wombs provides the example to be followed by the crocodile. Thus, the state of the goddesses' wombs as closed, stated in line 14, provides the mythic statement to which lines 15 through 18 are merely expansions or explanations.

The interpretation that Anat's womb traditionally remains closed posits a positive value to the role of Horus while Seth's action to open their wombs holds a negative value, consistent with other myths concerning Horus and Seth. That is, either Horus wins and their wombs remain closed, or Seth prevails and they are opened. The incantation context suggests that the former is true. Again, the meaning of the actions taken by Horus and Seth is rather unclear. The use of the phrase "mouth of the womb" rather than just "womb" suggests reference is being made to the vagina rather than the actual womb. If the "mouth of womb" refers to the vaginal opening, then its closure may refer to virginity, but if it refers to the womb itself, then perhaps parturition is referred to here. The difference becomes one of sexuality and procreativity. Hence, the closure of the vagina implies the virginity of Anat and Astarte—or at least sexual inactivity—and Seth's attempt to open them would imply seduction or rape. Perhaps the goddesses simply do not wish to engage in sex with the deviant Seth. Unfortunately, this interpretation of the "opened/closed" idea does not take into account the reference to the pregnancy of the goddesses.

A different interpretation of this text offered by te Velde (1977:28-9) in his study of Seth suggests a similar understanding of the roles of Seth and Horus. Following the suggestion of Barb (1959), te Velde argues that this passage refers to the role of Seth in causing unwanted abortions. That is, in closing the wombs of the goddesses, Horus is facilitating effective pregnancy through the cessation of menses, while Seth's "opening" is not defloration, but menorrhage and miscarriage. Here the point of the mythic precedent is not sexual, but procreative. Seth is associated with abnormal pregnancy and deviant sexuality in other Egyptian myths (te Velde 1977:53-9), and specifically associated with miscarriage in later Egyptian amulets (Barb 1959). Seth is sexually active, but more rarely procreative, and he remains more of a bachelor god than consort figure in Egyptian myth (te Velde 1977:29-30). Indeed, it would be most uncharacteristic of Seth to aid in the delivery of the goddesses, as some commentators conclude. Hence, even if Anat and Astarte are impregnated, they are not reproductive. If te Velde's interpretation of this reference is correct, it would certainly appear to be a native Egyptian tradition rather than anything recognizably Canaanite. Although the pregnancy of Anat would present another inconsistency with Ugaritic sources, its role here is simply in emphasizing the "normal" state of Anat's womb as closed.

In conclusion, the reference to Anat in the Harris Papyrus is much too enigmatic to be of any use in the description of Anat's sexuality. The Egyptian mythological context and the specific textual content include too many variables which we simply do not understand. To use this text in support of an argument concerning the difficult subject of Anat's sexuality and procreativity is cavalier, to say the least. Any paraphrase of this text adds its own interpretational bias while the meaning of the Egyptian remains unclear. Whatever the implication of the confusing passage, Anat and Astarte are depicted as not giving birth in this text. While there may be an implication of their sexual activity, this text should in no way contribute towards the depiction of Anat as sexually involved with Baal. In fact, the text seems to refer to the "mouth of the knife" rather than the "mouth of the womb" of the Canaanite goddesses. Finally, even if Egyptian evidence is a reliable source of information concerning Canaanite myth and religion—and this is a very difficult methodological position to defend—there is no clear evidence presenting Anat as procreative or sexually active with Seth. The complex relationship of deities in the mythological traditions concerning Seth further points to the Egyptian origin of mythic episodes involving the goddess Anat.

Anat as Wet Nurse

Scholars occasionally refer to Anat's role as a wet nurse in Ugaritic mythology as evidence for her sexuality and procreative function. Anat appears as a wet nurse for certain divine and human characters in both Ugaritic and Egyptian sources. The Ugaritic mythological texts portray

Anat suckling the heir of Kirta, Yassib, in *KTU* 1.15 ii 26-8. The text describes Yassib as

ynq. ḫlb. a[ṯ]rt	One who will suck the milk of Athirat,
mṣṣ. ṯd. btlt. [^{c}nt]	one who will drain the breasts of the Maiden [Anat],
mšnq[t. ilm (?) …]	the wet nurses [of the gods (?) …].

The reference to the gods Shahar and Shalim, "who suck the nipple of the breasts of the Lady" (*ynqm bap ḏd št*), in *KTU* 1.23, 61 may also refer to Anat's role as wet nurse. The identification of *št*, "the Lady," as Anat in this context, however, is based solely on the reference to Yatpan, Anat's henchman in the *Epic of Aqhat*, as *mhr št*, "the warrior of the Lady" (1.18 iv 27). Since "Lady" is an equally appropriate title for Athirat, *KTU* 1.23 does not provide decisive evidence for the traditional nature of Anat's status as a divine wet nurse. Finally, it is possible, although unlikely, that Anat serves as the wet nurse to the offspring of Baal and the heifer in *KTU* 1.10 iii 26-7.

Bowman (1978:225-34) surveys the Egyptian evidence for Anat as a wet nurse, paying special attention to the inscriptions in the temple of Anat at Tanis in which Ramses II refers to Anat as his mother and patroness (see Montet 1933). The symbolic reference to Anat as the mother of Ramses demonstrates his reliance on her for his warrior prowess and military success. In particular, Ramses II refers to himself as *mhr ^{c}nt*, an epithet that can mean either "suckling of Anat" or "warrior of Anat." The word is explained through either an Egyptian etymology as "suckling" from the root *hr*, "to suckle," or from the Semitic *mhr*, "warrior." Indeed, the term *mhr* appears to mean both "warrior" and "suckling" in various Egyptian texts (see Bowman 1978:228-34). Within the context of Egyptian royal ideology, Ramses' reference to himself as the "suckling of Anat" should identify the goddess as the pharaoh's patron and protector rather than a fertility goddess. She is responsible for imparting royal status to her human devotee and Ramses depicts his dependent relationship to the warrior goddess in familial terms. Clearly, this Egyptian portrayal of Anat should not be used as evidence for the maternal or procreative characteristics of the Ugaritic goddess.

The winged goddess suckling two male youths which is depicted on the famous ivory panel from Ugarit is frequently identified as the goddess Anat, as well.[70] Ward (1969) demonstrates the influence of Egyptian royal ideology upon the artistic motif employed in this scene. Ward (1969:235-7) notes that this ivory panel is actually one of a series of panels depicting the life of the Ugaritic king and concludes that kings symbolically imbibe the divine milk at their enthronement rather than in their infancy. Hence, if the winged goddess is in fact Anat then she is iconographically depicted as the wet nurse to the royal heir rather than as the generic divine wet nurse. The textual description of Anat suckling Yassib in *KTU* 1.18 iv 27 should also be recognized as royal rather than fertility imagery. That is, the common motif to each of her acts as divine nutrix is explicitly related to the royal line of Ugarit (cf. Wyatt 1984). A parallel tradition portraying Ishtar as the divine wet nurse of Neo-Assyrian kings is enlightening in this context. The motif of the Assyrian ruler having imbibed divine milk demonstrates his divine favor and royal status without necessarily attributing maternal characteristics to the erotic and martial Ishtar (see Weippert 1985:61-4, 71-8). Similarly, the virginal Athena is described as a wet nurse of warriors in Greek tradition without any connotation of fertility or sexual imagery (contra Kerényi 1978).

In summary, scholars have interpreted the identification of Anat as a wet nurse in Ugaritic myth as evidence for her function as a fertility or mother goddess. Taken within its own context, however, the information is better explained as evidence for Anat's association with royalty. Just as virtually all ancient Near Eastern deities have some association with the fertilizing powers of nature and life-sustaining forces, Anat's role as a divine nutrix does not identify her as a symbol of natural or human fertility. Thus, the procreative function often attributed to Anat by modern mythographers is not substantiated by her role as a divine wet nurse to royal figures.

III. CONCLUSION

Anat's sexuality remains ambiguous in the Ugaritic texts. It is possible that she serves as the consort of Baal or, less likely, El (1.23), but there is no clear evidence of her sexual involvement with any god.

---

70 Photographs of this ivory panel may be found as Plate VIII in *Syria* 31 (1954) and Plate XXIX (b) in Caquot and Sznycer (1980).

Her common epithet *btlt* does not necessitate that she is a virgin goddess although it does depict her as a youthful female, or "maiden," deity; its function as her primary epithet suggests its particular applicability to Anat among the goddesses. While some Ugaritic texts may be taken to describe Anat as sexually active—if approached with that presupposition—no text offers unambiguous support for this interpretative position. Anat's further characterization in a theriomorphic form is also unsubstantiated. Her portrayal as a winged goddess in *KTU* 1.10 ii 11 is consistent with the iconographic representations of winged goddesses from Ugarit, but there is neither textual nor iconographic evidence for Anat's bovine avatar. The strongest case for Anat's engaging in sex, perhaps in a bovine form, can be made for *KTU* 1.11 although even here the evidence is completely circumstantial. Similarly, *KTU* 1.13 has been interpreted to depict the active sexuality and procreative power of Anat. Unfortunately, this text is so difficult as to elude any definitive translation or exegesis. In his interpretation of *KTU* 1.13 as a mythological incantation against infertility, de Moor understands the bride to be too physically immature to engage in the sexual act. He (1980:309-10) accordingly explains Anat's role in the incantation: "It is perfectly natural for the supplicants to seek the help of the goddess of love in such a matter. According to the mythological passage quoted in lines 29ff. she herself once suffered from a similar handicap." Thus, he assumes that Anat must overcome this problem even though the extant myth gives no evidence of this event. His explanation elsewhere (1987:114) that the goddess can conceive and deliver only through her manifestation as a heifer robs the incantation of its efficacious mythic archetype and stretches the credulity of his readers. What kind of "goddess of love" is physically unable to engage in sex except in a nonanthropomorphic form?

While many scholars continue to describe Anat as a sexually active goddess, the opinions of de Moor are particularly amenable for analysis since he provides an articulate and systematic defense of this interpretative approach. De Moor (1987:7 n. 33) retains the translation of "virgin" for *btlt* but explains that there is no English term equivalent to the proper meaning of *btlt* as "a young woman who did not yet bring forth male offspring." Hence, Anat may be a *btlt* without necessarily being a virgin (cf. Gordon 1977:125). However, the very texts which are used to depict Anat as sexually active (1.10; 1.11; and 1.13) explicitly describe Baal's sexual partner as conceiving and delivering offspring.[71] While a divine "maiden" might engage in sex with males other than her "husband," the appellative *btlt* is completely inappropriate for a female who is both sexually active and procreative. Thus, if Anat is Baal's sexual partner in these texts then she is also a procreative goddess, a detail sufficient to disqualify her from the epithet *btlt.*

Similarly, de Moor's interpretation of Anat's epithet *ybmt limm* as "Wanton Widow of the Nations" is based explicitly upon the assumption that there is the obligation among Dagan's kin to marry her since Baal "had died without giving her a son" (de Moor 1987:14 n.70). That is, de Moor identifies *ybmt* as a widowed woman who has yet to bear a son. However, Baal does in fact engender a male heir by the heifer prior to his descent to the Netherworld (1.5 v) and if the goddess is not equated with Baal's heifer in this scene then what evidence is there to identify her as such in *KTU* 1.10 and 1.13? For Anat to qualify for the epithet *ybmt*, de Moor must assume that the impregnation of Anat depicted in *KTU* 1.10, 1.11, and 1.13 takes place temporally after the account of Baal's death and resurrection in the Baal Cycle. Of course, if Baal sires a son through Anat after his resurrection then she remains neither a *ybmt* nor a *btlt.* More importantly, de Moor's (1980:309) translation of *ybmt* as "Wanton Widow" is quite unconvincing and most speculative.

While there is certainly no consensus among Ugaritologists concerning the meaning of *ybmt limm*, many scholars implicitly agree with de Moor's conclusion that this epithet entails that Anat and Baal are spouses and that she becomes a "widow" upon his (annual) death (cf. Gray 1965:43; Pope 1965:240; Bowman 1978:189). Unfortunately, this fact is consistently assumed rather than defended. There is little evidence to support the identification of Anat as the formal spouse or consort of the Ugaritic storm god. Indeed, the connotation of widowhood required in the biblical occurrences of *ybmh* is not necessarily essential to the Ugaritic term *ybmt*. Given the discussion above, I would posit as the central element of Ugaritic and BH *ybmt*'s

71 Gordon's (1977:120, 125) opinion that Anat is not the heifer of Baal in *KTU* 1.5 v and 1.10, although she does engage in sex with Baal in 1.11, apparently in anthropomorphic form, also suffers from this weakness. Note Gray's (1979:319 n. 27) speculative suggestion that Anat's epithet *btlt* may indicate that "she came as a virgin to Baal."

semantic range the concept of a non-blood related female living in the household—a female affine. The attribution of widowhood to Anat is an interpretive assessment which conflicts with her attribution of maidenhood. It is hard to accept that the goddess Anat would retain the epithets of "widow" and "maiden" when she is, in fact, neither.

Finally, it is best to risk the charge of skepticism and to adopt a conservative interpretation of Anat's alleged sexual and procreative function in Ugaritic myth. The interpretation that Anat is sexually active and procreative is circumstantial and based upon a circular reading of the Ugaritic texts. Her description as a "maiden" goddess, on the other hand, is consistent with her narrative depiction as an independent and unrestrained goddess. Anat's identification as the *aḫt*, "sister," of Baal is also consistent with her behavior in the Baal Cycle wherein she faithfully supports Baal in his struggles and volunteers to fight his battles. Her active role as his companion and the aggressive executor of his desires suggests Anat's sororal rather than erotic involvements with Baal. While future discoveries of additional evidence may certainly prove that Anat does indeed participate in sexual relations with Baal, the texts presently available do not confirm Anat's role as sexually active or procreative. Therefore, the common portrayal of Anat as a "goddess of love" by modern scholars has a slim and unstable foundation. Certainly there is no evidence for her active patronage of sexual pleasure as in the case of Aphrodite and Ishtar.

The lack of definite information concerning the sexual component of Anat's mythic character is most unfortunate given the central importance of sexuality to feminine symbolism within androcentric mythologies. Anat's sexual abstinence, activity, or exploitation would provide important data for the proper analysis of her symbolic associations. Even without this information, however, much can be said concerning Anat's symbolic role in Ugaritic myth as a young female or "maiden." The evidence presented above concerning Anat's epithets *btlt* and *rḥm* establishes Anat's general depiction as a youthful female. Anat's gender and age attributes portray her as an adolescent character throughout the Ugaritic texts. Kirta alludes to Anat's nubility in his poetic reference to the beauty of a human woman, "whose loveliness is like the loveliness of Anat, whose beauty is as the beauty of Athtart," *dkn*ᶜ*m.* ᶜ*nt n*ᶜ*mh. km. tsm* ᶜ*ṯtrt. tsmh* (1.14 vi 26-7). Anat's qualifications as a wet nurse further suggest that she is a physically mature goddess. From these data one can further identify the mythic character of the goddess Anat as a woman of marriageable age according to ancient Near Eastern standards (see Roth 1987). Thus, she is physically equipped for marriage yet apparently chooses not to participate in this social institution. The importance of social position and sexual identity to feminine characters in polytheistic pantheons combines with the consistent depiction of Anat as an adolescent goddess in the Ugaritic corpus to suggest the symbolic importance of Anat's status as a female ripe for marriage.

The use of terms derived from the social sphere to describe Anat refers to social metaphors which are incorporated into the mythic character of this youthful goddess. Just as one has trouble discussing gender symbolism and "goddess biology" in any empirical sense, so one encounters difficulty in describing the social structure of ancient pantheons. However, the Ugaritic pantheon shows clear signs of a sociomorphic formation. That is, the members of the pantheon are described within the mythological material in terms applicable to human individuals and social structures. Hence, it is not improper to ascribe human age and gender attributes to the Ugaritic deities. In this sense we are employing social metaphors to identify social status within the divine society. This is not to suggest that the deities or pantheon are necessarily formed from these metaphors, but simply to note that these social terms and categories are purposefully incorporated into the literary description of the members of the divine realm.

As an adolescent goddess within an androcentric mythology one might expect Anat to be under the authority of some male. If she fits into the normative categories established for feminine characters in a patriarchal social structure, then Anat should to be under the dominance and authority of her father or husband. Yet Anat clearly rejects any attempts at dominance and preserves her independence. She is a liminal figure, both socially and sexually, in that she is outside of the normative feminine categories of mother, wife, or dependent daughter. In social terms, she is the adolescent female who has yet to accept the social position of a mature woman as wife and mother. Anat's role in procuring a heifer for Baal's amorous affairs (1.10), however, suggests her symbolic association with sex or fertility even though she is not herself sexually active. While conclusions to this discussion are deferred to the final chapter, the two themes of Anat's unrestrained behavior and her sexual ambiguity may both be intimately connected to her symbolic identity as a female of marriageable age who has maintained her independence from male dominance. For the present it is sufficient to conclude that Anat's consistent status as a maiden goddess in Ugaritic mythology provides a symbolic network combining themes of male authority and feminine sexuality. How these themes may be interpreted will be discussed in this study's final chapter.

CHAPTER 4
Violence and Passion

Scholars routinely interpret Anat's belligerence and combativeness soley in terms of her relationship to Baal and the promotion of natural fertility. Bowman (1978), in his unpublished dissertation concerning the goddess Anat, argues that Anat's role in Ugaritic myth and religion is based upon her identity as the hypostatic manifestation of Baal's will (cf. Albright 1953:195 n. 14). Implicit in this argument is the assumption that the mythic activity of Baal is intimately related to the agricultural cycle of ancient Canaan. Thus, Anat's "original" purpose in Ugaritic myth is to aid the storm god in causing natural fecundity (Bowman 1978:263-5); she is the feminine extension of Baal's identity as the fertility god who must defeat the forces of sterility. Unfortunately, this interpretation can not account for Anat's selfish actions which clearly work counter to Baal's purpose in the *Epic of Aqhat.* Indeed, Anat is frequently the initiator of actions in Ugaritic myth rather than the passive supporter of Baal's plans. She demands immediate gratification for her impulsive desires and fights tenaciously to realize her own goals. As argued below, this lack of self-restraint is perhaps more central to her mythic personality than her warlike attributes. More importantly, Bowman's interpretation reduces the goddess to a simplistic and one-dimensional function and neglects the multivalence of mythic symbols. While pointing out one aspect of Anat's role within the Baal Cycle, Bowman's analysis is inadequate in interpreting Anat's symbolic associations within Ugaritic myth.

Earlier scholars have been quite correct to note the important relationship between Baal and Anat and the subsequent link between Anat and natural fertility. In fact, the narrative motivation in both the Baal Cycle and *Aqhat* focuses on problems of fertility. While Anat works to correct these problems in the Baal Cycle, her actions cause the drought and the loss of the royal heir in *Aqhat*. In addition to the standard agricultural and seasonal interpretations of Ugaritic myth, however, mythographers must consider other symbolic uses of fertility, violence, and gender in the mythic identity of the goddess Anat. In particular, the results of the present study indicate that Anat's narrative actions and mythic symbolism are intrinsically related to her gender and social identity. Anat has a mythic personality apart from her brother, Baal, as well as an independent position within the Ugaritic pantheon. Thus, this chapter considers the themes of passion, violence and fertility in Ugaritic myth with special regard for the gendered symbolism of the goddess Anat. Particular attention is given to the symbolic significance of Anat's violent rage and her social status within the divine realm as an unmarried female.

I. VIOLENCE AND FERTILITY

The strongest influence on most interpretations of Anat's violent role in the Baal Cycle is clearly the Myth and Ritual school. This approach, with its emphasis on seasonal imagery and a necessary ritual component to myth, explains the violent actions of Anat as ritual prototypes and examples of her fertility function. As argued above, the common assumption that any goddess is a symbol of fertility based solely upon her gender should be discarded with the notion that all ancient Near Eastern goddesses were sexually active and functioned as fertile "mother goddesses" (e.g. Gray 1987:20). The assumption that the Baal Cycle has a ritual setting also remains unproven. Yet, the imagery of natural and seasonal fertility does pervade the Ugaritic myths and, thus, interpreters must confront the relation of Anat to this imagery and especially her relation to the role of Baal. The present section of this chapter offers a rather modest attempt to organize the available information concerning the relation of Anat to the actions of Baal in the Baal Cycle in order to evaluate her role in promoting natural fertility.

Anat's Violence And Fertility

Anat's Bloodbath. The bloodiest and most grisly depiction of Anat in Ugaritic myth actually constitutes her introduction to the Baal Cycle.[1] She is engaged in a frenzied massacre of apparently human warriors, with decapitated heads and hands flying about as she madly slaughters her hapless opponents. The bloodletting is so extensive that she is able to wade up to her thighs in the standing blood. Delighted by the carnage, Anat adorns herself with the dismembered parts of her defeated enemies. Although the meaning of the episode is unclear, Anat is apparently unsatisfied by her massacre on the battlefield and continues the butchery in her mansion. Unfortunately, Anat's motivation for this unrelenting slaughter is lost to a break in the tablet. The fragmentary beginning of the column, after approximately twenty-five lost lines, suggests that Anat has made herself up with henna and murex in preparation for her combat. The available text (1.3 ii 3–iii 2) reads:[2]

klat. ṯǵrt (4) bht. ᶜnt	Anat closed the gates of her mansion and
wtqry. ǵlmm (5) bšt. ǵr.	met the youths at the base of the
	mountain.
whln. ᶜnt. tm(6)tḫṣ. bᶜmq	Behold, Anat battled in the valley;
tḫtṣb. bn (7) qrytm	she slaughtered between the two cities.
tmḫṣ. lim. ḫp y[m]	She slew the people of the West;
8)tṣmt. adm. ṣat. špš	she silenced the men of the East.
9)tḥth. kkdrt. ri[š]	Beneath her like dirt clods were head(s),[3]
10)ᶜlh. kirbym kp.	above her like locusts were hand(s),
k.qṣm (11) ǵrmn. kp. mhr.	like destructive locusts (?) were the
	warriors' hand(s).[4]

---

1 Although there are numerous lacunae prior to this episode, there is no indication of Anat's activity prior to *KTU* 1.3 ii. Many scholars restore her name in *KTU* 1.2 i 40 as a poetic parallel to Athtart as she restrains Baal from attacking Yamm's messengers. While this is possible, such action would be inconsistent with Anat's usual character. Note also that Athtart alone admonishes Baal once he has defeated Yamm (1.2 iv 28ff). Regardless, Anat plays no active role in the extant myth prior to her bloody battle with the humans of the two cities.

2 On the massacre of Anat, see especially Gray (1979).

3 See Wehr (1976:817) for Arabic *kadara*, "clod of dirt." See also Mishnaic and BH (Isa 23:18) *kaddûr*, "ball." *TO* (158) reports Virolleaud's opinion that Arabic *kadara* means "grain of cereal," but I can not locate this term.

4 On the obscure phrase *qṣm ǵrmn* see Gray (1979) and de Moor (1987:5).

^{c}tkt (12) rišt. lbmth.	She attached the heads to her back;
šnst. (13) kpt. bḥbšh.	she bound the hands to her girdle.
brkm. tǵl[l] (14) bdm. d̲mr.	She plunged her knees into the soldiers' blood,
ḥlqm. bmm^{c} (15) mhrm.	her thighs (?) into the warrior's gore.[5]
mṭm. tgrš (16) šbm.	She drove out the foes (with her) arrows,
bksl. qšth. mdnt	the combatants with her bow-string.
17) whln. ^{c}nt. lbth. tmǵyn	Behold, Anat proceeded to her house;
18) tštql. ilt. lhklh	the goddess headed for her palace.
19) wl. šb^{c}t. tmtḫṣh. b^{c}mq	She was not satiated by her battle in the valley,
20) tḫtṣb. bn. qrtm.	(by her) slaughter between the cities.
tṯ^{c}r (21) ksat. lmhr.	She arranged (?) seats for the warriors;
ṯ^{c}r. ṯlḥnt (22) lṣbim.	she arranged tables for the troops,
hdmm. lǵzrm	footstools for the heroes.
23) mid. tmtḫṣn. wt^{c}n	She battled mightily and beheld (the scene);
24) tḫtṣb. wtḥdy. ^{c}nt	Anat slaughtered and gazed (upon the result).
25) tǵdd. kbdh. bṣḥq.	Her liver swelled with laughter,
ymlu (26) lbh. bšmḫt.	her heart was filled with joy,
kbd. ^{c}nt (27) tšyt.	the liver of Anat (with) victory (?),
kbrkm. tǵll. bdm (28) d̲mr.	as she plunged her knees into the soldiers' blood,
ḫlqm. bmm^{c}. mhrm	(her) thighs into the warrior's gore,
29) ^{c}d. tšb^{c}. tmtḫṣ. bbt	until she was satiated by battling in the house,
30) tḫtṣb. bn. ṯlḥnm.	(and) slaughtering between the tables.
ymḥ (31) bb(!)t. dm. d̲mr.	The soldiers' blood was wiped from the house;
yṣq. šmn (32) šlm. bṣ^{c}.	oil of well-being was poured from a bowl.
trḥṣ. ydh. bt(33)[l]t. ^{c}nt	Maiden Anat washed her hands,
uṣb^{c}th. ybmt. limm.	*Ybmt Limm*, her fingers.
34) [t]rḥṣ. ydh. bdm. d̲mr	She washed her hands of the soldiers' blood,
35) [u]ṣb^{c}th. bmm^{c}. mhrm	her fingers of the warriors' gore.

5 Cf. Rendsburg 1987:628.

36) [ṯ]ʿr. ksat. lksat.	Arranging chairs with chairs,
ṯlḥnt (37) bṯlḥn<t>.	tables with tables,
hdmm. tṯar. lhdmm	she arranged (?) footstools with footstools.
38) tḥspn. mh. wtrḥṣ	She scooped up water and washed,
39) ṭl. šmm. šmn. arṣ.	dew of the heavens and oil of the earth,
rbb (40) [r]kb. ʿrpt.	showers of the Rider of the Clouds.
ṭl. šmm. tskh	Dew the heavens poured on her;
41) [rb]b. nskh. kbkbm	showers the stars poured out upon her.
KTU 1.3 iii	
1) ttpp. anhb[m.]	She adorned herself with murex
[dalp. šd] (2) ẓuh. bym [...]	[whose] source [is one thousand tracts away] in the sea.

Despite the obscurity of many details in this grisly episode, the general portrayal of Anat as a bloodthirsty warrior is clear.

Anat's purpose and motivation for this ruthless slaughter of humans are unknown, as is the identity of her enemies. Undaunted by the lack of evidence, many scholars have offered interpretations which rely heavily upon the Myth and Ritual school of myth interpretation. Based upon the assumptions of this approach, Anat's actions must provide mythic archetypes for the fertility rituals performed by the religious leaders of Ugarit. Indeed, her most bloody exploits are conveniently explained by modern interpreters as rituals to induce the rain through sympathetic magic; as the blood flows so will the rain (Gray 1965:45). Scholars often appeal to the biblical portrayal of Baal's prophets lacerating themselves in order to stimulate rain (1Kings 18) to defend this interpretation. Gibson (1984:214) considers this slaying of humans "a mythical mirror image of a rite" to reduce anxiety during the change of seasons (cf. de Moor 1987:5 n. 21). Bowman (1978:263) illustrates the assumptions and prejudices at work when he states that Anat's "violence *must* have filled some function in the cult" (emphasis mine). While there certainly may be ritual associations or narrative functions for this particular massacre, the Ugaritic texts provide neither a reason nor a result of Anat's militant activities.

In fact, this episode may not play an important role in the mythic narrative but may simply provide a thematic introduction to the goddess herself. The scene of Anat reveling in the slaughter of her enemies and adorning herself with their dismembered parts appears to be a standard depiction of the goddess. This macabre episode apparently introduces Anat to both the Baal Cycle and *KTU* 1.13 i 5-7.[6] The grisly image evoked by this scene, similar to the iconography of Kali wearing a wreath of human heads, presents a striking image to humans both ancient and modern (see Pope 1977:605-12). Thus, Anat's motivation for this particular scene is perhaps not as significant as her general tendency towards violence in Ugaritic myth. In other words, while Anat's purpose in this bloody scene is lost to modern mythographers, the consistent portrayal of the maiden goddess in such violent exploits requires a comprehensive interpretation. The integration of her lethal temperament with the other aspects of her character demonstrates the importance of Anat's symbolic identity as an independent female of marriageable age. Thus, the symbolic matrix of gender, blood, and life and death receives particular attention throughout this chapter.

Anat's Fertility Ritual. While Baal is intimately associated with the fertility of the earth as the provider of rains (e.g. 1.16 iii 4-11), Anat's relation to natural fertility is more frequently assumed than defended by Ugaritologists. Given the crucial distinction between female sex, fertility and eroticism in the character of a goddess, one should not posit a fertility function for Anat without more explicit evidence from Ugaritic myth and religion.[7] In fact, virtually all ancient Near Eastern deities have some association with the fertilizing powers of nature. This is a standard divine attribute rather than any particular fertility function. Hence, the depiction of Anat as a fertility goddess requires textual support. Perhaps the most important textual evidence for the Maiden Anat's role as the provider of natural fertility is found in the series of enigmatic episodes in *KTU* 1.3 ii–iv.

The bloody introduction of Anat to the Baal Cycle in an active narrative role (1.3 ii 3-29) is immediately followed by a reference to the

---

6 The beginning of *KTU* 1.10 is missing, so it is unclear whether Anat is always portrayed in this manner.

7 Wyatt (1988:382-4), in his proposal of an Indian source for the Baal Cycle myths, is one of the few scholars to identify explicitly Anat as "the earth goddess" of Ugarit. He defends the etymology for her name based on the Ugaritic lexeme *ᶜnt*, "furrow," and links it to the apparent agricultural context of *KTU* 1.3 iv. Other scholars usually assume without elaboration the fertility function of this Ugaritic goddess.

goddess washing herself of her victims' blood and performing her toilette (1.3 ii 30–iii 2). After a gap of approximately twenty lines, the text continues with what is apparently Baal's dispatch of his messengers (1.3 iii 4-31) in which he describes Anat singing a "love song" concerning Baal, Pidray, Tallay, and Arsay (ll. 4-8). The message is essentially an invitation for Anat to hurry to Baal, but incorporated within it are the enigmatic instructions of lines 14-7. This message is delivered verbatim in 1.3 iv 8-10, and in the same column Anat repeats the instructions twice, once in the form of a question (ll. 22-5) and then in granting her assent upon the condition that Baal first display his lightning in the sky (ll. 25-31).[8] Although the extant text does not describe Anat actually performing these ritualistic actions, her conditional assertion is perhaps sufficient proof of her completion of the task. Baal's instructions provide the interpretive crux concerning Anat's fertility function:

qryy. barṣ (15) mlḥmt	Place (an offering of) bread in the earth!
št. b^{c} prm. ddym	Set mandrakes in the dust!
(16) sk. šlm. lkbd. arṣ	Pour out well-being into the heart of the earth,
(17) arbdd. lkbd. šdm	tranquility into the heart of the fields! (1.3 ii 14-17)

Anat's assent to these instructions, after setting the condition that Baal first display his lightning in the sky, follows in *KTU* 1.3 iv 27-31. She declares:

aqry (28)[an.] barṣ. mlḥmt	I will indeed place (an offering of) bread in the earth.
(29) ašt. b^{c} prm. ddym.	I will set mandrakes in the dust.
ask (30) šlm. lkbd. arṣ.	I will pour well-being into the heart of the earth,
arbdd (31) lkbd. šdm.	tranquility into the heart of the fields.

8 This short passage also occurs in *KTU* 1.1 ii 19-21 and 1.7, 26-8, heavily restored each time. In these two cases it appears that El, rather than Baal, is relating the instructions to Anat. Whether this is a mythological variant of the episode or whether the actions taken by Anat are recurrent (i.e., seasonal) is unclear.

The implications of Baal's message are quite significant for interpreting the role of Anat and her relationship to Baal. Unfortunately, the exact translation and meaning of this short section remain uncertain.

Scholars generally understand the pericope's initial line, *qryy barṣ mlḥmt*, in either one of two ways (see *TO* 163-5). In contrast to the translation adopted here, "Place (an offering of) bread in the earth," some scholars prefer, "Oppose war in the earth."[9] Disagreement over the correct translation of the verbal root *qry* concerns its biblical cognates. BH *qrᵓ* means "to call, invite" as well as "to happen, come (to someone)." The latter meaning of this root is frequently used with *mlḥmh* in the sense "to do battle." BH *qrh* also means "to come (upon)" and "to happen" in the G stem, but it is not combined with *mlḥmh*. However, Ugaritic distinguishes between the verbs *qrᵓ*, "to call, invite," and *qry*, "to meet; to sacrifice" (Gordon 1965:480). While Ugaritic *qry* clearly means "to meet, encounter" (e.g. 1.17 vi 43), the verbal root is not attested with the meaning "to oppose" in any other context.[10] Indeed, the attestation of *qry* in *qrym ab dbḥ lilm // šᶜly dǵṯh bšmym*, "My father has presented a sacrifice to the gods, // he has sent up incense to the heavens" (1.19 iv 29-30), demonstrates its sacrificial connotation. Thus, the D stem of *qry* means "to present; to cause to encounter," just as the G stem means "to encounter." Whether it can also mean "to encounter" in the sense of "to oppose" is unproven.

Given the difficulty of this passage, special attention is given to the poetic parallelism of Baal's instructions. Is Anat told to oppose war and place love in the earth, or is she instructed, with synonymous verbs, to offer sacrificial items? While BH *mlḥmh* clearly means "war," there is neither a verb *lḥm*, "to fight," nor a noun *mlḥmt*, "war," otherwise

---

9 Gibson (1978:49) and Gordon (1977:78), for example, support the sacrificial language while Ginsberg (1969:13) and de Moor (1987:9) prefer "Oppose war in the earth." The earlier understanding of *qryy* as "Come to me" is now generally abandoned (see van Zijl 1972:57 n. 2). Gray (1979:321) advocates a peculiar translation, "I am averse to strife on earth," for *qryy barṣ mlḥmt.* Finally, *TO* (163) offers the conjectural "Produits dans la terre des aliments," implying the fertility function of Anat in stimulating the crops (see also Bowman 1978:21).

10 It is possible that the beginning of Anat's bloodbath, *wtqry ǵlmm bšt ǵr*, should be read "(Anat) opposed the youths at the foot of the mountain" rather than "(Anat) met the youths at the foot of the mountain" (1.3 ii 4-5). Notably, even de Moor, who favors the translation of *qryy*, "oppose," in Baal's message, translates *wtqry* in this passage as "(she) went to meet" (see de Moor 1987:5, 9; de Moor and Spronk 1987:167).

attested in Ugaritic. The appearance of *mlḥmy*, apparently meaning "my bread," in the unfortunately broken context of *KTU* 1.5 ii 23 and the frequent use of the verbal root *lḥm,* "to eat," in various conjugations in Ugaritic texts (Whitaker 1972:397-8) further support the translation "bread" or "food" for *mlḥmt.* The poetic parallel of *mlḥmt* is the even more obscure lexeme *ddym*, but the verbal sense is clear: Baal instructs Anat to "set in the dust *ddym*," *št bᶜprm ddym.* Cognate terms and Ugaritic contextual evidence show the homograph *dd* can designate a "jar" (BH *dûd*), "(sexual) love" (BH *dôd*), and perhaps "mandrakes" (BH *dûdāʾîm*). While scholars generally avoid translating *ddym* as "a jar of sea water," opinion is split concerning the correctness of "love" and "mandrakes."

The primary obstacle to understanding *ddym* as "love" is the consistent writing with /y/. Goetze (1944:19) holds that *ddym* is connected with BH *dôdîm*, "(sexual) love," and that *-ayu* is an abstract ending "apparently with some pejorative connotation." Hence, Goetze (1944:20) translates, "Remove war from the earth! Do away with passion!"[11] Yet, there is no evidence for *-ayu* exhibiting a pejorative sense. De Tarragon (1980:46), in his study of Ugaritic ritual texts, concludes that there is an offering of *dd*, "love," in Ugaritic cultic sources.[12] Gray (1979:321) prefers to understand the term as "love tokens." While the writings *dd* (1.3 iii 4-8) and *ddm* could certainly refer to "love" (see Dietrich and Loretz 1981:142 n. 113), the orthography of *ddym* suggests that this is not the same term. Another proposed meaning of *ddym* is "mandrake," related to BH *dûdāʾîm*, an aphrodisiac in the biblical tradition (e.g. Gen 30:14-16; Cant 7:14) and throughout the ancient Near East (see Bosse-Griffiths 1983). The /y/ to /ʾ/ interchange in Ugaritic and BH is uncommon but not unprecedented. Fensham (1965:34-5) notes that the term *ddyt*, "red ochre" or "mandrakes," is used in the Egyptian myth of Sekhmet discussed above. In the Egyptian text, Re mixes *ddyt* in beer in order to give it the color

---

11 Goetze (1944:18-20) translates *qry* in the unattested sense, "to remove," and suggests that *št bᶜprt*, "to put in the dust," is an idiomatic expression meaning "to do away with (something)."

12 Acknowledging the ambiguity of the Ugaritic homograph *dd* and its meaning, "jar, pot," in certain economic texts, de Tarragon (1980:46) understands the reference to *dd ilš* in *CTA* 35, 6 as "bien aimé (dieu) *ilš*" rather than a reference to an offering contained in a pot.

of blood. Through this ruse, Re is able to pacify Sekhmet and save humanity from annihilation. Fensham notes that both the Egyptian and Ugaritic myths use *ddyt/m*, albeit in different manners, to bring peace to the human realm. Thus, I prefer to translate *ddym* as "mandrakes," in parallel to "bread," and understand Baal's message to Anat as instructions to place these concrete items in the ground as a ritualistic activity.

The latter two lines of Baal's instructions are generally clearer than the former, but the obscurity of intent remains. The scholarly discussion primarily concerns the possible allusions to Ugaritic ritual practices. That is, if Baal's instructions are in fact concerning sacrificial items rather than abstract ideas of "love" and "war," do Anat's actions reflect actual cultic practices from ancient Ugarit?

Recent studies of *šlmm* as "*šlm*-offerings" in Ugarit and Israel have advanced the understanding of this ritual form but do not aid in the interpretation of the present mythological text.[13] De Tarragon (1980:59) notes that the *šlm* sacrifice "est très bien attesté dans les textes de la pratique. C'est probablement le type de sacrifice le plus courant."[14] Admitting that "a clear rendering of the text eludes us," Levine (1974:12-3) concludes that *šlm* in this occurrence does *not* refer to a formal sacrifice, but simply means "peace." M. Smith (1986b:323 n. 58) suggests that this offering is in recognition of Baal's new status as king. Thus, Anat's libation may be either a reflection of actual cultic practice or simply a metaphor for "peace on earth."

The poetic parallel to Anat's pouring out of peace poses another philological difficulty in the term *arbdd*. Janowski (1980:239-41) reviews the earlier ideas concerning the treatment of *arbdd* as either one word or its separation into *ar bdd* or *arb dd*. De Moor (1986b:219 n. 8) has pointed out the problem with dividing a word which is consistently (six times) written without a word divider in the Ugaritic texts.[15] The explanation of *arbdd* as a verbal form (e.g. Gray 1979:321) is weakened by the apparent lack of morphological differentiation between Baal's

---

13 See Janowski (1980), de Tarragon (1980:59-62), Dietrich and Loretz (1981), and Levine (1974).

14 However, the Ugaritic texts often do not allow a definite distinction between an offering to the god Shalim and the *šlm*-sacrifice (de Tarragon 1980:159-60).

15 Goetze (1944:20) translates *arb dd* as "loving consideration," based upon Arabic cognates for *ʾrb*. Gibson (1978:49) reads *ar bdd*, "honey from a pot," based upon de Moor's (1975) earlier defense of *ar* as "honey-dew." *TO* (164) has a conjectural "des multitudes de délices."

instructions and Anat's speech. Although de Moor disagrees concerning the proper etymology of the term, he (1986b:219-20) now follows the suggestion of del Olmo Lete (1978:40-2) to translate *arbdd* as "calm, tranquility." The poetic parallelism of *arbdd* with *šlm* also supports such a meaning for this obscure lexeme. In opposition to earlier attempts to see this passage as cultic in nature, de Tarragon (1980:71) holds that *arbdd*, found only in literary texts, can not have a cultic significance. Hence, the reference to the pouring of *šlm* and *arbdd* is best understood as metaphorical rather than a sacrificial practice.

In summary, the initial bicolon of Baal's instructions to Anat is better translated, "Place (an offering of) bread in the earth; Set mandrakes in the dust," rather than "Oppose war in the earth; Place love in the dust." While the D stem of *qry* may possibly mean "to oppose," the attested meaning "to offer (a sacrifice)" in *KTU* 1.19 iv 29, as well as the poetic parallel *št*, "to set," better supports the reading "to place." The latter two lines of this passage, however, are more clearly metaphorical in nature. Significantly, the elements identified in Baal's message are not part of the actual Ugaritic cult, as far as we know; they are unattested in Ugaritic ritual texts. Yet, ancient Ugaritic cultic practices include the deposition of sacrificial items, especially liquids, into the ground (Schaeffer 1939:46-56). While it does not seem that Anat is here enacting a known ritual, her actions are indeed ritualistic. The general intent appears to be related to fertility and well-being on the earth. Anat's explicit association of this rite with Baal's lightning, perhaps a harbinger of rains, also suggests a fertility connection. Thus, Baal requests Anat to perform certain tasks which seem to promote natural fecunduty. This request is probably related to his new position as the divine king. In the final analysis, however, the scene and its possible cultic function remain obscure.

Since Baal's message is subsequent to Anat's bloodbath (1.3 ii), many commentators have argued that his instructions function to calm the violent goddess, lest her carnage run out of control. Gray (1979:321) and Kapelrud (1969:102), for example, understand Baal's message to Anat, "Oppose war in the earth; Place love in the dust," as a means to pacify the blood-thirsty goddess. In contrast to his earlier fertility interpretation (1977:9), Gibson (1984:215) has recently adopted Gray's view that Baal's instructions "merely use the metaphor of ritual language to call upon Anat, who was a goddess both of war and love, to abandon her first role as a slayer of gods and men and adopt her second as their benefactor and friend." Hence, this episode is understood as a striking parallel to Re's deliverance of humankind from destruction at the hands of Sekhmet in Egyptian myth (Gray 1979:321-2; Fensham 1965), as well as Shiva's action in calming the frenzied Kali in Hindu myth (Pope 1977:608). However, apart from its philological defense, this interpretation of Baal's message suffers from a serious flaw. Anat voluntarily ceases her carnage once she is satiated; she has already calmed down sufficiently to wash and play her lyre prior to Baal's commissioning of his messengers. Indeed, Baal himself describes Anat engaged in singing when the text resumes after a gap in *KTU* 1.3 iii. Thus, the most natural reading of the narrative would seem to exclude the interpretation advocated by Gray and Gibson. Anat is here acting independently of Baal.

Anat's Violence and Baal's Fertility. The enigmatic and complex succession of scenes in *KTU* 1.3 ii–iv have prompted numerous interpretations of Anat's violent nature and her relationship to Baal. The majority of scholars appears to understand the bloodletting of *KTU* 1.3 ii and the ritualistic instructions of 1.3 iii as a ritual process intended to prompt the gods to dispense fertility (e.g. Oldenburg 1969:89). Thus, this textual complex is said to confirm Anat's role as the Ugaritic goddess who brings fertility to the otherwise barren earth. To be sure, the sacrificial activities of Anat appear to aid Baal in promoting natural fertility. Apart from this scene, however, the evidence for Anat's direct association with natural fertility is scant. In particular, her violence in support of Baal's explicit quest for divine kingship does not necessarily reflect her fertility function. Since Anat is a volatile and combative deity by nature, the relation of her violent actions to the goals of Baal in the Baal Cycle must be considered individually.

Gray (1965:45) concludes that it is best to "explain the bloodbath of the goddess Anat as relating to a rite proper to the season of transition between the sterility of the late Syrian summer and the new season of fertility. It seems to us to indicate ... a rite of imitative magic to stimulate a liberal outpouring of fresh vitality, the blood being to the ancient Semite the life-essence." Even Anat's toilette is understood as a ritual to promote fertility, as Oldenburg (1969:89-90) explains that the people of Ugaritic believed that Anat's bathing caused the morning dew.

Bowman (1978:28) boldly affirms that Anat's bloodbath was a "ritual action of bloodletting designed to produce rain." Thus, this grisly scene is frequently explained as the mythic portrayal of an Ugaritic ritual in which Anat's worshipers play the role of her enemies. Citing the self-laceration of the Baalistic priests in 1 Kings 18, Bowman (1978:20) holds, "ᶜAnatu's violence may be considered one aspect of a ritual combat performed yearly at Ugarit, designed to instigate rainfall...."[16] This analysis is necessarily dependent upon the seasonal interpretation of the Baal Cycle and its ritual use in the Ugaritic cult. Like Gray, Bowman (1978:20) refers to Gaster, Hooke, and Eliade for support of the hypothetical role of ritual combat in the annual cultic cycle. The Frazerian conclusions of these scholars concerning ancient Near Eastern religion are suspect, to say the least. As discussed above, the Myth and Ritual approach, based upon the Pan-Babylonianism of an earlier generation, has suffered serious scholarly criticism and methodological invalidation.

Building upon Gray's understanding of Anat's support of Baal in the fertility cycle, Bowman (1978:29) argues that Anat "is not a goddess who instigates violent actions for her own ends in the Baᶜlu cycle, but the deity responsible for establishing fertility. Her relation to Baᶜlu is exemplified by her active role in bringing the rains." Bowman (1978:19, 263) insists that every time Anat sheds blood it is directly connected with Baal's fertility and, thus, his ability to provide rain.[17] This interpretive approach presumes that Anat is the hypostatic manifestation of Baal's active will. In a now classic explanation, Albright (1956:195 n. 14) argues that the name *ᶜanat* means "sign, indication of purpose, active will," and was "originally applied to the personified or hypostatized will of Baal." Based upon analogies drawn from Canaanite divine epithets, Albright (1968:117) proposes the hypothetical *ᶜAnat-panê-Baᶜal* as her original name in order to identify her explicitly as the "Wrath of Baal." Thus, Anat is the "active

---

16 Bowman (1978:20 n. 7) also applies his method of exegesis to *KTU* 1.13, which "is to be considered a prayer to ᶜAnatu that she carry out her violent actions to produce the rains."

17 Since the humans slaughtered in Anat's bloodbath (1.3 ii) do not overtly threaten Baal's position as divine king, this scene must bring "to the human sphere the significance of ᶜAnatu's actions elsewhere described on the divine plane" (Bowman 1978:19-20). In other words, since this violent scene does not fit Bowman's hypothesis, it must reflect a human fertility ritual intended to produce Baal's rains.

presence" of Baal who carries out his desires when he is absent; she is a hypostatic manifestation of Baal's will (see Bowman 1978:260-9; Gray 1979:324; Wyatt 1984:329). Scholars continue to construct interpretations of Anat's violent exploits as support for Baal in his struggle for cosmic fertility based upon this comprehensive theory of Anat's mythological identity.

However, Bowman's functional explanation for Anat's bellicose nature is ultimately insufficient. While Anat's violence does contribute to Baal's acquisition of divine kingship in the Baal Cycle, she is not limited to this one role in Ugaritic myth. Furthermore, Anat's support of Baal's kingship does not necessitate her participation in his role as a fertility deity. The circular nature of this argument results in the interpretation of obscure texts, such as Anat's bloodbath, so that they support the presumed function of Anat in Ugaritic myth. Finally, Anat's actions in *Aqhat* seriously undermine this theory, as even Bowman (1978:263) must concede. We will return to this discussion in the concluding chapter of this study. For the moment it is sufficient to note that Anat maintains a completely independent status in the extant Ugaritic literature and, in fact, occasionally allows her passions to lead her in opposition to Baal's goals. Even if Anat originated as a hypostatic manifestation of Baal's anger, the maiden goddess is clearly an independent deity within the Ugaritic religious tradition. Finally, the hypostatic explanation for Anat's narrative role severely limits her symbolic identity to a one-dimensional character inconsistent with her portrayal within the Ugaritic texts.

Anat and the Enemies of Baal

Anat's violence in the Baal Cycle is not restricted to her slaughter of humans in *KTU* 1.3 ii, discussed above. Additional examples of her bellicose temperament include her boasts concerning the conquest of monstrous sea dragons and her ruthless dispatch of Mot. These two cases provide evidence of Anat's vigorous support of Baal against his enemies, as Bowman points out. Anat's threatening ultimatum to El in the Baal Cycle is also considered under this heading. While this last scene is not actually a battle with Baal's enemy, Anat's position as Baal's intermediary in his bid for the divine kingship places her in a confrontational relationship with the divine patriarch, El. Since

Bowman (1978:263) argues that each act of Anat's violence in the Baal Cycle is related to Baal's fertility function, primary attention is given to the motivation for her lethal anger in each of these cases. My own interpretive approach suggests that it is Anat's generally unrestrained character which is at the base of her emotional outbursts rather than her concern with human or natural vitality.

Anat, Yamm, and the Dragon. One argument against Bowman's hypothesis that Anat fights Baal's battles is her conspicuous absence from Baal's conflict with Yamm in the Baal Cycle. Yet, while Anat is clearly not involved in the mythic battle as presented in *KTU* 1.2, she does claim to have defeated these watery foes of her brother. Whether Anat's boasts represent a variant tradition in which she does participate in Baal's conflict with Yamm or whether she is engaging in a bit of hyperbolic self-exaltation is unknown. Anat's anxiety at the approach of Baal's messengers motivates her boastful outburst in *KTU* 1.3 iii 32–iv 8:

32) hlm. ^{c}nt. tph. ilm.	Behold, Anat saw the gods
bh. p^{c}nm (33) ṭṭ.	Below, her feet shuffled,
b^{c}dn. ksl. tṯbr	behind, her loins collapsed,
34) ^{c}ln. pnh. td^{c}.	above, her face sweated.
tǵṣ. pnt (35) kslh.	The joints of her loins convulsed,
anš. dt. ẓrh.	the muscles of her back.
tšu (36) gh. w.tṣḥ.	She raised her voice and cried,
ik. mǵy. gpn. wugr	"Why have Gupan and Ugar arrived?
37) mn. ib. yp^{c}. lb^{c}l.	What enemy has risen against Baal,
ṣrt (38) lrkb. ^{c}rpt.	(what) foe against the Rider of the Clouds?
lmḫšt. mdd (39) il ym.	Did I not smite Yamm, the beloved of El,
lklt. nhr. il. rbm	did I not annihilate River, the great god?
40) lištbm. tnn. ištmdh	Indeed I conquered (?) the dragon; I destroyed it![18]
41) mḫšt. bṯn. ^{c}qltn	I smote the twisting serpent,
42) šlyṭ. d. šb^{c}t. rašm	the close-coiling one (?) with seven heads!
43) mḫšt. mdd ilm. arš	I smote Arsh, the beloved of the gods;
44) ṣmt. ^{c}gl. il. ^{c}tk	I silenced Attacker, the bull-calf of El!
45) mḫšt. k<.>lbt. ilm. išt	I smote Fire, the bitch of El;

18 On the reading and translation of this problematic line see Dietrich and Loretz (1982) and Pardee (1984).

46) klt. bt. il. ḏbb.	I annihilated Dbb, daughter of El!
imtḫṣ. ksp (47) itrṯ. ḫrṣ	I slew for silver; I possessed the gold of him
ṭrd. b^{c}l (iv 1) bmrym. ṣpn.	who would drive Baal from the heights of Sapon,
mšṣṣ. k.^{c}ṣr (2)udnh.	who would peck (?) his ear like a bird,[19]
gršh. lksi. mlkh	who would chase him from the seat of his kingship,
3) lnḫt. lkḥṯ. drkth	from his resting-place, from the throne of his dominion!
4) mnm. ib. yp^{c}. lb^{c}l.	What enemy has risen against Baal,
ṣrt. lrkb. ^{c}rpt	(what) foe against the Rider of the Clouds?"
5) y^{c}n. ǵlmm. y^{c}nyn.	The youths answered; they replied,
lib. yp^{c} (6) lb^{c}l.	"No enemy has risen against Baal,
ṣrt. lrkb. ^{c}rpt	(no) foe against the Rider of the Clouds.
7) tḥm aliyn. b^{c}l.	A message from Almighty Baal,
hwt. aliy (8) qrdm.	a word from the mighty warrior."

Lacking emotional self-control, Anat becomes overly excited when she sees the approach of Baal's lackeys. She glories in her prowess as a warrior and takes the credit for defending her brother against his enemies. Of course, the narrative shows that her anxiety is unwarranted, thus portraying her as a volatile and fractious character.

The text could also be understood as Anat addressing Baal and saying, "Did you not smite Yamm, the beloved of El," and so forth. However, the context suggests that Anat is taking credit for warding off those who challenge Baal's status, as does the use of the first person prefix verbal form in line 40. Moreover, the broken text of *KTU* 1.83:8-10, *tn*(!)*n lšbm tšt // trks lmrym lbnn*(!), "She placed the dragon on high, // She bound it to the heights of Lebanon," is best understood as a reference to Anat.[20] Whether Yamm is identified as Lotan (*ltn*) or the Dragon (*tnn*) who would chase Baal from his mountain home is unclear from the Ugaritic texts. John Day (1985:13-7) points out that while Yamm is not equated with Lotan in this text, Baal is also credited with defeating both Lotan and *šlyṭ* in *KTU* 1.5 i 1-3. Hence, Ugaritic texts

---

19 Cf. Dietrich and Loretz 1982:79-81.

20 Compare *TO* (168) and de Moor (1987:181-2). Note also the idiosyncratic interpretation of Wyatt (1987c), who claims that El, Athirat, Baal, and Anat should each be credited with killing the dragon in Ugaritic myth.

report that both Anat and Baal have defeated Yamm/Nahar, Lotan/Tnn, and an entourage of divine monsters.

Regarding this episode, Bowman (1978:41) states, "Although in other versions [i.e. *KTU* 1.2 iv] Ba^{c}lu participated in the conflict with Yammu, it is clear that Ba^{c}lu owes his position of dominance to ^{c}Anatu's actions. Her violence described in this section allows the storm god to continue providing his rains." Bowman's interpretation of the material is clearly influenced by his presuppositions. Indeed, the Baal Cycle clearly states that Kothar-wa-Hasis encourages Baal when he crumbles with despair in the face of his enemy. The divine craftsman then supplies Baal with two magic clubs which are necessary for his victory over Yamm (1.2 iv). Thus, Kothar, and not Anat, is primarily responsible for Baal's victory over Yamm. The application of Bowman's argument could thus conclude that Kothar is also only concerned with promoting Baal's rains. While Anat is credited with the defeat of Yamm, the Dragon, and other divine beasts in *KTU* 1.3 iii, the narrative depiction of this event in the Baal Cycle (1.2 iv) clearly excludes her. Indeed, *KTU* 1.82, 1-3, while broken, reads that Baal battles and defeats the Dragon (*tnn*) with the aid of Resheph the archer. These variant traditions illustrate Baal's need for aid in his cosmic battles, but they do not necessitate that his supporters be identified with him or his fertility function. It is worth repeating that the overt theme of the Baal Cycle is the establishment of the divine monarch and his rule, not natural fertility. Hence, Anat, Kothar, and Resheph may all aid Baal in his striving for the monarchy, yet none should be limited to a hypostatic manifestation of his fertility function.

Anat and El. The events leading up to Anat's confrontation with El begin with her reception of Baal's message. Although this invitation includes his ritual instructions, discussed above, and the proclamation of his lightning, Baal's primary intent in summoning Anat is apparently to procure her services as an intermediary. Baal wants his sister to approach El with his request for a palace, the mark of divine kingship. She is enthusiastic in her support for Baal's plan and volunteers her services. Indeed, she formulates her own means to win the acquiescence of El. The premeditation of her approach is striking in its overt violence. She tells Baal:

yṯb ly. ṯr. il[. aby]	He will attend to me, Bull El, my father,
yṯb. ly. wlh. [ ]	he will attend to me and [I?] to him….
[mṣḫ a]mṣḫ.nn. kimr. larṣ	[Surely I] will drag him like a lamb to the ground,
[ašhl]k. šbth. dmm.	I will make his grey hair run with blood,
šbt. dqnh [mm^{c}m]	the grey hair of his beard with gore,
[k]d. lytn. bt. lb^{c}l. kilm	if he does not give to Baal a house like the (other) gods,
[wḥẓ]r. kbn. aṯrt	a court like the sons of Athirat! (1.3 iv 54–v 4)

Anat proceeds immediately to El's abode. Unfortunately, the text concerning her entrance to El's court and his initial reaction to her approach is fragmentary. When the text is again coherent, Anat is beginning to speak.

19) wt^{c}n. btlt. ^{c}n[t.]	And Maiden Anat spoke,
[bnt.] bht(20)k.yilm.	"In the building of your mansion, O El,
bnt[.] bh[t]k. a[l. t]šmḫ	in the building of your mansion, do not rejoice!
21) al. tšmḫ. brm[. h]kl[k]	Do not rejoice in the raising of your palace,
22) al. aḫdhm. by[mn]y	lest I seize them with my right hand
[ ] (23) bgdlt. arkty.	… by the might of my long arm.
am[ḫṣ](24) qdqdk.	I will [strike] your head;
ašhlk. šbtk[. dmm]	I will make your grey hair run with blood,
25) šbt. dqnk. mm^{c}m[.]	the grey hair of your beard with gore!"
y^{c}ny (26) il. bšb^{c}t. ḥdrm.	El answered from the seven chambers,
bṯmnt (27) ap. sgrt.	from the eight compartments (?),
yd^{c}[tk.] bt. kan[št]	"I know that you, my daughter, are incorrigible,
28) kin. bilht. ql[ṣ]k.	and that among goddesses there is no restraining you.[21]
mh. taršn (29) lbtlt. ^{c}nt.	What do you desire, O Maiden Anat?"
wt[^{c}]n. btlt. ^{c}nt	And Maiden Anat answered,
30) tḥmk. il. ḥkm[.]	"Your decree, El, is wise,
ḥkmk (31) ^{c}m. ^{c}lm.	your wisdom is everlasting;
ḥyt. ḥẓt. tḥmk	a life of good fortune is your decree.

21 See the discussion below for the translation of this difficult bicolon.

32) mlkn. aliyn. bᶜl.	Our king is Almighty Baal,
ṯpṭn (33) in. dᶜlnh.	our judge, over whom is no one.
klnyy. qšh (34) nbln.	All of us (?) will indeed carry his chalice;
klnyy. nbl. ksh	all of us will carry his cup."
	(1.3 v 19-34)

Anat then communicates Baal's lack of a royal palace.

Although the opening of this scene is fragmentary, it appears that Anat dispenses with any formal salutation and launches directly into her threats upon entering El's palace. Indeed, her first statements are intended to quench any resistance on the part of El. Perhaps she expects him to be non-compliant; perhaps she simply lacks tact and diplomacy.[22] Anat's threat of physical violence to the person of El, striking in its graphic quality, is consistent with the volatile nature of the impetuous young goddess. El's initial response is interpreted variously by scholars. Many hold that he is cowed by the combative warrior goddess and immediately assents to whatever she will ask. The exact connotation of El's initial response is obscured by his vocabulary, but the sense that Anat is unrestrained and volatile is prominent. This fundamental description of Anat's character in Ugaritic myth is discussed further below. Unfortunately, El's response to Anat's actual demands concerning a palace for Baal is lost to a break in the tablet. When the text resumes, however, Baal and Anat are planning to importune Athirat for her support in Baal's plan. While it is possible that the approach of Anat alone (1. 3 v) and the approach of Anat and Athirat together (1.4 iv) illustrate divergent traditions, it is more likely that El denies Anat's initial request, thus requiring another delegation to gain his assent. If this is the case, then he cannot be genuinely afraid of Anat's bluff and bravado. Instead, El appears as the indulgent patriarch who tolerates the emotional outbursts of his young ward.

Athirat's reaction to the approach of the divine maiden also evidences Anat's violent nature. When Athirat sees Anat and Baal in the distance, she cries:

---

22 One can dismiss interpretations which claim that her threat to split El's skull and make his blood run is intended to stimulate rain (e.g. Bowman 1978:51 n. 23). Apart from the assumed fertility component of Anat's acts, there is no evidence to suggest that her threat is anything more than retributional violence.

[i]k (22) mǵy. aliyn. b[ᶜl]	Why is Almighty Baal approaching?
23) ik. mǵyt. b[t]lt (24) ᶜnt.	Why is the Maiden Anat approaching?
mḫṣy. hm[. m]ḫṣ (25) bny.	Are my enemies coming to slay my sons,
hm[. mkly. ṣ]brt (26) aryy	to annihilate the troops of my kinfolk?"
	(1.4 ii 21-6)

This passage associates Anat with the feud between Baal and Athirat's clan. It is unclear whether Athirat has cause to fear Anat as well, or whether it is simply Anat's bellicose nature and reputation which frighten her.

While one could interpret Anat's role as Baal's messenger as evidence for their hypostatic relationship, this is not necessarily accurate. To be sure, Anat acts as Baal's intermediary or messenger in the Baal Cycle and in *KTU* 1.10. Yet, Anat also acts as a messenger from El to Shapsh concerning the possibility of Baal's return (1.6 iv 22ff). Indeed, all deities seem to use intermediaries whenever possible. While minor deities usually play the role of messenger in ancient Near Eastern literature (e.g. Baal's two messengers Gupan and Ugar), this is not always the case. Baal acts as an intermediary for the human Danel in the *Epic of Aqhat* when he approaches El with Danel's request for a male heir. Furthermore, the role of Anat as Baal's messenger or intermediary is connected to her identity as a female. In fact, Baal uses only female intermediaries, Anat and Athirat, rather than his lackeys Gupan and Ugar when he desires El's acquiescence to his claim of divine kingship. This fact illustrates the importance and necessary subtlety of the mission to El, since only important deities were importuned. Moreover, the gender of the intermediaries is probably essential as they mediate between the two antagonistic males working out their new relationship.

Thus, Anat's role as Baal's intermediary does not necessitate their identity, nor does it necessitate any particularly intimate relationship between them. Anat actively takes Baal's side against El in his quest for a palace to legitimate his kingship. However, Athirat also enthusiastically exalts Baal before El, thus calling into question the hypostatic significance given to Anat's political support of her brother. Significantly, Anat is very unimportant after Baal receives permission to construct his palace. This permission entails El's formal acknowledgment of Baal's position as divine monarch. The lack of intimacy between Anat and Baal is also evident in Anat's absence from

Baal's discussion with Shapsh concerning his entrance into the Netherworld. Whatever advice Shapsh gives Baal is apparently unknown to Anat, who must scour the earth in search of her brother's corpse. Thus, it appears that Anat is not essential to Baal's rule but simply aids him in attaining certain goals. As Bowman (1978) emphasizes, Anat is instrumental to Baal's acquisition of the divine kingship. She frequently supports him in his battles, but she is most important when Baal is in transitional periods.

Anat and Mot. The most obvious support for Anat's passionate relationship to Baal is her actions after Baal acknowledges his submission to Mot and enters the Underworld. Anat's intense mourning activities on behalf of the slain Baal are discussed above. While she does voice her concern for the human followers of Baal who depend upon his fertilizing rain (1.6 i 6-7), Anat focuses her compassion on her deceased brother. Overwhelmed with grief at her loss, she entreats Mot to return her brother to her (1.6 ii 4-25).

[ym. ymm] (5) y^{c}tqn.	A day, days passed,
wr[ḥm. ^{c}nt] (6) tngṯh.	and the Damsel Anat sought him.
klb. ar[ḫ] (7) l^{c}glh.	Like the heart of a cow for her calf,
klb. ṯa[t] (8) limrh.	like the heart of a ewe for her lamb,
km. lb. ^{c}n[t] (9) aṯr. b^{c}l.	such was the heart of Anat after Baal.
tiḫd. mt (10) bsin. lpš.	She seized Mot by the hem of his garment;
tšṣqn[n] (11) bqṣ. all.	she grasped him by the edge of his robe.
tšu. gh. wt[ṣ](12)ḥ.	She raised her voice and cried,
at. mt. tn. aḫy.	"You, Mot, give (me) my brother!"
13) w^{c}n. bn. ilm. mt.	And Mot the divine answered,
mh (14) taršn. lbtlt. ^{c}nt	"What do you want (from me), O Maiden Anat?
15) an. itlk. waṣd.	I was going about to and fro, scouring
kl (16) ǵr. lkbd. arṣ.	every mount to the heart of the earth,
kl. gb^{c} (17) lkbd. šdm.	every hill to the heart of the fields.
npš. ḫsrt (18) bn. nšm.	My appetite was deprived of humans,
npš. hmlt. (19) arṣ.	my appetite, of the multitudes of the earth.
mǵt. ln^{c}my. arṣ (20) dbr.	I reached the pleasant place, the pasture,
ysmt. šd. šḥlmmt	the lovely field of *šḥlmmt.*
21) ngš. ank. aliyn b^{c}l	It was I who confronted Almighty Baal;

22) ^{c}dbnn ank. imr. bpy	I who made him a lamb in my mouth;
23) klli. bṯbrn q<n>y. ḫtu hw	Like a kid in my jaws he was crushed (?)."
24) nrt. ilm. špš. ṣḥrrt	The Lamp of the gods, Shapsh, blazed hot;
25) la. šmm. byd. bn ilm. mt	the heavens were wearied by the hand of divine Mot.

Anat's expectations upon her first entreaty of Mot are unclear. Does she really think that Mot can, or will, resurrect her brother whose corpse she buried? Significantly, Mot responds that he devoured Baal because of his hunger but avoids the issue of his ability to return Baal to life. Gray (1965:67) explains that the Ugaritic myths "are not metaphysical speculations, but are the outgrowth of ritual, where the fact of the death and burial of Baal and his revival correspond to rituals relating to the death and revival of vegetation." The rubric,"The Lamp of the gods, Shapsh, blazed hot; the heavens were wearied by the hand of divine Mot," emphasizes the lack of fertility precipitated by Baal's absence, but Anat's motivation for her approach to Mot is not her concern for earthly fertility. On the contrary, Anat is driven by her overwhelming grief at the loss of her brother.

Immediately following the above passage, the text continues:

26) ym. ymm. y^{c}tqn.	A day, days passed;
lymm (27) lyrḫm.	from days, to months.
rḥm. ^{c}nt. tngṯh	The Damsel Anat sought him.
28) klb. arḫ. l^{c}gl.	Like the heart of a cow for her calf,
klb (29) ṯat. limth.	like the heart of a ewe for her lamb,
km. lb (30) ^{c}nt. aṯr. b^{c}l.	such was the heart of Anat after Baal.
tiḫd (31) bn. ilm. mt.	She seized divine Mot,
bḥrb (32) tbq^{c}nn.	with a blade she split him,
bḫṯr. tdry(33)nn.	with a sieve she winnowed him,
bišt. tšrpnn	with a fire she burned him,
34) brḥm. tṭḥnn.	with millstones she ground him,
bšd (35) tdr^{c}.nn.	in the field she sowed him.
širh. ltikl (36) ^{c}ṣrm.	His flesh the birds did eat,
mnth. ltkly (37) npr[m].	his limbs the sparrows (?) did consume.
šir. lšir. yṣḥ	Flesh called to flesh.
	(1.6 ii 26-37)

Anat's purpose in so viciously dispatching Mot remains a matter of debate among commentators. Gray (1979:324), like Bowman (1978), argues that Anat's violence is related to Baal's quest for fertility, particularly when Baal is "in his periodic recession." Accordingly, Gray (1965:174) asserts, "It is precisely to restore Baal to life and vigour that Anat visits the underworld and deals so drastically with Mot, the inveterate enemy of Baal." However, Anat apparently fails to realize the significance of her own violent actions. While the fragmentary condition of the text between the slaying of Mot and the return of Baal prevents any definite conclusions, it appears that Anat is not motivated by a rational plan to bring back Baal from the dead. When her efforts at entreating Mot to return her brother fail, grief overwhelms Anat. She expresses this emotional rage by utterly destroying the agent of her brother's death. Her execution of Mot is not formal vengeance for her slain brother (contra Oldenberg 1969). Anat's restraint in her initial meeting with Mot indicates that this is no simple case of a blood feud. Indeed, Mot is not just another deity whose hands are stained with Baal's blood; rather, as Death personified, he is exempt from retribution.[23]

Clearly, Anat's primary intent is to annihilate the one responsible for separating her from her beloved brother. The thoroughness with which she extirpates Mot demonstrates her passionate feelings. Indeed, Anat's vicious behavior towards Mot demonstrates her unrestrained character rather than her fervent support for Baal and his fertility. The use of agricultural imagery in Anat's destruction of Mot, however, has sparked much discussion among Ugaritologists (see Healey 1983). One faction of scholars argues that Mot represents grain and that Anat's treatment of him represents the preparations for planting.[24] Another scholarly faction understands Anat's attack on Mot as the complete destruction of a hated enemy rather than fertility imagery. The latter view is more probable. Anat splits Mot (*tbq*^{c}*nn*) with a blade, winnows him (*tdrynn*) with a

---

23 In contrast to other ancient Near Eastern mythological traditions, the god of the dead is not a member of the Ugaritic pantheon. He neither receives sacrifices nor is included in any Ugaritic god list. Mot feeds on the bodies of the dead. Thus, he is Death personified—the Grim Reaper—rather than simply a deity whose realm is the Netherworld.

24 De Moor (1971:9-28) discusses the history of this interpretation and provides his own analysis (see 1971:245-9; 1987:86-90). Bowman (1978:80) argues that Anat is merely fulfilling "her role as the guarantor of fertility" in destroying Mot.

sieve, burns him with fire (*bišt tšrpnn*), grinds him (*ṭṭḥnn*) with millstones, and sows him (*tdrᶜnn*) in a field. Similarly, Exodus 32:20 describes Moses's extirpation of the golden calf with the verbs *śrp*, *ṭḥn* and *zrh*: Moses "took the calf that they had made, burned it with fire (*wyśrp bᵓš*), ground it to powder (*wyṭḥn ᶜd ᵓšr-dq*), sprinkled it upon the water (*wyzr ᶜl-pny-hmym*), and made the Israelites drink it." While BH *zrh*, "to scatter, winnow," and *zrᶜ*, "to sow," are not synonymous, BH *zrᶜ* can mean "to scatter" metaphorically, as in Zechariah 10:9. Thus, Anat's "sowing" of Mot refers to the scattering of his remains upon the ground. Furthermore, Mot himself recounts his harsh treatment at the hands of Anat and claims to have been "sown in the sea," *drᶜ bym* (1.6 v 19). Far from being horticultural imagery, this denotes the complete eradication of something. Thus, Mot does not represent grain nor does his destruction reflect the preparation of seed for planting and germination. On the other hand, there is apparently a direct connection between Anat's slaying of Mot and the return of Baal. In that the power of Mot keeps Baal in the Netherworld, Mot's demise has a vicarious significance for Baal.[25]

Apart from the narrative plot of the myth and its seasonal interpretation, the gender symbolism involved in Anat's defeat of Mot is significant. Pope (1977:228-9), among others, has made the biblical allusion to "Love is strong as death" (Cant 8:6). However, the defeat of Death by a maiden goddess calls for greater symbolic explication. Anat's motivation is her profound anxiety concerning the death of her brother, but her ability is perhaps rooted in her sexual identity. Indeed, Anat's mythic identity as a nubile young female is essential to her unique ability to defeat Death and restore fertility to the cosmos. While the male Baal willingly submits himself to Mot's servitude and descends to the Netherworld, Anat is apparently able to restore him to life through her defeat of Death. This symbolism aknowledges that females have the ability to create life—to overcome death—while males do not. Similarly, "maidens" are the source of life for a society. It is not the already fertile mother goddess who will guarantee the continuation of society, but the young girl who has not yet proven her procreative

---

[25] Of course, it is possible that Baal, not really dead, is just in hiding and returns once his rival is out of the way (see de Moor 1987:77-9). Regardless, Anat is responsible for the fertility god's return to the earth.

ability. Anat overcomes Death by the creative potential stored within her as an adolescent maiden. Thus, Anat's unchanneled energies unknowingly serve to restore fertility and life to the world. Even though Anat may try to deny her female sexuality and feminine identity, her own passions cause her to defeat Death and restore Baal, the source of life. Thus, she truly is the only deity capable of overcoming death in the Ugaritic pantheon.

Anat in the Baal Cycle

In conclusion, the role of Anat in the Baal Cycle centers on her violent disposition and coercive violence. While this mythic cycle remains largely impervious to comprehensive interpretation, Anat's function is crucial to the plot and imagery. Her active support of Baal is essential to his establishment as the divine sovereign. The conclusion of the Baal Cycle depicts Baal restored to his throne as the divine monarch. His antagonistic relationship with Mot has been resolved through compromise. Baal, as Lord of the earth, is not superior to Mot, the manifestation of death. Baal appoints the seasons and determines that the rains come at appropriate times for the fertilization of the earth, yet all creatures eventually die. Anat's support for Baal's kingship is crucial for the balance of cosmic power and the continuation of life. Her mythic identity as the divine maiden provides the symbolic justification for this important function. Yet, her sororal support for Baal does not define her simply as his lackey or a manifestation of his own identity. Anat's exuberance and enthusiasm reflect her basic nature. She is inherently headstrong, impatient, and demanding in her desires. In this sense, Anat's mythic identity as the adolescent tomboy is significant to her depiction as an independent female. Thus, her treatment of El and Mot are best understood as examples of her impetuous and unrestrained personality rather than simply as evidence for her relationship to Baal.

While Anat's loyalty to her brother provides the impetus for much of her violence, she is not merely his hypostatic presence. She is his steadfast supporter in the Baal Cycle, yet she maintains her independent identity. As one sees in her role in *Aqhat*, Anat is driven by her own desires rather than concern for the common good. It is perhaps merely fortuitous that Anat's capricious violence in the Baal Cyle results in a positive effect for the cosmos. In contrast to Albright's (1956:117) hypothetical identification of Anat as the "Wrath of Baal," the Ugaritic texts provide the epithet "Name of Baal," *^{c}ṯtrt šm b^{c}l*, only for the goddess Athtart (1.16 vi 54-7) (see McBride 1968:135-7). This epithet is used in the curse, "May Horon break your head; Athtart-Name-of-Baal your crown!" Indeed, in *KTU* 1.2 i 7-8 the curse is apparently uttered against Yamm, Baal's mortal enemy. By contrast, Anat does not appear until after the defeat of Yamm. Furthermore, if support of Baal in his battles necessitates a fertility function then one must posit Kothar as a fertility god, since he plays a critical role in Baal's defeat of Yamm. Those deities who support Baal in his struggles against his enemies can not be identified exclusively with his fertility function. Thus, Bowman (1978) simply overemphasizes one aspect of Anat's character at the expense of others.

Finally, Anat never fights at the side of Baal in Ugaritic myth. She apparently only wages war against his enemies when he can not actively engage his rival himself. Thus, Anat is most important during Baal's transitional periods. This function highlights her own liminal identity within the pantheon. Just as Artemis is associated with the marginal activities of Greek society (see Vernant 1987), so Anat's role in the Baal Cycle is most important at times of transition in the cosmic state. Anat's female identity qualifies her as an intermediary to approach El with Baal's request. More importantly, Anat is uniquely suited to overcome Mot during Baal's weakness. Her violence is dangerous but it is also constructive when properly channeled. Thus, Anat's own liminal identity and position within the Ugaritic pantheon contributes to the efficacy of her role during times of mythic anti-structure. Anat's gender and age are thus central to her symbolic identity as the adolescent tomboy.

II. ANAT AND AQHAT

In contrast to her secondary position in the Baal Cycle, Anat's portrayal as a passionate and violent goddess is central to the narrative of *Aqhat*.[26] The depiction of Anat's independence, capricious nature, and

---

26 Much research has been devoted to the *Epic of Aqhat*. The literary critical analysis of Parker (1989:99-144) provides an excellent summary of the text's structure and current trends in interpretation. Margalit (1989b) presents a thorough review of all literature and offers his own eccentric interpretation of the epic. In addition to the

sexual and gender identity in this Ugaritic epic supplies a wealth of primary information regarding her mythic character (contra Bowman 1978:263). Unfortunately, these elements are frequently neglected in analyses of the maiden goddess. Anat's encounter with Aqhat, charged with sexual tension, has many parallels in other ancient mythologies including but not limited to Ishtar's attempted seduction of Gilgamesh (see Parker 1989:107-12). The masculine symbolism of the warrior's bow also offers insight into the multivalent use of symbols in Ugaritic myth (see Hillers 1973). Thus, the present section focuses on the symbolic importance of gender, sexuality, and social expectations in the interpretation of Anat's role in *Aqhat.*

Anat and the Bow of Aqhat

Anat's Proposition. Anat appears in the story of *Aqhat* after substantial plot development in which Danel sires an heir and presents him with the divine hunting bow. Anat, engaged in a feast when she sights the youthful Aqhat sporting his new bow, is awe-struck by Aqhat's possession. She offers the crown prince gold and silver in exchange for his divine gift. Aqhat evades her request by suggesting that Kothar will make another bow for her if she provides the raw materials. Anat immediately raises the stakes with a counter offer of immortality. Aqhat derisively rejects this promise, however, and accuses Anat of attempting to deceive him. Whether Anat actually has the ability to grant immortality is unclear.[27] Finally, Aqhat insults the warrior goddess by saying that such weapons are not intended for females, anyway. Anat apparently breaks off negotiations in a huff and, after threatening Aqhat, proceeds to the palace of El.[28]

---

regular resources, philological commentary may be found in Dijkstra (1979), Margalit (1983), A. Cooper (1988), and their bibliographies.

27 Spronk (1986:151-61) argues that Anat promises Aqhat a prestigious role among the Netherworld dead rather than eternal life. His "non death" thus refers to the annual return of the dead to participate in the New Year festival. Spronk's argument, however, is unconvincing (see Pope 1987a).

28 Dressler (1979:211 n. 4) argues that Anat outwardly pretends to forgive Aqhat while inwardly scheming to destroy him (see also Gray 1965:113). While Anat may be capable of such deceit, it is more consistent with her character to understand her parting words as confrontational.

bnši. ^{c}nh. wtphn	Lifting her eyes, she perceived
11) [ ] kslh. kbrq	[the bow …], its string like lightning
12) [ ] xxx. thmt. brq	… oceans (?), lightning …
13) [ ] tṣb. qšt. bnt	… she coveted the bow …
14) [ ] ^{c}nh. km. bṯn. yqr	… her eyes, like a serpent hisses (?) …
15) [ ]larṣ.	…. to the earth.
ksh. tšpkm (16) [l^{c}pr]	She spilled her cup [in the dust].
[tšu. gh.] wtṣḥ.	She raised her voice and cried,
šm^{c}. m^{c} (17)[laqht. ǵzr.]	"Listen, O hero Aqhat!
[i]rš. ksp. watnk	Ask for silver, and I will give (it) to you,
(18) ḫrš. waš]lḥk.	gold, and I will bestow (it) to you!
wtn. qštk. ^{c}m (19)[btlt.] ^{c}n[t.]	(Just) give your bow to Maiden Anat,
qṣ^{c}tk. ybmt. limm	your arrows (?) to *Ybmt Limm*!
(20) wy^{c}n. aqht. ǵzr	But the hero Aqhat answered,
adr. ṯqbm (21) blbnn.	"Most splendid birches (?) from Lebanon,
adr. gdm. brumm	most splendid sinews from wild oxen,
22) adr. qrnt. by^{c}lm.	most splendid horns from wild rams,
mtnm (23) b^{c}qbt. ṯr.	tendons from bull's legs (?),
adr. bǵl il. qnm	most splendid reeds from a vast bed,
24) tn. lkṯr. wḫss.	Give (these) to Kothar-wa-Hasis!
yb^{c}l. qšt. l^{c}nt	He will construct a bow for Anat,
25) qṣ^{c}t. lybmt. limm	arrows for *Ybmt Limm*."
wt^{c}n. btlt (26) ^{c}nt.	Then Maiden Anat replied,
irš. ḥym. laqht. ǵzr	"Ask for life, O hero Aqhat;
27) irš. ḥm. watnk.	ask for life, and I will give (it) to you,
bl mt (28) wašlḥk.	immortality, and I will bestow (it) to you.
ašsprk. ^{c}m. b^{c}l (29) šnt.	I will cause you to count years with Baal;
^{c}m. bn il. tspr yrḫm	with the sons of El you will count months.
30) kb^{c}l. kyḥwy.	Like Baal when he gives life,
y^{c}šr. ḥwy.	he provides a banquet for the living one,
y^{c}š(31)r wšqynh.	he provides a banquet and serves him drink,
ybd. wyšr. ^{c}lh (32) n^{c}mn	The singer chants and sings over him,
[wt]^{c}nynn	and they respond to him;
ap. ank. aḥwy (33) aqht[. ǵz]r.	Thus will I myself give life to the hero Aqhat."
w.y^{c}n. aqht. ǵzr	But the hero Aqhat answered,
34) al. tšrgn. ybtltm.	"Do not deceive me, O Maiden,
dm. lǵzr (35) šrgk. ḫḫm.	for to a hero your lies are loathsome.
mt(!). uḫryt. mh. yqḥ	A man, what does he receive in the end;

36) mh. yqḥ. mt. aṯryt	what fate does a man receive?
spsg. ysk (37)[l]riš.	Glaze will be poured on (my) head,
ḥrṣ. lẓr. qdqdy	lime on the top of my pate.[29]
38) [ ]mt. kl. amt.	[Surely] the death of all will I die;
wan. mtm. amt	most certainly I will die.
39) [ap. m]ṯn. rgmm. argm.	And further words will I now speak:
qštm (40) [ ]mhrm.	Bows [are for] warriors;
ht. tṣdn. tinṯt (41) [bh.]	Will womenfolk now hunt [with one]?"
[g]m. tṣḥq. ^{c}nt.	Loudly laughed Anat,
wblb. tqny (42) [ ]	but in her heart she devised [a plan].
ṯb. ly. laqht. ǵzr.	"Hearken to me, O hero Aqhat,
ṯb ly wlk (43) [ ]	hearken to me and to you [I will speak (?).]
hm. laqryk. bntb. pš^{c}	If indeed I encounter you on the road of rebellion,
44) [ ]. bntb. gan.	... on the road of pride,
ašqlk. tḥt (45) [p^{c}ny. a]n(!)k.	I myself will trample you under [my feet],
n^{c}mn. ^{c}mq. nšm	most charming and strongest of men!"
46) [td^{c}ṣ. p^{c}]nm. wtr. arṣ.	She stamped her feet and the earth shook.
idk (47) [lttn. p]nm.	Then she indeed set her face
^{c}m. il. mbk(!) nhrm	towards El at the source of the rivers.
	(1.17 vi 10-47)

On the literal level of the narrative, the object of Anat's desire is the divine bow created by the craftsman Kothar-wa-Hasis. However, the sexual tension beneath the narrative is equally significant to the analysis of this mythological scene. Hillers (1973:72-4) demonstrates the important sexual symbolism of Aqhat's bow. The warrior's bow commonly symbolizes masculinity and warrior prowess in the ancient Near East (cf. Dressler 1975). As such a dominant masculine symbol, the bow carries various connotations of virility and sexual potency. Thus, Anat's desire for Aqhat's bow takes on these same symbolic ramifications of masculine gender and male sexuality. Yet, Anat's desire to possess this phallic symbol may be variously interpreted. Anat wishes to acquire the bow as a symbol of her own masculine attributes as the divine huntress. Hence, her desire represents her ambiguous gender and,

---

29 The reference to glaze and lime may refer to the Neolithic practice of plastering the heads of dead relatives (see Hendel 1987:80 n. 36; Margalit 1989b:347-9), but it also may simply be a metaphor for the greying of hair in old age.

in Freudian terms, a case of symbolic penis envy. Alternately, one may interpret the scene as the attempted seduction, or sexual conquest, of Aqhat, who must surrender to Anat's desires and entrust his "bow" to the aggressive female. In this case, Aqhat's suggestion that Kothar craft a bow for Anat is purposefully evasive. Indeed, if she desires a bow, why can she not have another one made? Symbolically, then, she desires *his* "bow" and none other. Lastly, perhaps Anat's jealousy prompts her to deprive Aqhat of this masculine symbol and, thus, symbolically castrate him. To be sure, Anat covets the actual bow in the text. The narrative result of the encounter, however, is the destruction of Aqhat's weapon. Aqhat is deprived of his phallic symbol and Anat is denied access to it. Hence, the bow—a symbol of masculine gender and sexuality—is an unobtainable goal for the impetuous goddess.

Thus, the interpretive crux concerns Anat's motivation for coveting the masculine symbol. Are her actions based upon her sexual drive or confused gender identity? Symbolically, of course, these are not mutually exclusive interpretations since one may posit unconscious drives to Anat. Sexual tension is certainly present in this encounter even if neither character is sexually active. While the phallic bow is clearly a gender symbol, the sexual connotation of Anat's desire in this scene remains subliminal. We will return to this discussion below.

Anat's Violent Response. After countering Aqhat's undiplomatic rebuff, Anat heads directly to the palace of El to demand satisfaction. In contrast to her approach in the Baal Cycle, she now offers obeisance to El prior to making her petition.

50) [lp^{c}n. il. t]hbr. wtql.	At the feet of El she fell and did homage,
tštḥ(51)[wy. wtkbd]nh.	she prostrated herself and did him honor.
tlšn. aqht. ǵzr	She denounced the hero Aqhat
52) [kdd. dn]il. mt. rpi	... the child of Danel, the man of *Rpi.*
wt^{c}n (53) [btlt. ^{c}nt.]	And [Maiden Anat] spoke,
[tšu.]gh. wtṣḥ.	[she raised] her voice and cried,
hwt (54) [ ].	"Him ...
aqht. yšxx (55) [ ]	Aqhat has ... "
	(1.17 vi 50-5)

Approximately ten lines are lost from the end of this column. Thus, we do not have Anat's actual complaint concerning Aqhat. El's initial reply to Anat is also lost in the fragmentary opening of the next tablet (1.18). The comparative evidence, discussed below, suggests that Anat slanders Aqhat for his insolence but that the patriarchal god initially defends the youth. Aqhat's refusal to surrender his bow, while impudent, is justified in that it was a gift of the gods. Indeed, Aqhat's reaction to Anat's proposition is most probably correct: Anat is not empowered to grant immortality and, finally, bows are reserved for male warriors in the ancient gender ideology.

Anat apparently begins her reply to El in line 6, *t^{c}n*. The remaining letters of lines 7-12 are consistent with Anat's threats to El in the Baal Cycle, in which she threatens to split his skull and make his hair run with his own blood. The reference to El's palace is out of place in the present context and suggests that the scene is formulaic in its depiction of the relationship between Anat and El.

wt^{c}n. [btlt. ^{c}nt]	And [Maiden Anat] replied,
7) [bnt. bht]k. yilm.	["In the building of your mansion,] O El,
[bnt. bhtk] (8) [al. tšmḫ]	[in the building of your mansion do not rejoice!]
al. tš[mḫ. brm. h(9)klk.]	Do not re[joice in the raising of your palace!]
[al.] aḫdhm. [bymny]	Lest I sieze them [with my right hand],
10) [b]gdlt. ar[kty.]	… in the strength of my long [arm]!
[ ] (11) [qdq]dk	… your [pat]e,
ašhlk[. šbtk. dmm]	I will cause [your grey hair] to run with [blood],
12) [šbt. dq]nk. mm^{c}m.	[the grey hair of your beard] with gore!
w[qra] (13) aqht. wyplṭk.	Then [call upon] Aqhat and let him deliver you,
bn[. dnil] (14) wy^{c}ḏrk.	the son [of Danel] and let him rescue you
byd. btlt. [^{c}nt]	from the hand of Maiden [Anat]!"
15) wy^{c}n. lṭpn. il dp[id]	And the kindly one, El the compassionate, replied,
16) yd^{c}tk. bt. kanšt.	"I know, my daughter, that you are incorrigible,
wi[n. bilht] (17) qlṣk.	and that [among the goddesses] there is no restraining you.
tb^{c}. bt. ḫnp. lb	Depart, my daughter, haughty is your heart.
[ti](18)ḫd. diṯ. bkbdk.	Take what is in your mind,
tšt. d[iṯ] (19) irtk.	carry out what is in your breast.

dṯ. ydṯ. m^{c}qbk	He who hinders you will be utterly destroyed."
[ttb^{c}] (20) [bt]lt. ^{c}nt.	Maiden Anat [departed] ....
	(1.18 i 6-20)

Various interpretations of this scene would present El as either amused, terrified, or indulgent in his reply to the threats of the belligerent goddess (see Margalit 1983:93-4). This is most unfortunate since El's response to Anat provides an important primary source of information concerning their relationship. As I argue above, *kanšt* does not refer to Anat being "like a man," but instead denotes her impetuous or desperate character.[30]

Since the root *qlṣ* does not appear in BH or Aramiac, philologists have turned to the Arabic lexicon for direction in translating this phrase. Arabic *qalaṣa* means "to contract, shrink, diminish, dwindle" (Wehr 1976:786; Lane 1863-93:2558-9). Rejecting this nuance for the Ugaritic root, many scholars (e.g. Gibson 1977:157) prefer to understand *qlṣ* as "scorn, contempt" based on BH *qlś.* However, *qalasa,* "to make fun of," and *qalaṣa,*"to shrink, diminish," are distinct verbal roots (Wehr 1976:786) in Arabic. This argues against the identification of Ugaritic qlṣ and BH qlś. Perhaps the best understanding of the Ugaritic term, based upon its Ugaritic context and an Arabic cognate, is "restraint" in the sense of "to shrink back" (see *UT* 478).[31] According to this reading, El is not terrified of the violent young goddess but indulgently allows her to do as she pleases.

Having received the acquiescence of the divine patriarch, Anat proceeds with her scheme to punish the insolent Aqhat.

[ttb^{c}] (20) [bt]lt. ^{c}nt.	Maiden Anat [departed],
idk. lttn. [pnm]	then she indeed set [her face]
21) [^{c}m. a]qht. ǵzr.	[towards] the hero Aqhat,
balp. š[d] (22) [rbt.]kmn.	from a thousand fields, ten thousand plots.

30 Some scholars take *anšt* to mean "companionable" or "gentle" (cf. Arabic *ᵓanīsa*) with a sense of irony in El's reply. Thus, Hackett (1989:19) translates El's attempt to soothe her, "I know, daughter, that you can be likeable, but goddesses have no restraint. Leave now, since you will do whatever blasphemous thing you want anyway." Ugaritic *anš* may mean "to be companionable," as in 1.16 vi 36, but the poetic parallel, *qlṣk*, suggests another meaning in this context.

31 Margalit (1983:94) claims that Arabic *qalaṣa* means "to rise up, become agitated" in Lane (1863-93:2559) (cf. *TO* 76) but this meaning appears only in an idiomatic phrase. The overwhelming evidence attests only "to diminish."

wṣḥq. btlt. [^{c}nt]	And Maiden Anat laughed,
23) [tšu.]gh. wtṣḥ.	she raised her voice and cried out,
šm^{c}. m[^{c}. la(24)qht. ǵz]r.	"Listen, [O hero Aqhat],
at. aḫ. wan. [aḫtk]	You are (my) brother and I am [your sister!]
25) [ ]. šb^{c}. ṯirk. [ ]	... your kin ...
	(1.18 i 19-25)

While the following text is fragmentary, a few words are clear. Anat apparently lures Aqhat to a distant region, *qrt. ablm*, with the promise to teach him some skill, *almdk* (1.18 i 29-30).

Many interpreters understand Anat's speech, *at. aḫ. wan.* [*aḫtk*], "You are (my) brother and I am [your sister!]," as a formal proposal of marriage. Accordingly, Gibson (1977:111) reads line 26 as [*lbt.*]*aby. ndt. ank*[ ], "I myself have fled [from] my father's [house...]," to suggest that Anat claims to have left her father's house in order to wed Aqhat. While this reading is possible, its plausibility is diminished by the poor condition of this line (see *KTU* 58). If Anat does in fact make a proposal of marriage to the youthful Aqhat than she is certainly attempting to seduce the crown prince. As Ishtar propositions Gilgamesh with erotic pleasure in the guise of marriage (Foster 1987:34), Anat may entice Aqhat with hints of her own erotic capacity.[32] As Athena has no compunction about parading nude before Paris in a divine beauty contest, so might Anat not be above using her own nubile charm to get what she wants. Such a proposition does not necessitate that Anat is actually prepared to engage in sex; her devious proposal would not conflict with her virginal character.

If Anat does promise marriage in order to lure Aqhat away from safety, then this is an example of her exploitation of her nubile sexuality. Dressler (1979), however, points out that the alleged proposal in this scene is based upon very little evidence. The text itself is incomplete, reading only *at. aḫ. wan.* [ ]. Furthermore, as Dressler (1979:213-6) argues, the formula "You are my brother and I am your sister" is not a

32 Such a motivation is certainly apparent to Gray (1965:111), who translates Anat's actions at first sighting Aqhat (1.17 vi 15), *larṣ kst tšrm*, as "She raises her skirts from the earth." The better reading is clearly *larṣ kst tšpkm [l^{c}pr]*, "...to the ground, she spilled her cup [in the dust]." In a peculiar and most fanciful interpretation, Margalit (1989b:324-7) understands *KTU* 1.18 i 22-7 as an explicit love scene between Anat and Aqhat.

formal proposal of marriage nor is it even a common reference to lovers in the ancient Near East. Thus, Dressler (1979) rejects any overt reference to Anat's sexuality here, and instead translates line 24 as "Come, my brother, and I myself will..." in connection with Anat's offer to teach Aqhat to hunt. Thus, Anat's deceptive seduction of Aqhat, while possible, remains speculative. Indeed, Anat's reconstructed statement, "You are my brother and I am your sister," may be only an affirmation of their common interests. Athena befriends human heroes in Greek literature without threat of sexual complications. Similarly, Anat may be (insincerely) proposing platonic friendship or patronage to the royal hunter.

Regardless of the specific means, Anat lures Aqhat into the countryside where she may have him killed without witnesses. Anat does not kill him herself but gets her henchman, Yatpan, "the Lady's warrior," *mhr št*, to carry out this task for her.

wy^{c}n. yṭpn. m[hr. št]	And Yatpan, the Lady's warrior, answered,
12) šm^{c}. lbtlt. ^{c}nt.	"Listen, O Maiden Anat,
at. ^{c}[l. qšth] (13) tmḫṣh.	For his bow you yourself should slay him;
qṣ^{c}th. hwt. lṭḥ[wy]	for his arrows you should not let him live!"
14) n^{c}mn. ǵzr. št. ṯrm.	The charming hero set a meal,
w[ ] (15) ištir. bḏdm.	... he was all alone in the pavilion.
wn^{c}rs[ ]	...
16) wt^{c}n. btlt. ^{c}nt.	The Maiden Anat answered,
ṯb. yṭp. w[ ] (17) lk.	"Pay attention, Yatpan, and [I will speak] to you.
aštk. km. nšr. bḫb[šy]	I will place you like a vulture in my girdle,
18) km. diy. bt^{c}rty.	like a bird (of prey) in my sheath.[33]
aqht. [km. yṯb] (19) llḥm.	Aqhat, as he sits down to eat,
wbn. dnil. lṯrm.	the son of Danel to dine,
[^{c}lh] (20) nšrm. trḫpn.	Above him vultures will soar,
ybṣr. [ḥbl. d](21)iym.	a flock of birds (of prey) will circle (?).

---

33 The term *nšr* is translated either as "vulture" or "eagle" by most commentators. The word most likely denotes a bird which eats both live prey and carrion. The placing of this bird in Anat's "girdle/sheath," *ḫbšy/t^{c}rty*, probably refers to the language of falconry. I have retained the translations "girdle" and "sheath" for consistency in the face of uncertainty, but perhaps one should understand these terms as designations for "bindings" and "hood."

bn. nšrm. arḫp. an[k.]	Among the vultures I myself will soar,
[^{c}]l (22) aqht. ^{c}dbk.	above Aqhat I will release you.
hlmn. ṯnm. qdqd	Strike him twice upon the head,
23) ṯlṯ id. ^{c}l. udn.	then three times over the ear.
špk. km. šiy (24) dm.	Make his blood run like a slaughterer (?),
km. šḫṭ. lbrkh.	like a butcher, (run) to his knees.
tṣi. km. (25) rḥ. npšh.	Make his life go out like wind,
km. iṯl. brlth.	his breath like spittle,
km. (26) qṭr. baph.	like smoke from his nostrils,
b(!)ap. mh(!)rh.	from his nostrils his strength.
ank (27) laḥwy.	Indeed, I will not let him live."
tqḥ. yṭpn. mhr. št	She took Yatpan, the Lady's warrior,
28) tštn. knšr. bḫbšh.	she placed him like a vulture in her girdle,
km. diy (29) bt^{c}rth.	like a bird (of prey) in her sheath.
aqht. km. yṯb. llḥ[m]	As Aqhat sat to eat,
30) bn. dnil. lṯrm.	the son of Danel to dine,
^{c}lh. nšr[m] (31) trḫpn.	Vultures soared above him,
ybṣr. ḥbl. diy[m.]	a flock of birds (of prey) circled.
[bn] (32) nšrm. trḫp. ^{c}nt.	Anat soared among the vultures,
^{c}l[. ahqt] (33) t^{c}dbnh.	above Aqhat she released him.
hlmn. ṯnm[. qdqd]	He struck twice his head,
34) ṯlṯ id. ^{c}l. udn.	then three times above his ear.
š[pk. km] (35) šiy. dmh.	He spilled his blood like a slaughterer,
km. šḫ[ṭ. lbrkh]	like a butcher, to his knees.
36) yṣat. km. rḥ. npš[h.]	His life went out like wind,
[km. iṯl] (37) brlth.	his breath like spittle,
km. qṭr. b[aph]	like smoke from his nostrils.
[ ] (38) ^{c}nt. bṣmt. mhrh.	… Anat, in destroying his strength,
[ ] (39) aqht. wtbk.	… Aqhat … And she wept.
yl[k. aqht(?)]	"Woe for [you, Aqhat!]
[ ] (40) abn. ank.	… I would create (?) …
w^{c}l. q[štk imḫṣk(?)]	… for your [bow I slew you],
41) qṣ^{c}tk. at. lḥ[wt]	(for) your arrows [I would] not let you live.
[ ] (42) wḫlq. ^{c}pmm[ ]	… and he perished ….

KTU 1.19 i

1) [l]aqht	(Of *Aqhat*)
2) tkrb. [ ]. lqrb[.] mym	The bow fell (?) into the midst of the waters,
3) tql. ^{c}[ ]lb. tṯbr	It fell … it shattered …

ṯṯbr (4) qšt[ ]nr.	The bow shattered …
yṯbr (5) ṯmn. [ ]	The precious … shattered.
btlt. ^{c}nt (6) ṯṯb. [ ]	Maiden Anat sat …
[t]ša (7) tlm. km [ ]. ydh.	She picked up the quiver in her hands like …,
kšr (8) knr. uṣb^{c} <t>h.	like a minstrel with a lyre at her fingers.
kḥrṣ. abn (9) ph. tiḫd.	Like … she clenched her teeth (?),
šnth. wakl. bqmm (10) tšt.	her teeth and food (?) … she placed
ḥrṣ. klb. ilnm	…
11) wṯn. gprm. mn.	And two heroes (?) recited,
gprh. šr 12) aqht.	his/her heroes sang (about) Aqhat.
y^{c}n. kmr. kmrm	They responded, "How bitter, how bitter!" (?)
13) kap^{c}. il. bgdrt.	"Like a great snake in a (stone) fence,
klb l (14) ḫṭh.	(like) a dog for its stick,
imḫṣh. kd. ^{c}l. qšth.	Thus I slew him for his bow,
15) imḫṣh. ^{c}l. qṣ^{c}th.	I slew him for his arrows.
hwt (16) l.aḥw.	I did not let him live.
ap. qšth. lttn (17) ly.	But his bow was not given to me,
wbmt[h y]ḥmṣ	and in his death it is spoiled."
ṣr[ ] 18) pr^{c}. qẓ. y[bl].	… The first fruits of summer withered,
šblt (19) bǵlph.	the ear of corn in its husk.
	(1.18 iv 11–1.19 i 19)

The first column of tablet 1.19 i is very difficult; lines 8-12 are particularly obscure (see A. Cooper 1988). Scholars generally translate this passage to describe either Anat's anxious reaction to Aqhat's demise or her grisly butchering of Aqhat's corpse.[34] While the text remains enigmatic, the former interpretation is certainly the more plausible on philological as well as contextual grounds. Anat apparently repents of

34 A. Cooper (1988:21) claims that *ḥrṣ, ṯn, mn,* and *šr* are "all verbs that pertain to butchering." Thus, he translates (1988:20):

kḫrṣ abn (9) ph.	While splitting open his jaws,
tiḫd. šnth.	She seizes his teeth,
wakl. bqmm (10) tšt	And she puts a butcher-knife in his maw.
ḥrṣ. klb. ilnm	She splits him open like a stag's innards,
11) wṯn. gprm.	And she cuts his carcass in two;
mn. gprh.	She cuts up his carcass;
šr (12) aqht.	She splits Aqhat down the middle.
y^{c}n. kmr. kmrm	He is abased like a poisonous snake, like two snakes.

her hostile and devious actions. As a result of her vendetta, the crown prince Aqhat is dead and the bow which she coveted is broken.

Comparative Mythemes

Ishtar and Gilgamesh. Ugaritologists routinely note the similarities between Anat's encounter with Aqhat and the attempted seduction of Gilgamesh by Ishtar in the *Epic of Gilgamesh.*[35] Each text portrays the impetuous young goddess whose desires are rebuffed by a mortal hero and who then gains permission from the patriarchal god to punish the insolent male. Anat's desire for the hunter's bow and Ishtar's more carnal attraction to Gilgamesh himself certainly differentiate the two scenes. Yet, it is surely not mere coincidence that Anat offers Aqhat the very thing for which Gilgamesh is seeking: immortality. Particular attention has been given to formal motifs and plot structure in the two ancient Near Eastern texts (see Parker 1989:113-6; Hackett 1989). However, the symbolic matrix which the two epics share provides numerous similarities in structure and interpretation.

Ishtar is introduced in the story of *Gilgamesh* after the hero's return from his successful battle with Humbaba. Gilgamesh is bathing when he catches the attention of Ishtar.

> ana dunqi ša Gilgamesh īnā ittaši rubûtu Ishtar
> alkamma Gilgamesh lu ḫāʾir atta
> inbīka yâši qāšu qīšamma
> atta lu mutēma anāku lu aššatka
>
> Princess Ishtar gazed with desire upon the beauty of Gilgamesh.
> "Come to me, Gilgamesh, (for) you are a lover!
> Give me freely of your love!
> You will be the husband and I will be your wife!"
> (Nineveh VI 6-9)

Ishtar follows her initial proposal with a long list of valuable gifts and honors she will bestow upon her prospective groom. Gilgamesh responds by ironically asking what he could give to his bride in return for such magnificent gifts. Gilgamesh then berates Ishtar with a series of unflattering comparisons (see Foster 1987:34-5). He recounts her

---

35 References to the *Epic of Gilgamesh* are made from the Nineveh recension, edited by Thompson (1930) (see Foster 1987:21 n. 1).

malicious treatment of past lovers, asking, "Which one did you love forever?" (VI 42). Detailing the baleful fate of these former paramours, Gilgamesh concludes his rejection by stating, "Thus, if you would love me, you would treat me like them" (VI 79). Evidently, Gilgamesh spurns Ishtar's seductive proposition because he recognizes his own vulnerability and the unavoidable consequences of intimacy with this capricious goddess.

Upon hearing Gilgamesh's litany of her spiteful treatment of past loves, Ishtar flies to the palace of her father, Anu.

> Ishtar uggugatma ana šamāmi [ēli]
> illikma Ishtar ana pānī Anim [abiša ibakki]
> ana pānī Antum ummiša illa[ka dīmāšša]
> abī Gilgamesh ittazzaranni
> Gilgamesh undennâ piššātiya
> piššātiya u errētiya
> Anum pâša īpušma iqabbī
> izzakkar ana rubûti Ishtar
> aba la atti tegrê ša ša[rri Gilgamesh]
> u Gilgamesh umannâ piššātiki
> piššātiki u er[rētiki]
>
> Ishtar became enraged and ascended to heaven.
> She went weeping to her father, Anu;
> Her tears flowed before her mother, Antum.
> "Father, Gilgamesh has insulted me incessantly!
> Gilgamesh has been recounting slander about me,
> slander against me and curses against me!"
> Anu opened his mouth and spoke;
> He replied to Princess Ishtar,
> "Well now, did you not incite King Gilgamesh,
> and then Gilgamesh recounted slander against you,
> slander against you and curses against you?"
> (Nineveh VI 80-91)

Ishtar ignores Anu's insinuation of her own culpability. She threatens to break down the gates of the Underworld, allowing the dead to return to earth where they will outnumber the living, if Anu does not cede her the Bull of Heaven to punish the impudent mortal. After reminding her of the dire consequences of such action, Anu grants her demands.

The similarity between this series of events in *Gilgamesh* and Anat's dialogues with Aqhat and El in *Aqhat* is clear. The patriarchal deity's compliance with the punishment of the human in each account demonstrates something of a divine whimsy at human expense. Hackett (1989:17-9) notes that while Ishtar and Anat are provoked by the heroes' charges of deceit, they nevertheless react with disproportionate fury. Each goddess essentially behaves like a spoiled child in running to her father and demanding satisfaction against the tactless male. In each case, the patriarchal god indulges his daughter and complacently allows the oppression of humans, thus demonstrating an abuse of absolute, divine power (Hackett 1989:22).

While the similarities of formalistic motifs and plot structure in *Gilgamesh* and *Aqhat* are informative, more attention should be devoted to the analysis of the symbolic matrix and relations in each text. In *Gilgamesh*, the hero seeks fulfillment of his life first in orgiastic revelry and heroic deeds and subsequently by seeking eternal life. The conflict between Gilgamesh's enjoyment of life and his fear of impending death is resolved only when he heeds the advice of certain (feminine) characters to accept his own mortality and find fulfillment through marriage and procreation. The meaning of life is found in social incorporation and social immortality through offspring rather than individual pursuits and personal immortality. Just as the text can be read as a rite of passage whereby Gilgamesh is transformed from a self-centered, hedonistic oppressor to a structure-supporting member of his society, a good shepherd to Uruk, so the conclusion also marks Gilgamesh's personal maturation into a well-adjusted individual. The answer to Gilgamesh's anxiety is found through procreation; the bipolar opposites of life and death are mediated by sex.

Ishtar's aborted seduction of Gilgamesh also fits into this structural analysis. While she offers sex—indeed, marriage—to the heroic king, it is obvious even to Gilgamesh that the result of a sexual encounter with her is fatal to the male. Foster's (1987:22) insight that Ishtar's sexuality is not the proper procreative sex of culture, but the erotic, unproductive sexuality of the harlot, underscores the danger which she presents to Gilgamesh. Ishtar's sexuality represents an anti-cultural activity which threatens the social structure of Uruk and Gilgamesh's psychological self-actualization. The contrast between the harlot's civilization of Enkidu through sex and Ishtar's attempted destruction of Gilgamesh through seduction is a strong theme in the Nineveh recension of this epic.[36] Foster (1987:36) concludes, "Through manipulation of person and number in speech, satire, and outright contempt, the Nineveh poet pictures the kind of sexual attraction represented by Ishtar first as a fundamental distortion of personal relationships and second as a surrender of dignity leading at once to childlessness and ultimately to debasement." Hence, the symbolic system of *Gilgamesh* distinguishes between the procreative sex of human culture, which is equated with life, and the animalistic, non-productive eroticism of Ishtar, which is equated with death.

The symbolic value of death in Ishtar's proposition to Gilgamesh is further analyzed by Abusch (1986), who points out, "Love and death are closely associated—be the relation one of identification, opposition, or ambivalence—and the text takes this association for granted; it is Gilgamesh who must decide how and where he will situate himself between the two" (1986:152 n. 17). Abusch understands Ishtar's proposal to be a thinly veiled description of Gilgamesh's glory as King of the Netherworld, rather than a description of his luxurious life on earth. Thus, Ishtar offers Gilgamesh death both symbolically and literally. Hendel (1987:73-81) sees this same theme reflected in the encounter of Anat and Aqhat. He submits that Anat's reference to the "life-given" at Baal's banquet refers to the banquet for the royal dead, the Rephaim, rather than to Aqhat's earthly immortality (cf. Spronk 1986:151-61). Thus, Aqhat's vehement rejection of her offer is based upon his insight into her treachery. Regardless of the correctness of Abusch and Hendel's analyses, the symbolic equivalence of submission to the goddess and death is clear in both texts. That is, even if Anat's offer of immortality does not convey an explicit reference to Netherworld existence, one may perceive the same symbolic triangle of immortality, death, and procreation in the story of Danel's heir and the maiden goddess. We will return to this subject below.

While the fragmentary condition of the narrative from Anat's encounter with Aqhat to his death precludes any definite conclusions, the general outline of events is clear. After the initial encounter between

---

36 Foster (1987:22) is careful to distinguish between the knowledge which sex initially brings to humans, as in Enkidu's acculturation, and its exploitation. He writes, "Once this knowledge is attained, continued non-productive sex is no longer acquisition of knowledge or affirmation of humanity but characteristic of the street, or, at worst, reversion to the animal state."

Anat and Aqhat, Anat again approaches the crown prince with an offer of friendship, perhaps of marriage. Aqhat's acceptance of this proposition ultimately leads to his death by order of Anat. While Ishtar is explicitly offering sex to the semi-divine hero, Anat makes no such overt proposition in the extant text. Indeed, the literal level tells only the tale of a maiden goddess who importunes a human warrior for his divine bow. However, the symbolic level of the epic certainly conveys a sexual tension within Anat and Aqhat's relationship. This sexual tension originates in the sexual nubility of the goddess and the charm of Aqhat, as well as the phallic symbolism of the bow. As a divine, nubile adolescent, Anat is erotic whether she intends to be or not. Indeed, her virginity actually accentuates her sexual availability. Thus, even if she does not actively entice Aqhat with her feminine charms, her nubility can not be denied. The erotic quality of her character is further emphasized by the relation of this scene with the traditional depiction of Ishtar's proposition to Gilgamesh.

Taking his cue from ancient Near Eastern and Classical texts which depict the emasculation of a young hero, Hillers (1973) proposes a thematic relation between *Aqhat* and various texts concerning the youth who loses his life after an encounter with an erotic female. Hillers cites examples from the myths and stories of Adonis, Attis, Eshmun, Bata, and Kombabos, as well as Gilgamesh and Aqhat. Conceding that Anat's proposition to Aqhat is not explicitly sexual, Hillers perceives the sexual tension behind the literal text. The theme expounded by Hillers includes the approach of an erotic female to a young man and the subsequent emasculation or death of the hero. Hillers' (1973:77) emphasis on the youth's emasculation supplies a common, but not universal, element to these traditions. Indeed, the centrality of the erotic female to these texts distinguishes them from *Aqhat*, in which the aggressive female is virginal. Hillers (1973:76) explains, "Only in Aqhat is the goddess's initial approach so undisguisedly hostile and threatening. The sexual theme is present ... in symbolic form, but only emasculation is stressed." In fact, the human's rejection of the goddess appears to be more central to the emasculation theme than the erotic nature of the female.[37] Regardless, Hillers' analysis clearly lends

---

[37] Hillers (1973:75-6) discusses five cases in which emasculation is explicit or likely in the text. Four of these five cases depict the youth emasculating himself; only

plausibility to the notion that Anat's murder of Aqhat is symbolically equivalent to his emasculation at the hands of the capricious goddess. Anat's ability to disarm Aqhat reflects the male's disempowerment and loss of masculine virility, just as Ishtar's attempted seduction of Gilgamesh would result in his death.

As discussed in a previous chapter, the symbolic association of castration, sex, and death should not be surprising. Niditch (1989:43) points out, "Associations between eroticism and death and between sex and violence are old and intimate ones reverberating in the various cultural artifacts of western and nonwestern tradition, reflecting and, in turn, affecting the essential nature of human self-consciousness." The similarity between the metaphorical language of seduction and battle suggests the equality, from an androcentric perspective, of the male submitting himself to the aggressive goddess and his surrender of his bow; either event results in the loss of his masculinity. In the case of *Aqhat*, the male engaged in the masculine role of predator becomes in fact the female's prey. Anat drains Aqhat of his life as she drains away his blood. The Freudian implications of this metaphor are clear (see O'Flaherty 1980:83-4). Ishtar changes warriors into women by taking away their bows and in *Aqhat* Anat actualizes the threat. Anat transforms Aqhat from a warrior into a non-warrior, from a virile male to a dead, asexual creature. Thus, even without an explicit sexual content, the motif of the threatening woman who promises pleasure but delivers only death is present in *Aqhat*. Here the motif is less striking because the dangerous female is not the erotic seductress, but the functionally androgynous maiden.

The Divine Huntress. Gilgamesh rejects Ishtar's erotic offer because he realizes that it will result in sterility and death rather than eternal life; Aqhat, on the other hand, turns down immortality in order to guard the

---

Adonis's fatal wound in his "thigh" is not self-inflicted. In this tradition the jealous husband of Aphrodite rather than the goddess herself kills the youth. By contrast, each of the four examples of self-inflicted emasculation tells of the complete lack of sexual contact between the youth and the aggressive female. In fact, Eshmun mutilates himself to avoid sexual contact with Astronoe. Similarly, Bata and Kombabos emasculate themselves in either evidence or proof of their innocence of an unjust accusation of sexual assault (see Hollis 1989). Finally, Attis is driven to castrate himself when he has broken his vow of chastity to Cybele.

symbol of his masculinity. This contrast between the relationship of procreative sex and eroticism in *Gilgamesh* and the emphasis on gender roles and sexual identity in *Aqhat* distinguish the two texts. When Anat covets the divine bow, Aqhat responds that bows are for males. This parting retort surely reflects the common gender ideology of the ancient Near East, but it is patently offensive to the divine huntress. Indeed, Anat's desire for the bow serves as a striking reminder of her ambiguous gender identity in Ugaritic myth. She is a female, yet she pursues male activities such as hunting and warfare and rejects the feminine roles of wife and mother.[38] Accordingly, scholars have noted the similarity of *Aqhat* and myths concerning the virgin huntress, Artemis, in Greek mythological literature. Studies by Xella (1976) and Fontenrose (1981:217-20) suggest that *Aqhat* incorporates the motif of the hunter confronted by the divine huntress (cf. Astour 1965:163-8). Fontenrose (1981) provides numerous examples of the hunter who is a favored companion of Artemis but is then killed because of his lack of chastity. This lack of chastity may be either his spurning the virgin goddess by taking a different lover or his sexual attraction to the goddess herself. While *Aqhat* appears to be distinct from the category of Classical texts in which the huntress is offended at the sexual behavior of a devotee, similarities remain.

Contrary to the assumption that simply attracting the attention of a goddess is dangerous to the male, Aqhat is actually threatened by the ambiguity of Anat's sexuality and gender. That is, it is her perverse desire for the masculine implement which brings about his death. Athena's sororal companionship with various human males contrasts with Anat's strained relationship with Aqhat. Athena is successful in repressing her own feminine sexuality and thus may enter the male domain without threat to males. On the other hand, the male companions of Artemis (e.g. Hippolytus, Actaeon) always end badly in Greek myth because of their chaste devotion to the maiden goddess. The human males inevitably are faithless to the goddess, falling in love with some other female, or they are persecuted by others for their celibacy. The woeful end of these males suggests the negative value attributed by

---

[38] In addition to her portrayal in *Aqhat*, Anat is perhaps depicted hunting in *KTU* 1.22 ii 11 and 1.114, 23. The relationship between Anat and Athtart in these episodes, as well as their connection to the "Lady of the Beasts" in Aegean and Levantine iconography, remains unclear (see also 1.92).

Greek social ideology to such exclusionary pursuits. In the same manner, Anat does not completely overcome her feminine identity in Ugaritic symbolism. She remains a female regardless of her striving towards androgyny in gender. Indeed, one may posit her confused sexual and gender identity as the root of her aggressive character and volatile emotions. Anat is the divine adolescent female trapped in her tomboy image.

Fontenrose (1981:252-3) concludes that hunting is symbolically related to both celibacy and sexual exploitation in that each reflects behavior which is not normative to human culture. Hunters are liminal figures who spend their time apart from the structures of society. This insight into the role of chastity and sexual abuse in the Classical myths concerning youthful hunters (e.g. Adonis, Actaeon, Orion, Hippolytus) also applies to Aqhat. He is a victim of Anat's confused gender and sexual identity. In his study of Amazons, Tyrrell (1984:73-84) discusses Adonis, Hippolytus, and Atalanta as examples of characters who flee marriage for the hunt. Hence, they remain in the limbo of adolescent transition and refuse to mature into their proper social category. This liminality erupts in various aberrant forms, including hypersexuality, celibacy, and feminized males who are "likened to worshipers of Eastern deities such as Cybele and Artemis of Ephesus, deities whose devotees were wild women and eunuchs" (Tyrrell 1984:76-7). Anat clearly fits into this model as the adolescent virgin huntress who refuses to accept an adult role within the divine society. Similarly, Aqhat's association with the maiden goddess of the hunt represents his own rejection of social and familial responsibilities. This lack of transition from youth to adulthood thus symbolizes death for society rather than continued life through marriage and procreation. The symbolic emasculation and death of Aqhat further link his tale to the fate of Classical devotees of the virgin huntress.

While Anat's violent energies are channeled in support of cosmic structure in the Baal Cycle, her role in *Aqhat* illustrates the dangerous qualities of the untamed maiden. Anat threatens the basic social fabric of the patriarchal culture as well as the life of Aqhat. Indeed, Anat's ambiguous gender results in the death of not just any masculine male but in the demise of the royal heir. The suffering of the entire society is reflected in *Aqhat* through the languishing of nature in sympathy with Aqhat's fate. The injustice of Anat's aggression further accentuates her irresponsible, unrestrained character. As a sexually mature female, Anat's sexual drives are assumed rather than emphasized in Ugaritic myth. She is portrayed as female, yet her actions contradict the normative female identity. Her adolescent status requires her integration into the androcentric social institutions, yet Anat rejects this world of culture for the natural realm of the hunt; hunting and bloodshed are surely Anat's substitute for sexual expression. From the perspective of the ancient social ideology, Anat's liminal position causes havoc within the accepted gender roles and structures of androcentric society. Life is found in females, but the maiden's rejection of her proper procreative role results in death and sterility for the society as a whole. Anat's retention of her virginal liminality is equated with Ishtar's sexual exploitation as the untamed, erotic female. In each case, the female independent of male control threatens the lives of males and the social structure which underlies social continuity. By refusing to accept a submissive position within the patriarchal culture, the independent female threatens the destruction of human culture and a return to the animalistic chaos of nature.

In conclusion, elements of sex, gender, and social ideology commingle in *Aqhat* to form a multi-layered web of symbolic meanings. The symbolism surrounding Anat in *Aqhat* combines both the erotic quality of Ishtar's proposition to Gilgamesh and the motifs of emasculation and gender distinction found in Classical texts.[39] In *Gilgamesh* and *Aqhat* the power of the independent female endangers the male, both personally and socially. The goddesses' eroticism threatens the males' sexual identity just as their social liminality undermines the stability of patriarchal culture in which females are controlled by androcentric institutions. *Aqhat* focuses upon two adolescent characters who are confused about their social roles and psychological identities. The inherent ambiguity of Anat's gender and sexuality is seen in the contrast between her roles in *Aqhat* and the Baal Cycle. Indeed, in

---

[39] This is not to suggest any necessary historical connection with the Classical traditions. The comparative analysis of Anat's role in Aqhat does not constitute a quest to uncover the "original" myth behind the literary text (see Parker 1989:137-8). These speculations are rarely convincing (e.g. Dijkstra 1979; Fontenrose 1981:117-20). By contrast, one may appeal to "fundamental traits of human sexual psychology" (Hillers 1973:75) and human social ideology for the recurrence of similar motifs in the texts under consideration.

Aqhat she represents the threat of emasculation, death, and social disruption, while the Baal Cycle portrays her unique ability as the maiden to overcome death. As Ortner (1974:86) has argued, the symbolic power of feminine characters lies in their ambiguity; by mediating between nature and culture, feminine symbols may function dynamically either to support or subvert culture. In fact, *Aqhat* prominently displays the social ambiguity of the adolescent female in its contrast between the roles of Anat and Pughat.

Anat and Pughat

We return to the plot of *Aqhat* with the discovery of Aqhat's murder and the recovery of his corpse from the vulture's stomach with the aid of Baal. After providing burial rites for the slain youth, Danel and his daughter Pughat mourn Aqhat for seven years during which a drought devastates the land (see Parker 1989:122-7, 131). Contrary to early attempts to interpret this epic text as a myth of the dying and rising god who personifies agriculture, this drought is in response to the injustice perpetrated against Aqhat. After observing the period of mourning for Aqhat, Pughat takes it upon herself to avenge the death of her brother.

28) wt^{c}n. pǵt. ṯkmt. mym	Pughat, she who shoulders water, spoke,
29) qrym. ab. dbḥ. lilm	"My father has offered a sacrifice to the gods;
30) š^{c}ly. dǵṯt. bšmym	he has sent up incense to the heavens,
31) dǵṯ. hrnmy. dkbkbm	incense of *Hrnmy* to the stars.
32) ltbrkn. alk. brktm	Now indeed bless me that I may go blessed;
33) tmrn. alk. nmrrt	consecrate me that I may go consecrated.
34) imḫṣ. mḫṣ. aḫy.	I will slay my brother's slayer;
akl[.]m (35) kly[. ^{c}]l. umty.	I will kill my sibling's killer."
wy^{c}n. dn(36 il. mt. rpi.	Danel, man of *Rpi*, answered,
npš. tḥ. pǵ[t]	"You will restore my life, Pughat,
37) ṯkmt. mym.	who shoulders water,
ḥspt. lš^{c}r (38) ṭl.	who brushes dew from the barley,
yd^{c}t. hlk. kbkbm	who knows the course of the stars.
[ ] (39) npš. hy. mḫ.	... my life, to her vigor ...
tmḫṣ. mḫṣ[. aḫk]	May you slay your brother's slayer;
40) tkl. mkly. ^{c}l. umt[k]	may you kill your sibling's killer."
41) [ ] bym.	... from the sea.

trtḫ[ṣ] (42)[wt]adm.	She washed and rouged herself,
tid(!)m. bǵlp ym	with rouge from seashells
43) dalp. šd. ẓuh. bym.	whose habitat is a thousand fields in the sea.
t[ḥt] (44) tlbš. npṣ. ǵzr.	Beneath, she put on a hero's garment.
tšt. ḫ[ ]b (45) nšgh.	She placed a k[nife] in its sheath (?);
ḥrb. tšt. bt^{c}r[th]	she placed a sword in its scabbard.
46) w^{c}l. tlbš. npṣ. aṯt.	On top, she put on a woman's garment.
[lm](47)ṣbi. nrt. ilm. špš.	At the setting of the sun, the divine luminary,
[ ] (48) pǵt. minš. šdm.	Pughat [entered] the place where fields meet (?).
lm ^{c}r[b] (49) nrt. ilm. špš.	At the entering of the sun, the divine luminary,
mǵy[t] (50) pǵt. lahlm.	Pughat approached the tents.
rgm. lyṭ[pn. y](51)bl.	Word was brought to Yatpan,
agrtn. bat. bḏdk.	"A hired woman has entered your pavilion
[ ] (52) bat. a(!)hlm.	… has come to your tents."
wy^{c}n. yṭpn. m[hr] (53) št.	Yatpan, the Lady's warrior, answered,
qḥn. wtšqyn. yn.	"Bring her in and let her serve me wine to drink,
qḥ (54) ks. bdy.	taking the cup from my hand,
qb^{c}t. bymny.	the mug (?) from my right hand!"
tq(55)ḥ. pǵt. wtšqynh.	Pughat was brought in and she served him drink;
tq(!)ḥ[. ks.] bdh	she took the cup from his hand,
56) qb^{c}t. bymnh.	the mug from his right hand.
wy^{c}n. yṭ[p]n[. mh]r (57) št.	And Yatpan, the Lady's warrior, spoke,
byn. yšt. iln(!).	"May our god drink of the wine,
il š[ ]il (58) dyqny. ḏdm.	El… El who owns the pavilion (?).
yd. mḫṣt. aq[h]t. ǵ(59)zr.	The hand that slew Aqhat the hero
tmḫṣ. alpm. ib. št	will slay thousands of the Lady's enemies!
[t]št (60) ḫršm. lahlm.	It will work magic against their tents,
p[ ]km (61) ybl. lbh.	… as … his heart
km. bṯn. y[ ]ah.	like a serpent …."
ṯnm. tšqy msk. hwt.	A second time she served him a mixture to drink;
tšqy	she served drink ….
	(1.19 iv 28-61)

While the conclusion to this scene is lost, it seems most likely that Pughat kills the drunken Yatpan with her concealed knife. Yatpan's role is essential to the plot of *Aqhat*, since a human could certainly not take vengeance upon the maiden goddess of the Ugaritic pantheon. Anat's henchman, however, is an appropriate target to illustrate the dynamic tension between the two liminal females.

The interpretive crux of this episode concerns the translation of the term *agrtn* in line 51 as either "our hired girl" or "our employer" (see *CAD* 1/1:151). Unfortunately, the poetic parallel of this term is effaced. At issue is whether Pughat is masquerading as Anat or a servant girl in order to infiltrate Yatpan's tent. Many commentators have noted the combination of masculine and feminine articles in Anat's costume described in Papyrus Chester Beatty VII. Thus, they interpret Pughat's mixed attire as an impersonation of the maiden goddess. However, Pughat appears to be hiding her knife and warrior's gear underneath her feminine gown rather than combining masculine and feminine articles of her wardrobe. The application of rouge is certainly not restricted to Anat's toilette. Hence, many interpreters hold that *agrtn* should be understood as "our hired girl" rather than "our mistress." Parker (1989:131) suggests that the lackey's reference to "our hired girl" refers to Pughat's appearance as a prostitute. Thus, she gains entrance to the banquet as an erotic female rather than as the impersonation of the militant Anat. Indeed, this interpretation fits well with the folkloristic motif of the dangerous seductress found in other texts.

Of particular relevance to Pughat's murder of Yatpan are the stories of Judith's decapitation of Holophernes, Jael's dispatch of Sisera, and Inara's deception of Illuyanka (see Parker 1989:131-3; Niditch 1989; Fontaine 1988). Named for the heroine of the Apocryphal book *Judith*, the "Judith theme" includes the deceptive eroticism of the Jewish woman and her murder of the drunken general in his effort to seduce her. This text may provide the closest parallel to Pughat's role in *Aqhat.* Fontaine (1988:96-7) emphasizes the usual banquet setting and common sexual components of these "female trickster" stories. Similarly, the best parallel to Anat's deception of Aqhat is the Hittite myth *Illuyankas* in which the goddess lures the dragon to a banquet in which her henchman aids in his execution (see Pritchard 1969:125-6). In each text, the deceptive female coaxes the male to relax his guard with alcohol so that she may overcome him (see also Niditch 1989). Fontaine (1988:97) notes that the banquet "set-up" gives the advantage to the host, although he is usually the one killed in the end. Similarly in *Aqhat*, Pughat avenges her brother in a banquet scene in which she is either the guest or servant. Yatpan's boasts further suggest his sexual designs on the "hired girl." The danger of these alluring yet lethal women is consistent with other erotic females discussed above, as is the irony of the seductress assassinating the warrior. Hence, while Yatpan's boasts may be intended to impress either Anat or a subservient female, the comparative evidence suggests the latter.

The inverse relationship between Anat and Pughat's roles in *Aqhat* is clear. Hillers (1973:80) summarizes the portrayal of the feminine characters: "One is the Virgin Anath, deceiving, violent, emasculating, the one who turns a man into a woman; opposing her and perhaps victorious in the end is Paghat, the sister, wise, compassionate, and loyal, who turns herself into a man in the cause of justice." Anat applies her cunning and power to kill the youthful hunter, thus depriving Danel of his heir and his people of a leader. The injustice of her violence is made more poignant by her failure to attain the bow. While Anat personifies the destructive and dangerous characteristics of the feminine, Pughat serves as the archetype of the obedient female who actively supports patriarchal structures. Hence, the submissive and rational Pughat is the perfect foil for the uncontrolled and violent Anat. In avenging her brother's murder Pughat temporarily takes on the masculine warrior characteristics of Anat. Like Judith, she enters a liminal period to avert tragedy to her people. Once her quest is completed, Pughat surely returns to her normative feminine role. Thus, the text of *Aqhat* communicates the necessary submission of young women to the patriarchal norm in order to avoid the chaotic effects of feminine liberation.

In conclusion, the *Epic of Aqhat* is primarily concerned with issues of procreation, social stability, and death rather than the resurrection of Aqhat.[40] Danel's uncertain procreative ability forms the central conflict of the first section of *Aqhat*, and Anat's promise of immortality in exchange for the phallic bow sets the scene for the next section. Danel overcomes his own mortality through begetting an heir. Aqhat, offered immortality by the virginal goddess Anat, is instead killed by her for not surrendering the symbol of his masculine identity. The maiden girl Pughat must then resolve this dilemma by taking on Anat's ambiguous gender and avenging her brother. Parker (1989:142-3) points out the

---

40 Parker (1989:100-7, 134-44) and Hackett (1989:23) also emphasize the theme of human existence in the face of divine power.

centrality of familial solidarity to the epic. Gender and procreation play important roles in the presentation of these familial needs. Anat here embodies the completely negative forces which disrupt the familial bonds. In contrast to Pughat's presentation as a proper daughter, Anat personifies the anti-social, anti-structural forces of the cosmos. In fact, Pughat's role in *Aqhat* is essentially the same as Anat's role in the Baal Cycle: each maiden mourns her slain brother and then avenges his death in support of cosmic stability. The ambiguity in Anat's character allows her to play either the positive or negative role, depending upon the symbolic context. It is precisely this ambiguous position of the adolescent maiden within the mythic structures which gives her symbol its potency. The maiden is at the threshhold of feminine sexuality and social maturity but has not crossed into her adult role. Anat is female yet retains her childish lack of gender distinction in her social and psychological identities. Thus, she mediates the bipolar opposites of life and death, male and female, and social continuity and social disintegration. Anat's juxtaposition with Pughat in *Aqhat* subtly, but clearly, expresses this ambiguity in the symbol of the divine maiden.

III. THE PASSIONS OF ANAT

Ugaritic myth consistently portrays Anat as a violent and unrestrained goddess whose emotions frequently overwhelm her. Anat's reaction to the approach of Baal's messengers and her spiteful remarks to the divine assembly after Baal's death illustrate her combativeness. Her heartfelt mourning for Baal reveals her compassionate side. Aggressive in attaining her own goals, Anat threatens the divine patriarch with physical abuse if he does not acquiesce to her demands and actualizes her threats concerning the hapless Aqhat. Her bloodbath and murderous treatment of Mot also display her exuberance and frenzied zeal. Similarly, Anat's behavior in *Aqhat* reflects her compulsive nature. Her quick transition from fury to regret over Aqhat's death demonstrates her capricious character. Included in this litany of Anat's passionate behavior should be the enigmatic text *KTU* 1.96 (RS 22.225).[41] The opening lines (1-6) read:

---

41 On this text see especially Virolleaud (1960), Astour (1963; 1988), Lipínski (1965), Caquot (1985), and de Moor (1987:109-10).

1) ^{c}nt(!). hlkt. wšnwt	Anat (!) was wandering about (?).
2) tp. aḫh. wn^{c}m.	She saw her brother and he was lovely;
aḫh (3) kysmsm	her brother was very beautiful.
tspi. širh (4) l. bl ḥrb.	She ate his flesh without a knife;
tšt. dmh (5) lbl. ks.	she drank his blood without a cup.
tpnn. ^{c}n (6) bṯy.	She turned to the spring of *Bṯy* (?),

Unfortunately, the text following these lines is unintelligible to most philologists (cf. de Moor 1987:109-10). Commentators unanimously read the opening word of *KTU* 1.96 as *^{c}nt* although the text clearly shows *^{c}nh.*[42] While one may thus dismiss this enigmatic text as providing no evidence for the goddess Anat, the scholarly literature concerning Anat's alleged role in this text must be considered in any comprehensive discussion of Anat in Ugaritic myth.

The interpretation of this fragmentary mythic episode is especially difficult given the obscurity of both its vocabulary and content. The reference to "her brother" in line 2 is not specified, although Ugaritologists routinely assume that it is Baal. In general, two approaches to understanding this text are favored by Ugaritic specialists.[43] The first refers to the Dionysiac cult of sparagmos and

---

42 *^{c}nh* is hardly a simple orthographic error for *^{c}nt*, and one would not expect the scribe to make a mistake in the first word of a composition. Scholars have apparently not made sense of the actual writing, and thus "correct" the text in order to provide a logical subject for the feminine verbal forms. Accordingly, the unspecified "brother" of the subject in line 2 is identified as Baal. In a private communication, however, P. Kyle McCarter, Jr., has suggested to me that the actual subject of this enigmatic text is, in fact, "his/her eye." Thus, the reference to "its brother" refers simply to the other eye, as in certain Mesopotamian riddles. Egyptian myths concerning the "eye of Re," Hathor, provide obvious parallels to this interpretation. Indeed, *KTU* 1.96 may be an Ugaritic version of an Egyptian tradition. McCarter's suggestion is more plausible than any interpretation which involves the goddess Anat and does not require altering the text.

43 Of course, other interpretations have been offered. In keeping with the fertility emphasis of the Myth and Ritual school, Oldenburg (1969:89-90) holds that *KTU* 1.96 reflects "how in case of drought the last drops of rain (= Ba^{c}al) are absorbed by the underground springs, which then by the function of ^{c}Anat well up again. The function of ^{c}Anat in connection with springs indicates that she is the specific goddess of springs." Oldenberg further associates Anat's bathing ritual with fertility by explaining that the people of Ugaritic believed that this caused the morning dew. Oldenberg does not reveal his evidence for these statements.

Taking a different approach, Løkkegaard (1982:134) links *KTU* 1.96 with the myth of *KTU* 1.12 in which Baal is killed by the Devourers, *aklm*. He argues that the */t/* verbal prefix on *tspi. širh … tšt. dmh* denotes the third masculine plural verbal form

homophagy—a frenzied tearing apart and cannibalism of a live victim—while the second explains this as a love scene between Anat and Baal. The obscure vocabulary of this short mythological fragment further complicates its accurate translation. The verb *šnwt* appears to be cognate with Syriac *šĕnâ*, "to depart, be dislocated." This verbal root is attested in Anat's formulaic reply to Baal's messengers (1.3 iv 33) meaning "to depart." Since the meaning "to depart (from a location)" combines the verb with the prepositional /b/ (Pardee 1976:281), the verbal hendiadys with *hlk* may mean "to go forth, wander." In addition to its primary meaning "to depart," Syriac *šĕnâ* can mean "be insane, frenzied" (Payne Smith 1903:586-7; Brockelmann 1928:789-90). Pope (1977:358) apparently bases his translation, "Anat went wild," on this Syriac verb. While either reading is acceptable, the attestation of the root *šnw* in Ugaritic meaning "to depart" persuades me to accept the less specific meaning "to wander" or "depart" in this context.

Following the suggestion of Virolleaud (1960), Astour (1988) prefers to translate *šnwt* as "to admire," cognate to the Arabic verb *sanā*, "to shine, gleam, radiate, flash" (Wehr 1976:436). Astour (1988:14) translates *tp. aḫh. wn*ᶜ*m. aḫh* as "her brother's timbrel, her brother's melodious voice" based on the depiction of Baal as a singer in *KTU* 1.108. The Ugaritic and BH word *tp*, "tamborine," is certainly well attested. Astour's criticisms of explaining *tp* as a nominal form of the root *ypy*, "to be beautiful," are also cogent. Thus, Astour (1988:16) reads, "Anat went and admired her brother's timbrel and her brothers lovely voice, for he/it was beautiful." However, the meaning "melodious voice" for *n*ᶜ*m* is otherwise unattested and the relation of Baal's musical ability to Anat's cannibalism is found only in Astour's

---

rather than the second feminine singular. He states, "Ysmsm is no doubt identical with or a miswriting for Ysmm, the 'beautiful ones,' well-known from the SS text [*KTU* 1.23], their name being euphemistic for tearing monsters roaming on the desert boarder." Thus, Løkkegaard (1982:134) translates, "Anat ascends little by little, she comes up with her brother, yea, her brother's grace. Certainly the 'Fair Gods' are eating his flesh without a sword, and they are drinking his blood without a cup." To the contrary, *ysmsm*, meaning "beautiful," is clearly the reduplicated form (see GKC §55e; §84b) of the common Ugaritic root *ysm*. The reduplicated form of *ysm* is attested elsewhere in Ugaritic literature (1.17 ii 42; 1.4 iv15; 1.19 ii 60).

reference to Dionysiac frenzies. Contrary to Astour, the reading "she sees" for *tp* seems most likely.[44]

Astour champions the attempt to link this fragmentary mythic episode with the Dionysian practice of sparagmos and homophagy.[45] While there is literary evidence for the frenzied Maenads and Bacchic worshipers tearing apart their live victims, there is no evidence for any relation to Canaanite practices. The consumption of raw flesh is common to the Dionysiac cult and 1.96, but no other links are evident. Astour (1965:178-81) claims that there is abundant evidence for these practices in West Semitic cultures, but he is able to list only one example of humans eating an animal raw (1Sam 14:32) and a few examples of ritual dismemberment in ancient Syria-Palestine. Indeed, none of these alleged practices is similar to Anat's cannibalistic treatment of Baal. Moreover, Astour's (1965:181) interpretation assumes a ritual expression of this myth in which the worshipers commune with their god through partaking of his body and blood. The Frazerian analogy with the Christian Eucharist is obvious but ultimately unconvincing. In conclusion, the value of Astour's comparative work lies in the similarity of motif which he perceives rather than in historical connections between the Dionysiac cult and the Ugaritic text.

The eccentric translation of Lipínski (1965) reads *KTU* 1.96 as an explicit sexual encounter between Anat and Baal involving culinary metaphors for sexual activity. Lipínski (1965:47-8) explains *šnwt* as "to be inflamed; to be in heat; to be passionate," also based upon Arabic *sanā*, "to shine." His speculative translation, founded upon the assumed sexual relationship of Anat and Baal, is ingenious in its metaphorical references to genitalia and sexuality. De Moor (1987:109-10) concurs with the sexual interpretation while providing a less explicit translation. However, the use of *tspi širh ... tšt dmh* as sexual metaphor is unprecedented in Northwest Semitic literature. The clarity of the verbs suggests that they be taken literally.

---

44 While Astour (1988:16) is correct to note that the common Ugaritic verb *ph*, "to see," should be written with the /h/ (see also Gordon 1965:91), his verdict is far from final. The writing *ypn* in *KTU* 1.19 iii 14 clearly means "he saw" and as such is an example of the omitted /h/ in the verb *ph*. The writing *tp* may be explained as a jussive in which the final /h/ is etymologically correct but phonetically unnecessary. Regardless, one could posit haplography in this school tablet and read *tp<h>*.

45 Astour 1963; 1965:176-94; 1988.

Also relevant to the discussion of *KTU* 1.96 is the so-called *Cannibal Hymn* from the Pyramid texts (see Simpson 1973:269-73) in which the deceased king eats the flesh of the gods in order to assimilate their attributes into himself. While there is no direct connection between this Egyptian text and the Ugaritic mythological fragment, it is interesting to note the concept of one deity partaking of the body of another in an effort to assimilate its attributes. Unfortunately, the motivation for Anat's devouring of Baal's flesh, apart from its attractiveness, is completely lacking in *KTU* 1.96.[46]

Given the lack of context for this mythic scene, perhaps the best explanation for Anat's activity is her intense mourning for her slain brother. In opposition to the insistence of Astour (1988), there is no evidence that Baal is alive in this scene. To the contrary, the passive role of Baal suggests that Anat encounters Baal's corpse. Overwhelming grief at the discovery of Baal's corpse provides a plausible explanation for Anat's macabre actions. There is certainly anthropological evidence for the ritual cannibalism of dead relatives. Sanday (1986:7) explains that in "endocannibalism (the cannibalism of relatives) human flesh is a physical channel for communicating social values and procreative fertility.... Endocannibalism recycles and regenerates social forces that are believed to be physically constituted in bodily substances or bones at the same time that it binds the living to the dead in perpetuity." In her distress over her brother's death, Anat moans that she would follow him into the Netherworld (1.6 i 7-8). Similarly, Anat's mourning for Baal might incorporate such frenzied behavior (cf. Burkert 1983:48-52). Granted, there are no other examples for this type of mourning activity from the ancient Near East (see Lewis 1989). However, this explanation of Anat's role in *KTU* 1.96, while speculative, is at least consistent with her passionate mourning for Baal in the Baal Cycle.

In conclusion, parallels from Greece, Egypt, and modern ethnography are intriguing but they contribute little to a definite interpretation of Anat's role in *KTU* 1.96. A ritual connection for this mythological scene is completely speculative. Ultimately, *KTU* 1.96 must remain enigmatic and contextually unique among the Ugaritic

---

46 Margalit (1989a:67) argues that *KTU* 1.96 depicts Anat's unwitting consumption of her brother. He suggests that she does not recognize Baal in his theriomorphic manifestation as a bull. In a highly speculative interpretation, Margalit (1989a) identifies *KTU* 1.92 as another Ugaritic theophagy.

texts. However, each of the suggested interpretations—sexual, Bacchic, mourning—is exemplary of Anat's passionate nature. Regardless of Anat's apearance in *KTU* 1.96, then, the unrestrained and emotional quality of her behavior is consistent throughout the Ugaritic corpus, as discussed in this chapter. While each of Anat's violent actions in the mythological literature may have its own cause or motivation, such as the death of Baal, her overexuberance and volatile personality remain unexplained in the myths. That is, why is she so fundamentally capricious and temperamental that she explodes with only slight provocation? Her mythic identity as an independent female certainly accounts for some of her character, but it is also her particular age and gender as the hoyendish adolescent which provides the key to her symbolic persona.

CHAPTER 5

Conclusion: Violence and the Maiden

The Maiden Anat is a complex symbol which can not be typologically reduced to an ancient Near Eastern "goddess of love and war." In contrast to this modern reduction of an ancient symbol, Anat presents the mythographer with an individual identity as a maiden goddess, embodying the tensions and paradoxes of feminine power in an androcentric world. Analysis of Anat's sexuality and gender, essential components of many goddesses within androcentric mythologies, reveals the symbolic particularity of her mythic character. As this study argues, Anat is neither sexually active nor procreative. She is, in fact, a virginal female within the Ugaritic pantheon. Yet, while Anat is a female character, her gender is ambiguous. The adolescent Anat refuses to submit to the patriarchal institutions of marriage and the social expectations of feminine behavior. Disdaining feminine social roles and domestic responsibility, Anat engages in the masculine activities of hunting, warfare, and politics. This rejection of the normative social position as wife and mother forces Anat into a liminal position within the ancient gender and social ideology. Anat's liminal identity is a source of discord and strife within the pantheon: she threatens the patriarchal authority with physical abuse, destroys the royal heir, and defies normative gender roles. As the unrestrained maiden she personifies one form of the feminine threat to androcentric culture and patriarchal society.

The literary descriptions of Anat consistently portray her as an adolescent female. Her qualification as a wet nurse emphasizes her female pubescence. Thus, Anat's unwillingness to accept the social role and identity of an adult female even though she is physically mature places her in an ambiguous position within the ancient social ideology. Modern discussions of adolescence contribute toward our understanding of Anat as a mythic symbol. Dalsimer (1986:4) comments on adolescence as a period of "heightened sexuality, intensified irritability and belligerence, of violating rules, and of disrespect for the older generation." Rather than identifying adolescence as a modern problem, historical evidence suggests the universality of the problems of emerging adulthood. Indeed, lesser mobility and stricter social roles could even intensify the social repression of young females in the pre-industrial world. Ugaritic myth depicts Anat caught up in the turbulent emotions and desires of female adolescence. The maiden goddess struggles with her self-identity in terms of gender, sexuality, and social role. The tension between Anat's physical maturity and her rejection of a normative feminine identity remains unresolved in Ugaritic myth. However, Anat's liminal identity in Ugaritic myth is made clearer by understanding her as an unrestrained, adolescent female with an unresolved self-identity.

This study concludes that Anat's actions in Ugaritic myth are intrinsically related to her identity as an adolescent female independent of male authority. Under the ancient social ideology, Anat should be a submissive wife and mother active within the domestic sphere. As the adolescent tomboy, Anat is outside of the normative categories of feminine social positions. The symbolic significance of her character in the Ugaritic pantheon is most clearly reflected in the *Epic of Aqhat* in which her confused gender plays a central role in the destruction of the royal heir. The subtle symbolic significance of Anat's desire for Aqhat's bow is heightened by reference to comparative mythemes of goddesses either seducing or castrating human males. Ultimately, Anat's rejection of her feminine gender and confused sexuality forces Aqhat symbolically to forfeit his own masculine identity in death.

Similarly, Anat's attraction to Baal in the Baal Cycle is informed by the importance of friendships in early adolescence as a means to see oneself reflected in the qualities of one's companions (see Dalsimer 1986:8-9, 25). Just as Athena befriends heroes in Greek myth, so Anat's sororal relationship to Baal may reflect her desire to emulate his masculine qualities. Anat's association with Baal is consistent with her own identity as the adolescent tomboy. Her interest in Baal's sexual escapades (e.g. *KTU* 1.10), but lack of recognition of her own sexuality, is also consistent with the portrayal of emergent feminine sexuality in early adolescence (see Dalsimer 1986:32-9). Rather than indulge her own libidinous desires, Anat denies her undiscovered sexuality. The result is a strong sexual tension in Anat's character. Hence, her violent temperament and lack of self-restraint manifest her own confused gender, sexual, and social identity rather than a real malevolence or aggressively martial function. While this study argues that Anat is a virginal figure in Ugaritic myth, it is certainly possible that she is sexually involved with Baal, as de Moor and others hold. Such an interpretation would not undermine the ambiguity of Anat's sexual and gender identity, as seen in *Aqhat*. Rather than admit this realization of Anat's feminine sexuality, however, the Ugaritic myths appear to emphasize the strong sexual tension of her liminal character—a tension which I think remains unresolved.

Hence, Anat's tantrums symbolically represent the feelings of confusion and frustration common to early adolescence. Friedrich (1978:160-1) notes a relation between traditional stories of helpless females being given in marriage by their fathers as a reflection of the anxieties of adolescent females within repressive androcentric societies. Similarly, the modern folkloristic association of adolescent girls with disruptive poltergeists attests to the turbulence of emerging sexuality and confusion over social and psychological identities (see Price 1945:4-5, 36). Thus, Anat is perhaps representative of feminine rage at repressive androcentric social and gender ideology. Denied access to legitimate political power because of her sex, she remains disenfranchised. Since Anat chooses not to be a submissive wife and mother confined to the domestic sphere, she is left with no socially acceptable alternative identity. Anat's use and abuse of her violent power may reflect her frustration with the patriarchal social system. As adolescent girls in ancient Ugarit were most probably given by their fathers in arranged marriages as young teenagers (see Roth 1987; Saporetti 1979:4-5), it should not be surprising to see mythic concern with the need for "maidens" to capitulate to the expectations of the androcentric society. The need for proper control of women is not an uncommon theme in myth (see Devereux 1982; Ortner 1974; Bamberger 1974). Anat's independence of male dominance in the mythic pantheon may have symbolic importance to her violent nature as a female who retains her independence from all male authority.

The social process of maturation and role assumption is central to the perpetuation of human societies and a common theme of ritual and mythic importance (see Turner 1969; Tyrrell 1984). As the independent female, Anat is marginal to the pantheon's society, just as an independent female is liminal to ancient Near Eastern cultures. In this sense, Anat's structural position is very similar to that of Inanna/Ishtar in Mesopotamian mythology. Both Anat and Inanna/Ishtar represent non-normative forms of female sexuality within androcentric ideology: Inanna exploits her sexual nature while Anat denies hers. Inanna's excessive eroticism and Anat's repressed sexuality are symbolic equivalents in their overt rebellion against the patriarchal norm of submissive, procreative wives. In each case, the goddess maintains strict control of her own sexual availability rather than surrendering her sexual and procreative abilities to patriarchal control. Thus, the rage and violence of Inanna and Anat mythically demonstrate the uncontrolled nature of adolescent females who do not accept social responsibility and subsequent male dominance (see also Vanstiphout 1984).

Mythically, Anat's violent nature may represent an androcentric fear of uncontrolled women. Male ambivalence towards feminine sexuality in androcentric ideology results in the perceived need for male control of feminine energies to avert social chaos. Anat's freedom from male control, in the form of a husband or dominant father, provides a symbolic explanation for her uncontrolled passions in Ugaritic myth. Indeed, the fear of powerful women is not an uncommon element in many myths (e.g. Lederer 1968; Devereux 1982), and so is a plausible source for Anat's bloody and violent image. Bottéro (1987) reaches similar conclusions in his study of Inanna/Ishtar as warrior and prostitute. Anat's threatening figure thus may embody the danger of the uncontrolled female within the patriarchal symbolic system. Myth and folktales often include elements which transgress societal norms in order to show the negative or disastrous effect they would have if implemented (see Sasson 1981:95-6; Oden 1979:51-5). In this context, Fontaine (1988:98-9) notes,

> The [independent] goddess who acts on her own behalf rather than for others is too frightening a figure to appear with any frequency in myth or cult. The ambivalent and terrifying figure of the powerful divine female is domesticated into the Helper of the gods and Donor to the city-state. In this fashion

patriarchy finds a literary method for absorbing female power and making it acceptable (i.e. subservient) to the dominant ideology.

Anat's anti-social role is clearly seen in her inverse relationship to the maiden Pughat in the *Epic of Aqhat.* In this text Anat's destructive actions are ameliorated by the actions of the submissive and structure-supporting Pughat. As the unrestrained and rebellious female, Anat is a threat to patriarchal culture and its social insititutions.

From within this social context, then, one may provide a symbolic interpretation of aspects of Anat's mythic role and character as the adolescent tomboy. The importance of gender to Anat's liminal character is seen in her bloody image as warrior and huntress. The symbolic association of females and blood provides a powerful and mutlivalent symbolic complex associated with danger, sexuality, and fertility. King (1983) points out the symbolic association of Artemis with feminine bleeding and maturity in ancient Greek thought. Women bleed at the loss of their virginity, during their menstrual cycle, and at childbirth, thus providing the symbolic relationship of women's bleeding and active fertility. Yet, contrary to these feminine attributes of procreation, Anat consistently utilizes her powerful energies for death rather than life. In contrast to goddesses of fertility and "mother goddesses," Anat spills others' blood and deprives them of their lives rather than spilling her own blood as a procreative female. Thus, Anat's role as a life-taker rather than a life-giver communicates an important element of her gender symbolism. In discussing the symbolic values of masculine and feminine images, Ortner (1974:72) explains that while females provide life through their miraculous powers of procreation, males are capable only of creation through the symbolic or technical manipulation of external objects. Hence, craftsmen deities are usually male. Furthermore, within the symbolic system of androcentric culture,

male activities involving the destruction of life (hunting and warfare) are often given more prestige than the female's ability to give birth, to create life.... It is not the killing that is the relevant and valued aspect of hunting and warfare; rather, it is the transcendental (social, cultural) nature of these activities as opposed to the naturalness of birth.....

Thus, Anat's role as life-taker demonstrates a masculine aspect of her character which directly contrasts with the feminine role of natural procreation. These contradictions between her female sex and her masculine actions result in a definite gender ambiguity from the ancient androcentric perspective; Anat causes men to bleed in death without herself bleeding in procreative sex and childbirth.

While Anat's violent actions in Ugaritic myth consistently lead to the death of her opponents, her exercise of lethal force nonetheless results in fertility and cosmic order in the Baal Cycle. In slaying Death, Anat's life-taking is actually life-giving. Significantly, Anat does not bestow life through the female process of childbirth, but through the masculine act of depriving her male enemy of his life. She can not deny her natural procreative ability no matter how hard she attempts to adopt masculine gender traits; Anat reserves the female creative potential within herself as the pubescent goddess. However much she may reject her feminine identity as a nubile female, the Maiden Anat is, in fact, the symbolic source of life. Symbolism of Anat's female adolescence may also be inferred from the bloodbath (*KTU* 1.3 ii) in which she wades in blood "up to her knees, ... up to her thighs." The language of this text may allude to menarche or menstruation in the pubescent goddess. An encounter with the bloodied Anat is clearly lethal to human males; virtually all of her violent hostility in Ugaritic myth is directed against male characters. Here Anat hacks off the warriors' heads and hands, clear phallic euphemisms. In her analysis of Premenstrual Syndrome (PMS) in Late Industrial societies, Emily Martin (1988) notes the association of PMS with women's lack of conformity to male expectations (see also Delaney, Lupton, and Thoth 1988:83-103). Martin (1988:173-81) discusses the rage which overcomes many women at this point in the menstrual cycle, asking why "women might feel extreme rage at a time when their usual emotional controls are reduced" (1988:175). She suggests (1988:177) that "the source of this diffuse anger could well come from women's perceptions, however inarticulate, of their oppression in society." Similarly, Delaney, Lupton, and Thoth (1988:76) state that while normal adolescents value menarche as a mark of maturity, the adolescent who rejects her female identity is traumatized by the physiological changes of puberty since they defy her ambiguous gender identity. Thus, the hoydenish girl may "increase her efforts to gain a penis or castrate a male—at least symbolically" (Delaney, Lupton, and Thoth 1988:76). This is exactly what one sees in Anat's attempt to deprive Aqhat of his bow and her beheading of the warriors in the bloodbath. Anat's violence may represent her rage as the maiden rebelling against her feminine identity within the androcentric culture. Hence, it would be appropriate for Anat to be depicted in this lethal frenzy during her menstrual period. Even without explicit menarcheal or menstrual symbolism, however, Anat's bloodbath may depict the goddess's feminine rage against males and masculine power in the androcentric culture.

While Greek myth presents Athena as a female who rises above her sex through her rational capacity and suppression of feminine sexuality, Ugaritic myth, by contrast, depicts Anat as ultimately unsuccessful in her efforts to adopt a masculine identity. Indeed, Anat functions in Ugaritic myth as a dangerous female who deprives men of their lives. The Ugaritic myths communicate the inevitability of Anat's biological nature and the futility of her bid for a masculine identity. Like Inanna (Groneberg 1986), Anat may combine feminine and masculine attributes in her character but she may not completely reject her female identity. As the divine maiden, Anat embodies the sexual and procreative power of adolescent females even within her ambiguous gender. While Anat continually defies proper feminine roles with none to admonish her in Ugaritic myth, she is a source of conflict and strife in the divine realm. The ambiguity of her liminal role demonstrates its necessary function in the symbolic system. In structural terms, the Maiden Anat mediates the contradictions of male and female, fertility and sterility, and eroticism and procreation.

In conclusion, the symbolic analysis of the goddess Anat reveals the individuality of her character as an adolescent female who maintains her independence in the face of patriarchal authority. Anat rebels against the androcentric repression of females by rejecting the normative roles open to one of her sex. As the adolescent tomboy, the Maiden Anat embodies one form of feminine threat to patriarchal society: the maiden's rebellion against her prescribed roles as procreative wife restricted to the domestic sphere. The multivalence of gender and sexual symbolism within the androcentric symbolic system illustrates the complexity of symbolic communication in the ancient mythic texts. As an adolescent maiden, Anat retains in herself the creative potential of the female sex, but this power becomes lethal if not properly channelled into creative acts. Hence, Anat's violent function in Ugaritic myth both supports and threatens the cosmic balance of power. The divine maiden provides the necessary energy to overcome death in the Baal Cycle, yet she causes chaos in an otherwise balanced world in *Aqhat* through her misdirected passions. As an independent female Anat poses a threat to both the patriarchal social structure and individual males who encounter her in her unrestrained freedom. This ambiguity in Anat's character illustrates the powerful mythic potential of feminine symbols in androcentric myth.

WORKS CITED

Aartun, Kjell

1984 Neue Beiträge zum ugaritischen Lexicon I. *UF* 16:1-52.

1986 Neue Beiträge zum ugaritischen Lexicon II. *UF* 17:1-47.

Abusch, Tzvi

1986 Ishtar's Proposal and Gilgamesh's Refusal. *HR* 26:143-87.

Aistleitner, J.

1969 *Wörterbuch der ugaritischen Sprache*, ed. O. Eissfeldt. Berlin: Akademie-Verlag.

Albright, William F.

1925a The Evolution of ᶜAn-ᶜAnat-ᶜAttâ. *AJSL* 41:73-101.

1925b Further Observations on the Name ᶜAnat-ᶜAttah. *AJSL* 41:283-5.

1927 Notes on the Goddess ᶜAnat. *AJSL* 43:233-6.

1938 Recent Progress in North-Canaanite Research. *BASOR* 70:18-24.

1950 Baal-zephon. Pp. 1-14 in *Festschrift Alfred Bertholet*, ed. W. Baumgartner et al. Tübingen: J. C. B. Moor.

1953 *Archaeology and the Religion of Israel.* 3rd ed. Baltimore: The Johns Hopkins University Press.

1968 *Yahweh and the Gods of Canaan.* Winona Lake, IN: Eisenbrauns.

Alster, Bendt

1972 *Dumuzi's Dream.* Copenhagen: Akademisk Forlag.

1976 On the Interpretation of the Sumerian Myth 'Inanna and Enki'. *ZA* 66:20-34.

1983 The Mythology of Mourning. *Acta Sumerologica* 5:1-16.

Andersen, Jörgen

1977 *The Witch On the Wall: Medieval Erotic Sculpture in the British Isles.* London: Gearge Allen & Unwin.

Aschkenasy, Nehama
1986 *Eve's Journey: Feminine Images in Hebraic Literary Tradition.* Philadelphia: University of Pennsylvania Press.

Ashley, Elana
1977 *The "Epic of AQHT" and the "RPUM Texts": A Critical Interpretation.* Unpublished Ph.D. Dissertation, New York State University.

Astour, Michael
1963 Un texte d'Ugarit récemment découvert et ses rapports avec l'origine des cultes bachiques grecs. *RHR* 164:1-15.
1965 *Hellenosemitica.* Leiden: E. J. Brill.
1966 Some New Divine Names from Ugarit. *JAOS* 86:277-84.
1969 Le triade de déesses de fertilité à Ugarit et en Gréce. Pp. 9-24 in *Ugaritica VI*, ed. C. F. A. Schaeffer. Paris: Imprimerie Nationale.
1988 Remarks on *KTU* 1.96. *SEL* 5:13-24.

Attridge, Harold W., and Robert A. Oden, Jr.
1981 *Philo of Byblos. The Phoenician History.* CBQMS 9. Washington, D. C.: Catholic Biblical Association of America.

Babb, Lawrence A.
1975 *The Divine Hierarchy: Popular Hinduism in Central Asia.* New York: Columbia University Press.

Bamberger, Joan
1974 The Myth of Matriarchy. Pp. 263-80 in Rosaldo and Lamphere.

Barb, A. A.
1959 Seth or Anubis? *Journal of the Warburg and Courtauld Institutes* 22:367-71.

Barnett, R. D.
1969 ^{c}Anat, Ba^{c}al, and Pasargadae. *MUSJ* 45:407-22.
1978 The Earliest Representation of ^{c}Anath. *Eretz-Israel* 14:28-31.

Barr, James
1987 *Comparative Philology and the Text of the Old Testament.* Winona Lake, IN: Eisenbrauns.

Barrelet, M.-Th.
1955 Les déesses armées et ailées. *Syria* 32:222-60.
Baumgarten, A. I.
1981 *The Phoenician History of Philo of Byblos.* Leiden: E. J. Brill.
Beane, Wendell Charles
1977 *Myth, Cult and Symbols in Śākta Hinduism.* Leiden: E. J. Brill.
Bhattacharyya, Narendra Nath
1977 *The Indian Mother Goddess.* 2nd ed. Columbia, MO: South Asia Books.
Biggs, Robert D.
1967 *Ša.zi.ga. Ancient Mesopotamian potency incantations.* Locust Valley, NY: J. J. Augustin.
Bleeker, C. J.
1963 Isis and Nephthys as Wailing Women. Pp. 190-205 in *The Sacred Bridge.* Leiden: E. J. Brill.
1973 *Hathor and Thoth.* Leiden: E. J. Brill.
1988 Isis and Hathor: Two Ancient Egyptian Goddesses. Pp. 29-48 in C. Olson.
Bonnet, Hans
1952 *Reallexikon der ägyptischen Religionsgeschichte.* Berlin: Walter de Gruyter.
Boose, Lynda E., and Betty S. Flowers, eds.
1989 *Daughters and Fathers.* Baltimore: The Johns Hopkins University Press.
Bosse-Griffiths, Kate
1983 The Fruit of the Mandrake. Pp. 62-74 in *Fontes Atque Pontes: Eine Festgabe für Hellmut Brunner*, ed. M. Görg. Wiesbaden: Otto Harrassowitz.
Bottéro, Jean
1987 La femme, l'amour et la guerre en Mésopotamie ancienne. Pp. 165-83 in *Poikilia. Études offertes à Jean-Pierre Vernant.* Paris: Ecole des Hautes Études en Sciences Sociales.

Bowman, Charles Howard
1978 *The Goddess ᶜAnatu in the Ancient Near East.* Unpublished Ph.D. Dissertation, University of California at Berkeley.

Brockelmann, Carl
1928 *Lexicon Syriacum.* Halle: Niemeyer.

Brown, C. Mackenzie
1988 Kālī, the Mad Mother. Pp. 110-44 in C. Olson.

Brown, Norman O.
1953 *Theogony.* New York: Bobbs-Merrill.

Brubaker, Richard L.
1988 The Untamed Goddesses of Village India. Pp. 145-60 in C. Olson.

Buckley, Thomas, and Alma Gottlieb, eds.
1988 *Blood Magic: The Anthropology of Menstruation.* Berkeley and Los Angeles: University of California Press.

Burkert, Walter
1979 *Structure and History in Greek Mythology and Ritual.* Berkeley and Los Angeles: University of California Press.
1983 *Homo necans.* Trans. Peter Bing. Berkeley and Los Angeles: University of California Press.
1985 *Greek Religion.* Trans. John Raffan. Cambridge: Harvard University Press.

Burrows, Millar
1940 The Ancient Oriental Background of Hebrew Levirate Marriage. *BASOR* 77:2-15.

Bynum, Caroline Walker
1986 Introduction: The Complexity of Symbols. Pp. 1-20 in Bynum, Harrell and Richman.

Bynum, Caroline Walker, Stevan Harrell, and Paula Richman, eds.
1986 *Gender and Religion: On the Complexity of Symbols.* Boston: Beacon.

Cameron, Averil, and Amélie Kuhrt, eds.
1983 *Images of Women in Antiquity.* Detroit: Wayne State University Press.

Caquot, André

1978 Remarques sur la Tablette ougaritique RS 1929 No 6 (*CTA* 13). *Eretz-Israel* 14:14*-18*.

1979 Une épisode peu connu du mythe de Baal et de la Génisse (19.54 = *PRU* V, 124 = *KTU* 1.93). *UF* 11:101-4.

1985 Une nouvelle interprétation de *KTU* 1.19 i 1-19. *SEL* 2:93-114.

Caquot, A., and M. Sznycer

1980 *Ugaritic Religion.* Leiden: E. J. Brill.

Caquot, A., M. Sznycer, and A. Herdner

1974 *Textes Ougaritiques.* Tome 1: *Mythes et Légendes.* Paris: Les Éditions du Cerf.

Cassuto, Umberto

1971 *The Goddess Anath.* Trans. I. Abrahams. Jerusalem: Magnes.

Cazelles, Henri

1956 L'hymne ugaritique à Anat. *Syria* 33:49-57.

Clifford, Richard J.

1972 *The Cosmic Mountain in Canaan and the Old Testament.* Cambridge: Harvard University Press.

Cohen, Mark

1981 *Sumerian Hymnology: The Eršemma.* Cincinatti: Ktav.

Cohen, Percy S.

1969 Theories of Myth. *Man* 4:337-53.

Colpe, Carsten

1969 Zur Mythologischen Struktur der Adonis-, Attis- und Osiris- Überlieferungen. Pp. 23-44 in *lišān mitḫurti.* AOAT 1. Neukirchen-Vluyn: Neukirchener and Kevelaer: Butzon & Bercker.

Cooper, Alan

1988 Two Exegetical Notes on *Aqht.* *UF* 20:19-26.

Cooper, Jerrold S.

1980 Review of *Enlil und Ninlil*, by Hermann Behrens. *JCS* 32:175-88.

Craigie, P. C.

1978 Deborah and Anat: A Study in Poetic Imagery. *ZAW* 90:374-81.

Craven, Toni

1983 *Artistry and Faith in the Book of Judith.* SBLDS 70. Chico, CA: Scholars Press.

Cross, Frank M.

1952 Ugaritic *dbᵓat* and Hebrew Cognates. *VT* 2:162-4.

1973 *Canaanite Myth and Hebrew Epic.* Cambridge: Harvard University Press.

Cunchillos, J.-L.

1985 Le dieu Mut, guerrier de El. *Syria* 62:205-18.

Cutler, B., and J. Macdonald

1982 On the Origin of the Ugaritic Text *KTU* 1.23. *UF* 14:33-50.

Dahood, Mitchell

1958 Ancient Semitic Deities in Syria and Palestine. Pp. 65-94 in *Le Antiche Divinità Semitiche*, ed. S. Moscati. Rome: Centro di Studi Semitici.

1979 Review of M. Dietrich and O. Loretz, *Die Elfenbeininschriften und S-texte aus Ugarit* (1976). *Or* 48:448.

Dalsimer, Katherine

1986 *Female Adolescence: Pyschoanalytic Reflections on Works of Literature.* New Haven: Yale University Press.

Daumes, François

1977 Hathor. *LÄ* 2:1024-33.

Day, John

1985 *God's conflict with the dragon and the sea.* Cambridge: Cambridge University Press.

Day, Peggy, ed.

1989 *Gender and Difference in Ancient Israel.* Minneapolis: Fortess.

Deem, Ariella

1978 The Goddess Anath and Some Biblical Hebrew Cruces. *JSS* 23:25-30.

Delaney, Janice, Mary Jane Lupton, and Emily Thoth

1988 *The Curse: A Cultural History of Menstruation.* 2nd ed. New York: E. P. Dutton.

Delcourt, Marie

1961 *Hermaphrodite.* Trans. Jennifer Nicholson. London: Studio.

Detienne, Marcel

1977 *The Gardens of Adonis: Spices in Greek Mythology.* Trans. Janet Lloyd. Atlantic Highlands, NJ: Humanities.

1979 Violentes "eugénies." Pp.183-214 in *La cuisine du sacrifice en pays grec*, ed. M. Detienne and J.-P. Vernant. Paris: Gallimard.

Devereux, Georges

1982 *Femme et Mythe.* Paris: Flammarion.

Dickason, Anne

1982 The Feminine as a Universal. Pp. 10-30 in Vetterling-Braggin.

Dietrich, M., and O. Loretz

1975 Der keilalphabetische *šumma izbu*-Text RS 24.247+265+268+328. *UF* 7:133-40.

1977 *gzr* "abschneiden, abkneifen" im Ugar. und Hebr. *UF* 9:51-6.

1980a Ämter und Titel des Schreibers *ilmlk* von Ugarit. *UF* 12: 387-9.

1980b Der Tod Baals als Rache Mot's für die Vernichtung Leviathans. *UF* 12:404-7.

1980c Anats grosse Sprünge. Zu *KTU* 1.13 iv 31-40 *et par.* *UF* 12:383-6.

1981 Neue Studien zu den Ritualtexten aus Ugarit (I). *UF* 13:63-100.

1982 *šb, šbm* und *udn* im Kontext von *KTU* 1.3 iii 35b - iv 4 und *KTU* 1.83:8. *UF* 14:77-81.

1986 Sieges- und Thronbesteigungslied Baals (*KTU* 1.101). *UF* 17:129-46.

Dietrich, M., O. Loretz, and J. Sanmartín

1976 *Die Keilalphabetischen Texte aus Ugarit.* AOAT 24. Neukirchen-Vluyn: Neukirchener and Kevelaer: Butzon & Bercker.

van Dijk, Jacobus

1986 ᶜAnat, Seth and the Seed of Prēᶜ. Pp. 31-51 in *Scripta Signa Vocis*, ed. H. Vanstiphout et al. Groningen: Egbert Forsten.

1989 The Canaanite God Hauron and His Cult in Egypt. *Göttinger Miszellen* 107:59-68.

Dijkstra, Meindert

1979 Some Reflections on the Legend of Aqhat. *UF* 11:199-210.

1986 An Ugaritic Fable (*KTU* 1.93). *UF* 18:125-8.

Donahue, Charles

1941 The Valkyries and the Irish War-Goddesses. *Publications of the Modern Language Association of America* 56:1-12.

Donner, H., and W. Rollig

1962-4 *Kanaanäische und Aramäische Inschriften.* Wiesbaden: Otto Harrassowitz.

Dossin, G.

1950 Le panthéon de Mari. Pp. 41-50 in *Studia Mariana*, ed. A. Parrot. Leiden: E. J. Brill.

Doty, William G.

1986 *Mythography: The Study of Myths and Rituals.* Birmingham: University of Alabama Press.

Douglas, Mary

1966 *Purity and Danger.* New York: Praeger.

Dressler, Harold H. P.

1975 Is the Bow of Aqhat a Symbol of Virility? *UF* 7:217-20.

1979 The Metamorphosis of a Lacuna. *UF* 11:211-7.

Driver, G. R.

1956 *Canaanite Myths and Legends.* Edinburgh: T. & T. Clark.

DuBois, Page

1982 *Centaurs and Amazons.* Ann Arbor: University of Michigan Press.

Dundes, Alan, ed.

1984 *Sacred Narrative: Readings in the Theory of Myth.* Berkeley and Los Angeles: University of California Press.

Eaton, Alfred Wade

1964 *The Goddess Anat: The History of Her Cult, Her Mythology, and Her Iconography.* Unpublished Ph.D. Dissertation, Yale University.

Edzard, Dietz Otto

1965 Mesopotamien. *WMyth* 1:19-139.

Eichler, B. L.

1977 Another Look at the Nuzi Sistership Contracts. Pp. 45-9 in Ellis.

Ellis, Maria, ed.

1977 *Essays on the ancient Near East in memory of J. J. Finckelstein.* Hamden, CN: Archon.

El-Sayed, Ramadan

1982 *La déesse Neith de Saïs.* 2 vols. Paris and Cairo: Institute français d'Archéologie orientale.

Emerton, J. A.

1978 A Further Note on *CTA* 5 i 4-6. *UF* 10:73-7.

Engnell, Ivan

1943 *Studies in Divine Kingship in the Ancient Near East.* Uppsala: Almqvist and Wiksell.

Farber, W.

1977 *Beschwörungsrituale an Ištar und Dumuzi.* Weisbaden: F. Steiner.

1989 (W)ardat-lilî(m). *ZA* 79:14-35.

Farber-Flügge, G.

1973 *Der Mythos 'Inanna und Enki' unter besonderer Berücksichtigung der Liste der ME.* Rome: Pontifical Biblical Institute.

Faulkner, F. O.

1936 The Bremner-Rhind Papyrus -- I. *JEA* 22:121-40.

Fauth, Wolfgang

1981 Ištar als Löwengöttin und die löwenköpfige Lamaštu. *WO* 12:21-36.

1986 Lilits und Astarten in aramäischen, mandäischen und syrischen Zaubertexten. *WO* 17:66-94.

Fensham, F. C.
1965 The Destruction of Mankind in the Near East. *Annali dell'Istituto Universitario Orientale di Napoli* 15:31-7.

Foley, C. M.
1987 Are the "Gracious Gods" *bn šrm*? *UF* 19:61-74.

Fontaine, Carole
1988 The Deceptive Goddess in Ancient Near Eastern Myth: Inanna and Inaraš. *Semeia* 42:84-102.

Fontenrose, Joseph
1971 *The Ritual Theory of Myth.* Originally 1966. Berkeley and Los Angeles: University of California Press.
1981 *Orion: The Myth of the Hunter and the Huntress.* Berkeley and Los Angeles: University of California Press.

Foster, Benjamin R.
1977 Ea and Ṣaltu. Pp. 79-84 in Ellis.
1987 Gilgamesh: Sex, Love, and the Ascent of Knowledge. Pp. 21-42 in Marks and Good.

Frazer, James G.
1911-5 *The Golden Bough.* 12 vols. 3rd ed. London: Macmillan.

Friedrich, Paul
1978 *The Meaning of Aphrodite.* Chicago: University of Chicago Press.

Frymer-Kensky, Tikva
1984 The Tribulations of Marduk. The So-Called "Marduk Ordeal Text." Pp. 131-41 in *Studies in Literature from the Ancient Near East,* ed. Jack M. Sasson. New Haven, CT: American Oriental Society.

Gardiner, Alan H.
1935 *Hieratic Papyri in the British Museum. Third Series.* Vol I. London: British Museum.

Gaster, Theodor H.
1936 The story of Aqhat. *Studi e materiali di storia delle religioni* 12:126-49.
1966 *Thespis: Ritual, Myth and Drama in the Ancient Near East.* New York: Harper and Row.

Geertz, Clifford

1966 Religion as a Cultural System. Pp. 1-46 in *Anthropological Approaches to the Study of Religion*, ed. Michael Banton. London and New York: Tavistock Publications.

Germond, Philippe

1981 *Sekhmet et La Protection du Monde.* Aegyptiaca Helvetica 9. Faculté des Lettres de l'Université de Genève.

Gese, H.

1970 Die Religion en Altsyriens. Pp. 1-232 in *Die Religionen Altsyriens, Altarabiens und der Mandäer*, ed. H. Gese, M. Höfner, and K. Rudolph. Stuttgart: W. Kohlhammer.

Gibson, J. C. L.

1975 Myth, Legend, and Folk-lore in the Ugaritic Keret and Aqhat Texts. Pp. 60-8 in *Congress Volume, Edinburgh, 1974.* VTSup 28. Leiden: E. J. Brill.

1977 *Canaanite Myths and Legends.* Edinburgh: T. and T. Clark.

1984 The Theology of the Ugaritic Baal Cycle. *Or* 53:202-19.

Ginsberg, H. L.

1941 Did Anat Fight the Dragon? *BASOR* 84:12-14

1945a The North-Canaanite Myth of Anath and Aqhat (I). *BASOR* 97:3-10.

1945b The North-Canaanite Myth of Anath and Aqhat (II). *BASOR* 98:15-23.

1969 Ugaritic Myths, Epics, and Legends. Pp. 129-55 in Pritchard.

Goetze, Albrecht

1944 Peace on Earth. *BASOR* 93:17-20.

Goldman, Bernard

1961 The Asiatic Ancestry of the Greek Gorgon. *Berytus* 14:1-23.

Good, Robert M.

1987 Exodus 32:18. Pp. 137-42 in Marks and Good.

Gordon, Cyrus H.
1956 Ugaritic ḫrt/ḫirîtu "cemetery." *Syria* 33:102-3.
1965 *Ugaritic Textbook.* AnOr 38. Rome: Pontifical Biblical Institute.
1977 Poetic Legends and Myths from Ugarit. *Berytus* 25:5-133.

Gordon, R. L., ed.
1981 *Myth, Religion and Society.* Cambridge: Cambridge University Press.

Gould, J. P.
1980 Law, custom and myth: aspects of the social position of women in classical Athens. *JHS* 100:38-59.

Grabbe, L. L.
1976 The Seasonal Pattern and the Baal Cycle. *UF* 8:57-63.

Graefe, Erhart
1980 Nephthys. *LÄ* 4:457-60.

Gray, John
1965 *The Legacy of Canaan.* 2nd ed. VTSup 5. Leiden: E. J. Brill.
1979 The Bloodbath of the Goddess Anat. *UF* 11:315-24.
1985 *Near Eastern Mythology.* New York: Peter Bedrick.

Greenfield, Jonas C.
1966 Studies in West Semitic Inscriptions I. *AcOr* 29:1-18.

Greenstein, Edward L.
1982a The Snaring of the Sea in the Baal Epic. *Maarav* 3:195-216.
1982b "To Grasp the Hem" in Ugaritic Literature. *VT* 32:217-8.

Griffiths, J. Gwyn
1970 *Plutarch's De Iside et Osiride.* Cambridge: University of Wales Press.
1980 *The Origins of Osiris and His Cult.* Leiden: E. J. Brill.

Groneberg, Brigitte
1981 Philologische Bearbeitung des Agušaya-Hymnus. *RA* 75:107-34.
1986 Die sumerisch-akkadische Inanna-Ištar: Hermaphroditos? *WO* 17:25-46.

Gruber, Mayer
1986 Hebrew *qĕdēšāh* and Her Canaanite and Akkadian Cognates. *UF* 18:133-48.

Gurney, O. R.
1962 Tammuz Reconsidered: Some Recent Developments. *JSS* 7:147-60.

Hackett, Jo Ann
1984 *The Balaam Text from Deir ᶜAllā.* HSM 31. Chico, CA: Scholars Press.
1989 Rehabilitating Hagar: Fragments of an Epic Pattern. Pp. 12-27 in P. Day.

Hallo, William W., and J. J. A. van Dijk
1968 *The Exaltation of Inanna.* New Haven: Yale University Press.

Harding, Esther
1972 *Woman's Mysteries Ancient and Modern: A Psychological Interpretation of the Feminine Principle as Portrayed in Myth, Story and Dream.* New York: Putman.

Haussig, H. W., ed.
1961- *Wörterbuch der Mythologie.* Stuttgart: Ernst Klett Verlag.

Healey, J. F.
1980 Ugaritic *ḥtk*: A Note. *UF* 12:408-9.
1983 Burning the Corn: new light on the killing of Mōtu. *Or* 52:248-51.
1985 The Akkadian "Pantheon" List from Ugarit. *SEL* 2:115-25.
1986 The Ugaritic Dead: Some Live Issues. *UF* 18:27-32.

Heimpel, Wolfgang
1982 A Catalogue of Near Eastern Venus Deities. *Syro-Mesopotamian Studies* 4:9-22.

Helck, Wolfgang
1971a *Betrachtungen zur grossen Göttin und den ihr verbundenen Gottheiten.* Munich and Vienne.
1971b *Die Beziehungen Aegyptens zu Vorderasien im 3. und 2. Jahrtausend v. Chr.* 2nd ed. Wiesbaden: Otto Harrassowitz.

Hendel, Ronald S.
1987 *The Epic of the Patriarch: The Jacob Cycle and the Narrative Traditions of Canaan and Israel.* HSM 42. Atlanta: Scholars Press.

Herdner, Andrée
1963 *Corpus des tablettes en cunéiformes alphabétiques découvertes à Ras Shamra-Ugarit de 1929 à 1939.* Mission de Ras Shamra,10. 2 vols. Paris: Imprimerie Nationale.

Herrmann, W.
1969 Aštart. *Mitteilungen des Instituts für Orientforschung* 15:6-55.
1982 Die Frage nach Göttergruppen in der religiösen Vorstellungswelt der Kanaanäer. *UF* 14:93-104.

Hertz, Neil
1985 *The End of the Line.* New York: Columbia University Press.

Hillers, Delbert R.
1964 *Treaty-Curses and the Old Testament Prophets.* Rome: Pontifical Biblical Institute.
1973 The Bow of Aqhat: The Meaning of a Mythological Theme. Pp. 71-80 in Hoffner (1973a).

Hoch-Smith, Judith, and Anita Springs, eds.
1978 *Women in Ritual and Symbolic Roles.* New York: Plenum.

Hoffner, Harry A., Jr.
1973a *Orient and Occident*, ed. H. A. Hoffner, Jr. AOAT 22. Neukirchen-Vluyn: Neukirchener and Kevelaer: Butzon & Bercker.
1973b Incest, Sodomy and Bestiality in the Ancient Near East. Pp. 81-90 in Hoffner (1973a).

Hollis, Susan Tower
1989 The Woman in Ancient Examples of the Potiphar's Wife Motif, K2111. Pp. 28-42 in P. Day.

Hooke, Samuel H., ed.
1933 *Myth and Ritual.* London: Oxford University Press.
1935 *The Labyrinth.* London: Oxford University Press.
1958 *Myth, Ritual, and Kingship.* Oxford: Clarendon.

Huehnergard, John
1987 *Ugaritic Vocabulary in Syllabic Transcription.* Harvard Semitic Studies 32. Atlanta: Scholars Press.

Huffmon, Herbert B.
1965 *Amorite Personal Names in the Mari Texts.* Baltimore: The Johns Hopkins University Press.

Hutter, Manfred
1985 *Altorientalische Vorstellungen von der Unterwelt.* OBO 63. Freiburg: Universitätsverlag and Göttingen: Vandenhoeck & Ruprecht.

Hvidberg, Flemming Friis
1962 *Weeping and Laughter in the Old Testament.* Originally 1938 in Danish. Leiden: E. J. Brill.

Hvidberg-Hansen, F. O.
1979 *La déesse Tnt, une étude sur la religion canaanéo-punique.* 2 vols. Copenhagen: Gad.

Irving, Dorothy
1978 *Mytharion: The Comparison of Tales from the Old Testament and the Ancient Near East.* AOAT 32. Neukirchen-Vluyn: Neukirchener and Kevelaer: Butzon & Bercker.

Jacobsen, Thorkild
1970 The Myth of Inanna and Bilulu. Pp. 52-71 in *Toward the Image of Tammuz,* ed. Wiliam L. Moran. Cambridge: Harvard University Press.
1976 *The Treasures of Darkness: A History of Mesopotamian Religion.* New Haven: Yale University Press.
1987 *The Harps That Once….* New Haven: Yale University Press.

James, E. O.
1959 *The Cult of the Mother Goddess.* London: Thames and Hudson.
1958 *Myth and Ritual in the Ancient Near East.* New York: Praeger.

Janowski, Bernd
1980 Erwägungen zur Vorgeschichte des israelitischen *šelamîm-Opfers.* *UF* 12:231-59.

Jung, C. G.
1973 *Four Archetypes.* Trans. R. F. C. Hull. Princeton: Princeton University Press.

Kapelrud, Arvid S.
1969 *The Violent Goddess: Anat in the Ras Shamra Texts.* Oslo: Universitetsforlaget.

Kautzsch, E., ed.
1985 *Gesenius' Hebrew Grammar.* Trans. A. E. Cowley. 2nd English ed. Oxford: Clarendon.

Kerényi, Karl
1969 Kore. Pp. 101-55 in *Essays on a Science of Mythology,* by C. G. Jung and C. Kerényi. Trans. R. F. C. Hull. Princeton: Princeton University Press.
1978 *Athene: Virgin and Mother.* Trans. Murray Stein. Zurich: Spring Publications.

Kessler, Suzanne J., and Wendy McKenna
1978 *Gender: An Ethnomethodological Approach.* New York: John Wiley and Sons.

King, Helen
1983 Bound to Bleed: Artemis and Greek Women. Pp. 109-27 in Cameron and Kuhrt.

Kinsley, David R.
1975 *The Sword and the Flute; Kālī and Kṛṣṇa.* Berkeley and Los Angeles: University of California Press.
1986 *Hindu Goddesses: Visions of the Divine Feminine in the Hindu Religious Tradition.* Los Angeles and Berkeley: University of California Press.
1989 *The Goddesses' Mirror.* Albany: State University of New York Press.

Kippenberg, Hans G., ed.
1984 *Struggles of Gods: Papers of the Groningen Group for the Study of the History of Religions.* Berlin: Mouton.

Kirk, G. S.
1970 *Myth: Its Meaning and Functions in Ancient and Other Cultures.* Berkeley and Los Angeles: University of California Press.

Kramer, Samuel Noah
1969 *The Sacred Marriage Rite.* Bloomington: Indiana University Press.
1972 *Sumerian Mythlogy.* Philadelphia: University of Pennsylvania Press.
1979 *From the Poetry of Sumer.* Berkeley and Los Angeles: University of California Press.
1980 The Death of Dumuzi: A New Sumerian Version. *Anatolian Studies* 30:5-13.
1982 Lisin, the Weeping Mother Goddess. Pp. 133-44 in *Zikir Šumim,* ed. G. van Driel. Leiden: E. J. Brill.
1983 The Weeping Goddess: Sumerian Prototypes of the Mater Delorosa. *BA* 46:69-80.
1985 BM 23631: Bread for Enlil, Sex for Inanna. *Or* 54:117-32.
1987 By the Rivers of Babylon: A Balag-Liturgy of Inanna. *Aula Orientala* 5:71-90.

Kutsch, E.
1986a *ḥtn. TDOT* 5:270-7.
1986b *ybm. TDOT* 5:367-73.

Lackenbacher, S.
1971 Note sur l'*ardat-lilî. RA* 65:119-154.

Lambert, W. G.
1985 The Pantheon of Mari. *MARI* 4:525-39.

Landsberger, B.
1968 Jungfraulichkeit: Ein Beitrag zum Thema 'Beilages und Eheschliessung'. Pp. 41-105 in *Symbolai Juridicae et Historicae Martino David Dedicatae.* Leiden: E. J. Brill.

Lane, Edward William
1863-9 *An Arabic-English Lexicon.* London and Edinburgh: Williams and Norgate.

Lange, H. O.
1927 *Der magische Papyrus Harris.* Copenhagen: Danske.

Leclant, Jean
1960 Astarté à cheval d'après les représentations égyptiennes. *Syria* 37:1-67.
1975 Anat. *LÄ* 1:253-8.

Lederer, Wolfgang
1968 *The Fear of Women.* New York: Harcourt Brace Jovanovich.

Lefkowitz, Mary R.
1986 *Women in Greek Myth.* Baltimore: The Johns Hopkins University Press.

Levine, Baruch
1974 *In The Presence of the Lord.* SJLA 5. Leiden: E. J. Brill.

Lévi-Strauss, Claude
1958 The Structural Study of Myth. Pp. 50-66 in Sebeok.
1964-7 *Mythologiques I-IV.* Paris: Plon.
1969 *The Raw and the Cooked.* New York: Harper and Row.

Lewis, Theodore J.
1989 *Cults of the Dead in Ancient Israel and Ugarit.* HSM 39. Atlanta: Scholars Press.

L'Heureux, Conrad E.
1979 *Rank Among the Canaanite Gods.* HSM 21. Missoula, MO: Scholars Press.

Lichtheim, Mariam
1980 *Ancient Egyptian Literature: A Book of Readings. Vol. III.* Berkeley and Los Angeles: University of California Press.

Limet, H.
1971 Le poème épique "Inanna et Ebiḫ": Une version des lignes 123 à 182. *Or* N.S. 40:11-28.

Lipínski, E.
1965 Les conceptions et couches merveilleusses de ᶜAnath. *Syria* 42:45-73.
1967 Le dieu Lim. Pp. 151-60 in *Compte Rendu de la XVe Rencontre Assyriologique Internationale.* Liège.
1971 El's Abode. Mythological Traditions Related to Mount Hermon and to the Mountains of Armenia. OLP 2:13-69.

Lipman-Blumen, Jean
1984 *Gender Roles and Power.* Englewood Cliffs, NJ: Prentice-Hall.

Littleton, C. Scott

1982 *The New Comparative Mythology.* 3rd ed. Berkeley and Los Angeles: University of California Press.

Locher, Clemens

1986 *Die Ehre einer Frau in Israel.* Freiburg: Universitätsverlag and Göttingen: Vandenhoeck & Ruprecht.

Loewenstamm, Samuel E.

1972 The Killing of Mot in Ugaritic Myth. *Or* 41:378-82.

1975 Anat's Victory over the Tunnanu. *JSS* 20:22-7.

1982 Did the Goddess Anat Wear Side-whiskers and a Beard? *UF* 14:119-23.

Løkkegaard, F.

1953 A Plea for El, the Bull, and Other Ugaritic Miscellanies. Pp. 219-35 in *Studia Orientalia Ioanna Pedersen.* Copenhagen: Einar Munksgaard.

1982 Review of Hvidberg-Hansen (1979). *UF* 14:129-40.

McBride, S. Dean

1969 *The Deuteronomic Name Theology.* Unpublished Ph.D. Dissertation, Harvard University.

Maier, Walter A., III

1986 *ʾAšerah: Extrabiblical Evidence.* HSM 37. Atlanta: Scholars Press.

Marcus, David

1972 The Verb "To Live" in Ugaritic. *JSS* 17:76-82.

1977 The Term "Chin" in the Semitic Languages. *BASOR* 226:53-60.

Margalit, Baruch

1980 *A Matter of "Life" and "Death". A Study of the Baal-Mot Epic (CTA 4-5-6).* AOAT 206. Neukirchen-Vluyn: Neukirchener and Kevelaer: Butzon & Bercker.

1983 Lexicographical Notes on the *Aqht* Epic (Part I: *KTU* 1.17-18). *UF* 15:65-103.

1984 *KTU* 1.93 (= *PRU* 5:124): The Prayer of a Sick Cow. *SEL* 1:89-101.

1989a *KTU* 1.92 (Obv): A Ugaritic Theophagy. *Aula Orientalis* 7:66-80.

Margalit, Baruch (Continued)

1989b *The Ugaritic Poem of AQHT*. BZAW 182. Berlin: de Gruyter.

Marglin, Frédérique Apffel

1985 Female Sexuality in the Hindu World. Pp. 39-60 in *Immaculate and Powerful: The Female in Sacred Imagery and Social Reality*, ed. C. W. Atkinson, C. H. Buchanan, and M. R. Miles. Boston: Beacon.

Marks, John, and Robert M. Good, eds.

1987 *Love & Death in the Ancient Near East: Essays in Honor of Marvin H. Pope*. Guilford, CT: Four Quarters.

Martin, Emily

1988 Premenstrual Syndrome: Discipline, Work, and Anger in Late Industrial Societies. Pp. 161-81 in Buckley and Gottleib.

Massart, A.

1954 *The Leiden Magical Papyrus I 343 + I 345*. Leiden: E. J. Brill.

May, L. A.

1984 Above Her Sex: The Enigma of the Athena Parthenos. *Visible Religion* III:106-30.

Mead, Margaret

1935 *Sex and Temperament in Three Primitive Societies*. New York: William Morrow.

Medicine, Beatrice

1983 "Warrior Women" - Sex Role Alternatives for Plains Indian Women. Pp. 267-80 in *The Hidden Half: Studies of Plains Indian Women*, ed. Patricia Albers and Beatrice Medicine. New York: University Press of America.

du Mesnil du Buisson, Robert

1970 *Études sur les dieux phéniciens hérités par l'Empire Romain*. Leiden: E. J. Brill.

1973 *Nouvelles études sur les dieux et les mythes de Canaan*. Leiden: E. J. Brill.

Middleton, John

1967 *Myth and Cosmos: Readings in Mythology and Symbolism*. Garden City: Natural history Press.

Miller, Patrick D., Jr.
1971 Animal Names as Designations in Ugaritic and Hebrew. *UF* 2:177–86.
1981 Ugarit and the History of Religions. *JNSL* 9:119-28.
Montet, P.
1933 *Les Nouvelles Fouilles de Tanis (1929-1932)*. Paris: Les Belles Lettres.
Montley, Patricia
1978 Judith in the Fine Arts. *Anima* 4:37-42.
de Moor, Johannes C.
1964 Ugaritic *ṯkḥ* and South Arabian *mṯkḥ*. *VT* 14:371-2.
1969 Studies in the New Alphabetic texts from Ras Shamra. *UF* 1:167-88.
1970 The Semitic Pantheon of Ugarit. *UF* 2:187-228.
1971 *The Seasonal Pattern in the Ugaritic Myth of Baᶜlu.* AOAT 16. Neukirchen-Vluyn: Neukirchener and Kevelaer: Butzon & Bercker.
1972 *New Year with Canaanites and Israelites.* Kampen: J. H. Kok.
1975 *ᵓar* "Honey-dew." *UF* 7:590-1.
1979 Contributions to the Ugaritic Lexicon. *UF* 11:639-53.
1980 An Incantation Against Infertility (*KTU* 13). *UF* 12:304-10.
1986a The Crisis of Polytheism in Late Bronze Age Ugarit. *OTS* 24:1-20.
1986b Ugaritic Smalltalk. *UF* 17:219-23.
1987 *An Anthology of Religious Texts from Ugarit.* Leiden: E. J. Brill.
de Moor, J. C., and Klaas Spronk
1987 *A Cuneiform Anthology of Religious Texts from Ugarit.* Leiden: E. J. Brill.
Moore, Carey A.
1985 *Judith.* AB 40. New York: Doubleday.
Mullen, E. Theodore, Jr.
1980 *The Divine Council in Canaanite and Early Hebrew Literature.* HSM 24. Chico, CA: Scholars Press.

Nakata, Ichiro
1974 *Deities in the Mari texts.* Unpublished Ph.D. Dissertation, Columbia University.

Neumann, Erich
1954 *The Origins and History of Consciousness.* Bollinger Series 43. Princeton: Princeton University Press.
1956 *The Great Mother: Analysis of the Archetype.* Bollinger Series 54. Princeton: Princeton University Press.

Niditch, Susan
1989 Eroticism and Death in the Tale of Jael. Pp. 43-57 in P. Day.

Nilsson, Martin P.
1957 *The Dionysiac Mysteries of the Hellenistic and Roman Ages.* Lund: CWK Gleerup.

Nougayrol, Jean
1956 *Textes accadiens des archives sud. PRU* IV. Paris: Imprimerie Nationale.
1968 Le panthéon d'Ugarit. *Ugaritica V*, ed. J. Nougayrol et al. Paris: Geuthner.

Ochshorn, Judith
1981 *The Female Experience and the Nature of the Divine.* Bloomington: University of Indiana Press.

Oden, Robert A., Jr.
1977 *Studies in Lucian's De Syria Dea.* HSM 15. Missoula, MO: Scholars Press.
1979 Theoretical Assumptions in the Study of Ugaritic Myths. *Maarav* 2:43-63.
1987 *The Bible Without Theology.* New York: Harper and Row.

O'Flaherty, Wendy Doniger
1973 *Asceticism and Eroticism in the Mythology of Śiva.* London: Oxford University Press.
1980 *Women, Androgynes, and Other Mythical Beasts.* Chicago: University of Chicago Press.

Oldenburg, Ulf
1969 *The Conflict Between El and Baᶜal in Canaanite Religion.* Leiden: E. J. Brill.

Olender, Maurice

1987 Baubo. *EncRel* 2:83-4.

del Olmo Lete, G.

1978 Notes on Ugaritic Semantics IV. *UF* 10:37-46.

1981a *Mitos y leyendas de Canaan.* Valencia: Institución San Jeronimo.

1981b Le Mythe de la Vierge-mère ᶜAnatu. Une nouvelle interprétation de *CTA/KTU* 13. *UF* 13:49-62.

1982 Notes on Ugaritic Sematics V. *UF* 14:55-69.

1984 *Interpretación de la Mitología Cananea.* Valencia: Institución San Jeronimo.

1986 The 'Divine' Names of the Ugaritic Kings. *UF* 18:81-95.

Olson, Alan, ed.

1980 *Myth, Symbol, and Reality.* Notre Dame: University of Notre Dame Press.

Olson, Carl, ed.

1988 *The Book of the Goddess Past and Present.* New York: Crossroad.

Olyan, Saul M.

1988 *Asherah and the Cult of Yahweh in Israel.* SBLMS 34. Atlanta: Scholars Press.

Ortner, Sherry

1974 Is Female to Male as Nature is to Culture? Pp. 67-87 in Rosaldo and Lamphere.

Ortner, Sherry, and Harriet Whitehead, eds.

1981 *Sexual Meanings: The Cultural Constructions of Gender and Sexuality.* Cambridge: Cambridge University Press.

Padel, Ruth

1983 Women: Model for Possession by Greek Daemons. Pp. 3-19 in Cameron and Kuhrt.

Page, S.

1968 The Tablets from Tell al-Rimah 1967. *Iraq* 30:87-97.

Pardee, Dennis

1975 The Preposition in Ugaritic. *UF* 7:329-78.

1976 The Preposition in Ugaritic. *UF* 8:215-322.

1984 Will the Dragon Never Be Muzzled? *UF* 16:251-5.

Parker, Simon B.

1977 The Historical Composition of *KRT* and the Cult of *EL*. *ZAW* 89:161-75.

1987 Death and Devotion: The Composition and Theme of *Aqht*. Pp. 71-83 in Marks and Good.

1989 *The Pre-biblical Narrative Tradition.* Resources for Biblical Studies 24. Atlanta: Scholars Press.

Patai, Raphael

1959 *Sex and Family in the Bible and the Middle East.* New York: Doubleday.

1967 *The Hebrew Goddess.* New York: Ktav.

Patton, John H.

1944 *Canaanite Parallels in the Book of Psalms.* Baltimore: The Johns Hopkins University Press.

Paul, Shalom

1969 Exod. 21:10: A Threefold Maintenance Clause. *JNES* 28:48-53.

1982 Two Cognate Semitic Terms for Mating and Copulation. *VT* 32:492-4.

Payne Smith, J., ed.

1903 *A Compendious Syriac Dictionary.* Oxford: Clarendon.

Perlman, Alice, L.

1978 *Asherah and Astarte in the Old Testament and Ugaritic Literature.* Unpublished Ph.D. Dissertation, University of California at Berkeley.

Petersen, David L., and Mark Woodward

1977 Northwest Semitic Religion: A Study of Relational Structures. *UF* 9:233-48.

Pomeroy, Sarah B.

1975 *Goddesses, Whores, Wives, and Slaves: Women in Classical Antiquity.* New York: Shoken Books.

Pope, Marvin

1955 *El in the Ugaritic Texts.* VTSup 2. Leiden: E. J. Brill.

1965 Anat. *WMyth* 1:235-41.

1966 Review of Gray (1965). *JSS* 11:228-41.

1971 Review of Gese et al. *UF* 3:375-6.

1977 *Song of Songs.* AB 7C. Garden City: Doubleday.

Pope, Marvin (Continued)

1983 Review of L'Heureux (1979). *BASOR* 251:67-9.

1987a Review of Spronk (1986). *UF* 19:452-63.

1987b The Status of El at Ugarit. *UF* 19:219-30.

Pötscher, Walter

1987 *Hera: Eine Strukturanalyse im Vergleich mit Athena.* Darmstadt: Wissenschaftliche Buchgesellschafte.

Preston, James J., ed.

1982 *Mother Worship: Theme and Variations.* Chapel Hill: University of North Carolina Press.

Preuss, H. D.

1984 *lĕʾom.* *TWAT* 4:411-3.

Price, Harry

1945 *Poltergeist Over England.* London: Country Life LTD.

Pritchard, James B.

1943 *Palestinian Figurines in Relation to Certain Goddesses Known Through Literature.* AOS 24. New Haven: American Oriental Society.

1969 *Ancient Near Eastern Texts Relating to the Old Testament.* 3rd ed. Princeton: Princeton University Press.

1974 *The Ancient Near East in Pictures.* 2nd ed. Princeton: Princeton University Press.

Redford, Donald B.

1973 New Light on the Asiatic Campaigning of Ḥoremheb. *BASOR* 21:36-49.

Rendsburg, Gary A.

1987 Modern South Arabian as a Source for Ugaritic Etymologies. *JAOS* 107:623-8.

Renfroe, F.

1980 Methodological Considerations Regarding the Use of Arabic in Ugaritic Philology. *UF* 12:33-74.

Reisner, G. A.

1896 *Sumerisch-babylonische Hymnen nach Thontafeln griechischer Zeit.* Berlin.

Roberts, J. J. M.

1972 *The Earliest Semitic Pantheon.* Baltimore: The Johns Hopkins University Press.

Robertson, N.
1982 The Ritual Background of the Dying God in Cyprus and Syro-Palestine. *HTR* 75:313-59.

Robins, Gay
1988 Ancient Egyptian Sexuality. *Discussions in Egyptology* 11:61-72.

Roccati, Alessandro
1972 Une Légende égyptienne d'Anat. *Revue d'Égyptologie* 24:154-9.

Rogerson, J. W.
1974 *Myth in Old Testament Research.* Berlin: Walter de Gruyter.

Rosaldo, Michelle Zimbalist, and Loise Lamphere, eds.
1974 *Woman, Culture, and Society.* Stanford: Stanford Universty Press.

Roth, Martha
1987 Age at Marriage and the Household. *Comparative Studies in Society and History* 29:715-47.

Rowe, Alan
1930 *The Topography and History of Beth-Shan.* Philadelphia: University of Pennsylvania Press.
1940 *The Four Canaanite Temples of Beth-Shan.* Philadelphia: University of Pennsylvania Press.

Sanday, Peggy Reeves
1981 *Female Power and Male Dominance.* Cambridge: Cambridge University Press.
1986 *Divine Hunger.* Cambridge: Cambridge University Press.

Sanmartín, J.
1976 *arbdd* "Liebes-Opfer": Ein Hurrisches Lehnwort im Ugaritischen. *UF* 8:461-4.
1980a Die Haartracht der ᶜnt. *UF* 12:341-4.
1980b Glossen zum ugaritischen Lexikon (IV). *UF* 12:335-44.
1980c Lexikographisches zu *Mt*'s Spruch *KTU* 1.5 i 1ff. *UF* 12:438-9.

Saporetti, Claudio
1979 *The Status of Women in the Middle Assyrian Period.* Trans. B. Boltze-Jordan. Malibu: Undena.

Sasson, Jack M.

1981 Literary Criticism, Folklore Scholarship, and Ugaritic Literature. Pp. 81-98 in *Ugarit in Retrospect*, ed. Gordon Douglas Young. Winona Lake, IN: Eisenbrauns.

Schaeffer, Claude F. A.

1939 *The Cuneiform Texts of Ras Shamra-Ugarit.* London: Oxford Unversity Press.

Sebeok, Thomas A., ed.

1958 *Myth: A Symposium.* Bloomington: Indiana University Press.

Segal, Robert A.

1980 In Defense of Mythology: The History of Modern Theories of Myth. *Annals of Scholarship* 1:3-49.

Seidl, U.

1980 Inanna, Ištar. B. In der Bildkunst. *RlA* 5:87-9.

van Selms, A.

1954 *Marriage and Family Life in Ugaritic Literature.* London: Luzac.

1975 A Systematic Approach to *CTA* 5,I,1-8. *UF* 7:477-82.

Shulman, David

1976 The Murderous Bride: Tamil Versions of the Myth of Devī and the Buffalo-demon. *HR* 16:120-46.

1980 *Tamil Temple Myths: Sacrifice and Divine Marriage in the South India Saiva Tradition.* Princeton: Princeton University Press.

Simpson, William K., ed.

1973 *The Literature of Ancient Egypt.* New Haven: Yale University Press.

Sjöberg, Åke W.

1976 in-nin šà-gur$_4$-ra. A Hymn to the Goddess Inanna by the en-Priestess Enḫeduanna. *ZA* 65:161-254.

1977 Miscellaneous Sumerian Texts, II. *JCS* 29:3-45.

Slater, Philip E.

1968 *The Glory of Hera. Greek Mythology and the Greek Family.* Boston: Beacon.

Smith, Jonathan Z.

1969 The Glory, Jest and Riddle: James George Frazer and *The Golden Bough.* Unpublished Ph.D. Dissertation, Yale University.

1973 When the Bough Breaks. *HR* 12:342-71.

1987 Dying and Rising Gods. *EncRel* 4:521-7.

Smith, Mark S.

1984 Divine Travel as a Token of Divine Rank. *UF* 16:359.

1986a Baal in the Land of Death. *UF* 17:311-4.

1986b Interpreting the Ba^{c}al Cycle. *UF* 18:313-39.

von Soden, Wolfram

1955 Gibt es ein Zeugnis dafür, dass die Babylonier an die Wieder-auferstehung Marduks geglaubt haben? *ZA* 17:130-66.

1965-81 *Akkadisches Handwörterbuch.* 3 vols. Weisbaden: Otto Harrasssowitz.

Spronk, Klaas

1986 *Beatific Afterlife in Ancient Israel and in the Ancient Near East.* AOAT 219. Neukirchen-Vluyn: Neukirchener and Kevelaer: Butzon & Bercker.

Stadelmann, Rainer

1967 *Syrisch-Palästinensische Gottheiten in Ägypten.* Probleme der Ägyptologie 5. Leiden: E. J. Brill.

Stamm, Johann J.

1939 *Die akkadische Namengebung.* MVAG 44. Leipzig.

Starr, Omega Means

1984 An Apotropaic Incest Ritual in the Baal and Anath Cycle. *Folklore* 95:231-44.

de Tarragon, Jean-Michael

1980 *Le Culte à Ugarit.* Cahiers de la Revue biblique 19. Paris: Gabalda.

Teixidor, Javier

1977 *The Pagan God.* Princeton: Princeton University Press.

Thompson, R. Campbell

1930 *The Epic of Gilgamesh.* Oxford: Oxford University Press.

Tiwari, J. N.

1985 *Goddess Cults in Ancient India.* Delhi: Sundeep Prakashan.

Tolkien, J. R. R.

1985 *The Return of the King.* Originally 1956. New York: Ballantine.

Trebilcot, Joyce

1982 Two Forms of Androgynism. Pp. 161-9 in Vetterling-Braggin.

Tropper, J., and E. Verreet,

1988 Ugaritisch *ndy, ydy, ndd* und *d(w)d.* *UF* 20:339-50.

Trujillo, J. Ivan

1973 *The Ugaritic Ritual for a Sacrificial Meal Honoring the Good Gods (Text CTA: 23).* Unpublished Ph.D. Dissertation, The Johns Hopkins University.

Turner, Victor

1967 *The Forest of Symbols: Aspects of Ndembu Ritual.* Ithaca: Cornell University Press.

1969 *The Ritual Process.* Ithaca: Cornell University Press.

1975 Symbolic Studies. *Annual Review of Anthropology* 4:145-61.

Tyrrell, William Blake

1984 *Amazons: A Study in Athenian Mythmaking.* Baltimore: The Johns Hopkins University Press.

Vanstiphout, H. L. J.

1984 Inanna/Ishtar as a Figure of Controversy. Pp. 225-38 in Kippenberg.

de Vaux, Roland

1972 *The Bible and the Ancient Near East.* Trans. Damian McHugh. London: Darton, Longman & Todd.

te Velde, H.

1977 *Seth. God of Confusion.* 2nd ed. Leiden: E. J. Brill.

1984 Relations and Conflicts between Egyptian Gods, particularly in the Divine Ennead of Heliopolis. Pp. 239-58 in Kippenberg.

Vernant, Jean-Pierre

1980 *Myth and Society in Ancient Greece.* Trans. Janet Lloyd. Atlantic Highlands, NJ: Humanities Press.

1981a The union with Metis and the sovereignty of heaven. Pp. 1-15 in R. L. Gordon.

1981b The myth of Prometheus in Hesiod. Pp. 43-56 in R. L. Gordon.

1981c Sacrificial and alimentary codes in Hesiod's myth of Prometheus. Pp. 57-79 in R. L. Gordon.

1987 Artemis. *EncRel* 2:420-1.

Vetterling-Braggin, Mary, ed.

1982 *"Femininity," "Masculinity," and "Androgeny."* Totowa, NJ: Rowman and Littlefield.

Vickery, John B.

1973 *The Literary Impact of The Golden Bough.* Princeton: Princeton University Press.

Vincent, A.

1937 *La religion des Judéo-Araméens d'Elephantine.* Paris.

Virolleaud, Charles

1936 ᶜAnat et la gènisse. *Syria* 17:150-73.

1937 La déesse ᶜAnat-Astarté dans les poémes de Ras-Shamra. *Revue des Études Sémitiques* 1:4-22.

1938 *La deésse ᶜAnat.* Paris: P. Geuthner.

1944-5 Fragments mythologiques de Ras-Shamra. *Syria* 24:1-23.

1960 Une nouvel épisode du mythe ugaritique de Baal. *CRAIBL* (June, 1960) 180-6.

Wagner, Günter

1967 *Pauline Baptism and the Pagan Mysteries.* Trans. J. P. Smith. Edinburg: Oliver & Boyd.

Walcot, Peter

1966 *Hesiod and the Near East.* Cardiff: Wales.

1969 The Comparative Study of Ugaritic and Greek Literatures. *UF* 1:111-18.

1984 Greek attitudes towards women: the mythological evidence. *Greece & Rome* 31:37-47.

Ward, William A.

1969 La déesse nourricière d'Ugarit. *Syria* 46: 225-39.

Waterston, Alastair

1988 The Kingdom of ᶜAṯtar and His Role in the AB Cycle. *UF* 20:357-64.

Watson, Wilfred G. E.

1977 Ugaritic and Mesopotamian Literary Texts. *UF* 9:273-84.

1984 Internal Parallelism in Ugaritic Verse. *SEL* 1:53-67.

1989 What does Ugaritic *gmn* mean? *Aula Orientalis* 7:129-31.

Wehr, Hans

1976 *Arabic-English Dictionary*, ed. M. J. Cowan. 3rd ed. Ithaca: Spoken Languages Services.

Weippert, Manfred

1985 Die Bildsprache der neuassyrischen Prophetie. Pp. 55-93 in *Beiträge zur prophetischen Bildsprache in Israel und Assyrien*, ed. H. Weippert et al. OBO 64. Freiburg: Universitätsverlag and Göttingen: Vandenhoeck & Ruprecht.

Wenham, Gordon J.

1976 *bᵉtûlāh* 'A Girl of Marriageable Age.' *VT* 22:326-48.

Westbrook, Raymond

1988 *Old Babylonian Marriage Law*. Archiv für Orientforschung Beiheft 23. Horn, Austria: Berger & Söhne.

Whitaker, Richard E.

1972 *A Concordance of the Ugaritic Language*. Cambridge: Harvard University Press.

Wilcke, Claus

1980 Inanna, Ištar. A. Philologisch. *RlA* 5:74-86.

1986 Familiengründung im alten Babylonien. Pp. 213-317 in *Geschlechtsriefe und Legitimation zur Zeugung*, ed. Ernst W. Müller. Freiburg and Munchen: Karl Alber.

Willis, Wendell Lee

1985 *Idol Meat in Corinth*. Chico, CA: Scholars Press.

Winter, Urs

1986 *Frau und Göttin*. OBO 53. Freiburg: Universitätsverlag and Göttingen: Vandenhoeck & Ruprecht.

Witt, R. E.

1971 *Isis in the Graeco-Roman World*. Ithaca: Cornell University Press.

Wyatt, Nicholas

1980 The Relationship of the Deities Dagan and Hadad. *UF* 12:375-9.

1983 The Stela of the Seated God from Ugarit. *UF* 15:271-7.

1984 The ᶜAnat Stela from Ugarit and Its Ramifications. *UF* 16:327-37.

1987a Sea and Desert: Symbolic Geography in West Semitic Religious Thought. *UF* 19:375-89.

1987b Baᶜal's Boars. *UF* 19:391-8

1987c Who Killed the Dragon? *Aula Orientalis* 5:185-98.

1988 The Source of the Ugaritic Myth of the Conflict of Baᶜal and Yam. *UF* 20:375-85.

Xella, Paolo

1976 Un 'Rilettura' del poema di Aqhat. Pp. 61-91 in *Problemi del mito nel Vicino Oriente antico.* Naples: Istituto orientale di Napoli.

van Zijl, Peter J.

1972 *Baal.* AOAT 10. Neukirchen-Vluyn: Neukirchener and Kevelaer: Butzon & Bercker.

1975 A Discussion of the words *anš* and *nšy* in the Ugaritic Texts. *UF* 7:501-14.